WHEN
ENGLAND
RULED
THE
WORLD

WHEN ENGLAND RULED THE WORLD

Four Years That Shaped the Modern Game

STEVE MINGLE

First published by Pitch Publishing

Pitch Publishing
A2 Yeoman Gate
Yeoman Way
Worthing
Sussex
BN13 3QZ
www.pitchpublishing.co.uk
info@pitchpublishing.co.uk

© 2016, Steve Mingle

A CIP catalogue record is available for this book
from the British Library.

ISBN 978-1-78531-159-8

Typesetting and origination by Pitch Publishing

Printed by TJ International Ltd, Padstow, Cornwall

Contents

Acknowledgements/Bibliography 7

Introduction 8

1966/67:
United's Stepping Stone 13

1967/68:
Manchester: A City United In Glory 83

1968/69:
Triumph of the Dark Side 157

1969/70:
Return of the School of Science 230

Four Years that Shaped the Modern Game? 297

Acknowledgements/Bibliography

Material for the book has been derived from a wide range of sources, the most important of which were the digital archives of the *Times*, *Guardian* and *Observer* together with the author's 'I knew they would come in useful sometime' collection of *Soccer Star* and *Football League Review* magazines. The archives of the *Daily Mirror* and *Daily Express* were also invaluable, especially in reflecting more emotional responses to the national team's fluctuations in form over the period. Collections of *Shoot*, *Goal* and *Jimmy Hill's Football Weekly* magazines all provided much helpful material, despite provoking all too frequent non-productive interludes of nostalgic reminiscence. Of particular help amongst the vast array of websites visited were www.englandfootballonline.com, and www.11v11.com.

Additional club and individual specific material came from

Sir Alf, Leo McKinstry, Element (2007)
Ossie: King Of Stamford Bridge, Martin King and Martin Knight, Mainstream (2004)
Greavsie, Jimmy Greaves, Sphere (2004)
Ball Of Fire, Alan Ball, Pelham (1967)
www.mightyleeds.co.uk
Match Of The Day, John Motson, BBC Books (1992)

Apologies to any source inadvertently omitted; some facts and anecdotes have become so embedded in the author's memory that the origin has long been forgotten...

Introduction

England. The summer of 1966. The sixties might have been getting into their swing, but the optimistic mood hadn't spread to football. Attendances for the 1965/66 season had fallen again, with the league programme attracting the lowest aggregate of spectators since the war. In an era full of strikes and pay freezes, life was tough for the working man, with many concluding that even the relatively cheap admission prices would instead be better spent on beer and fags. At least these were sources of guaranteed pleasure: on the pitch, there had been a marked trend towards a more negative, unappealing style of football, with many teams, particularly away from home, setting up in an increasingly defensive formation and showing little inclination to entertain. There had also been sporadic instances of trouble on the terraces, a further deterrent to all but the most committed supporters.

Since the previous World Cup in Chile, English club football had been almost wholly dominated by the industrial North. Liverpool (twice), Manchester United and Everton had won the four division one titles, whilst Leeds United, emerging as a dark force under Don Revie, had finished second in the previous two seasons. The last two FA Cup finals had both seen Lancashire v Yorkshire shoot-outs. There was an abundance of talent to be found in teams elsewhere, but nowhere near enough consistency for any of them to mount a serious title challenge.

It seemed as though the best that London clubs could hope for was a decent cup run, and West Ham had shown what was possible by winning the cup in 1964 and following it up with another Wembley triumph, in the 1965 European Cup Winners' Cup Final. Spurs and Chelsea also had star names with obvious talent and potential, but the era had been one of the darkest in Arsenal's history. Under Billy Wright's stewardship, the Gunners had become well acquainted with the bottom half of the table, and the fans had voted with their feet in the face of football which was both unattractive and unsuccessful. Their May 1966 home game against Leeds attracted just 4,500 to Highbury. The North East was also a region in footballing decline, with none of its teams having had a sniff of a trophy throughout the decade. The Midlands had fared little better.

Although English clubs had tasted success in Europe, no English side had ever reached the final of the premier competition, the European Cup. Exits were often accompanied by tirades against the Machiavellian ways of the victors, with more than a few suggestions that some officials had been incentivised to favour the continentals. For all the flamboyant brilliance of the Real Madrid and Brazil sides of recent years, the average British fan still regarded many aspects of foreign football with deep suspicion, not necessarily the ideal mentality for hosting a successful international competition.

But of much greater concern as the tournament approached was the state of our own team, and optimism was thin on the ground. The increasingly pragmatic style favoured by Alf Ramsey had delivered a series of workmanlike but uninspiring performances, leaving observers to conclude that England would be overwhelmed should they meet the exotic Brazilians or the highly fancied West Germans, to name but two.

Eric Batty, eccentric contributor to *World Soccer* and *Soccer Star* magazines, was at the extreme end of the pessimists but there were few who argued with his core sentiment. 'One thing is absolutely sure: the first time England meet a talented, well-balanced team, they will go out.' But worse still, and Batty was hardly unique amongst serious journalists, came the almost treacherous 'I do not want England to win!' His rationale was his 'certain knowledge that English football needs to be reformed and reorganised at almost every point, and to win the World Cup would set back these reforms.'

So whilst the tabloids were full of the jingoistic optimism that inevitably accompanied sporting events on home soil, there were plenty who had dismissed England's chances of serious progress and who felt it would be best for all concerned if we flopped dismally, took a long hard look at ourselves, and went back to the drawing board.

Some of this negativity emanated from the cool relationship between Ramsey and the press. Not naturally forthcoming and scarcely able to conceal his contempt for the Fleet Street pack and their lack of enthusiasm for his methods, Ramsey had exacerbated the position with his famous 'We will win the World Cup' quote shortly after his appointment in 1963. It wasn't made in a remotely boastful way, rather in defiance and irritation at journalists who even at the outset were doubting his and his team's credentials, but there were evidently more than a few in Fleet Street itching to throw the quote back in his face.

Of course, they never got the chance. England's triumph was met by incredulity by much of the press, many of whom had been forced to eat humble pie. And even the most positive reaction was often tempered by an element of disappointment at the team's style of play. For some, it still wasn't enough to have brought home football's greatest prize; what was needed was to have done it by playing a scintillating brand of football. There were acknowledgments aplenty for England's teamwork, effort, strength, fitness and courage, but through the superficial euphoria there was a clear sense of damning the team with faint praise. 'England's endeavour is enough' said one headline, with another broadsheet claiming that 'whatever the team may have lacked in skill it more than made up for it with the type of display that owed more to the British character than any special footballing prowess...' But at least we had played fair, and even the broadsheets couldn't resist a little dig at those nasty foreign types. 'Forgotten were the snivelling South Americans and their niggling football...'

More considered reflection led to the general conclusion that England had been worthy winners, even if it couldn't be denied that plenty of things had gone their way. Apart from having had home advantage, they benefitted from a crucial, controversial and probably incorrect decision in the final, from a refereeing display which incensed their Argentinian opponents in the quarter-final and from being drawn in what was widely reckoned to be the weakest qualifying group. They were also able to play all their matches at Wembley via a FIFA-approved loophole which allowed them to switch venues for the semi-final from Goodison Park, a ground with which their Portuguese opponents had by then become very familiar.

In terms of tactics, the cliché most associated with Ramsey's team is 'wingless wonders'. But whilst it's true that his team in the knockout stages may not have contained orthodox wingers as we knew them, the team certainly didn't lack width. The spaces on the flanks made available by his preferred formation were exploited time and again by the runs of Peters and Ball in particular, with Cohen and Wilson also frequently moving forward to overlap. Four of England's goals from open play throughout the tournament came from crosses, most tellingly Hurst's header from Peters' cross in the quarter-final and his 'was it over the line?' goal from Ball's surge down the right and low cross. The difference was that these crosses were provided by players moving into open space, rather than from the conventional touchline huggers who offered little to the team effort away from their own strictly demarcated zone.

It can instead be argued that the most significant call made by Ramsey wasn't the lack of wingers; instead it was the omission of possibly the most gifted player at his disposal in favour of one with a far greater work ethic. Yes, Jimmy Greaves had initially been injured; yes, Geoff Hurst had immediately made an impact with his quarter-final winner, and it made it easier for Ramsey to make what at the start of the tournament would have been a tumultuous decision. But Greaves' omission from the Final XI was still a hugely significant landmark, defining the shift in mentality from teams being selected as the best eleven players to the eleven players who would best fit into the system chosen by the manager.

An illustration of Ramsey's approach came when, after being selected for an important match, no-frills centre-half Jack Charlton reportedly asked, 'What am I doing here, Alf? I'm not the best centre-half in the country.' Ramsey responded: 'You're right, Jack, you're nowhere near the best centre-half. But you can do what I want you to do.' As did every one of England's players on that momentous July day.

But now, after recognising our achievement, however churlishly, it was time to look forward, and *The Guardian* set the tone. 'England, who gave the game to the world, are at last its champions and with it comes the challenge to set the lead.' So, month by month, at international, club, and individual level, how did we do?

1966/67:

United's Stepping Stone

AUGUST 1966

The nation's football fans had just two weeks to recover from the World Cup celebrations before the domestic programme got under way with the Charity Shield. The all-Merseyside affair took place at Anfield in front of a capacity 63,000 crowd, who were treated to the sight of the Jules Rimet trophy being paraded around the ground before the game began. Roger Hunt settled the issue with a fierce twenty-five-yarder, with champions Liverpool running out more comfortable winners than the 1-0 scoreline indicated. Reports on the match suggested that Everton needed strengthening in midfield if they were to become serious players again, and Harry Catterick evidently shared the sentiment; just two days later, they signed Alan Ball from Blackpool, reportedly from under Leeds United's noses, for a handsome £110,000. Even though the fee was a record between British clubs, there were few if any who queried whether Ball would deliver value for money. At just twenty-one, he had been one of England's major successes of the tournament and was clearly destined for many more great things.

The real action began seven days later and hopes that the World Cup feelgood factor would bring the fans flocking back received a serious reality check. Overall attendances throughout the four divisions were down 70,000 on the previous year, producing the lowest opening-day aggregate since the war. There were mitigating features – it was a swelteringly hot day and the Oval Test match between England and Gary Sobers' West Indies was being televised live – but there were a number of disappointing turnouts, even at grounds where members of Ramsey's triumphant XI would be on display.

At Upton Park, the golden triumvirate of Moore, Hurst and Peters took the field alone to receive the thunderous applause of the crowd. Once the other nineteen players entered the arena, Chelsea rather spoiled the occasion by chalking up a 2-1 victory, due largely to the brilliance of Peter Bonetti in goal. 'We will not meet him every week,' observed Ron Greenwood with undeniable accuracy. Some were surprised that they had even met him at all, given Chelsea's signing of Alex Stepney during the summer, but it was a great start for Bonetti in his battle to retain his place in the side.

At Old Trafford, just 41,000 turned up to recognise World Cup winners Charlton and Stiles, but this wasn't the only thing on the pre-match agenda – Charlton had also been named as the previous season's Footballer Of The Year. United generously chose to mark his achievement by presenting him with a coffee table, a silver coffee set and a canteen of cutlery. The prospect of a few gentle afternoons on Nescafe and Battenburg *chez* Bob and Norma clearly inspired his team-mates, as with just twenty minutes on the clock they had romped into a 4-1 lead, en route to a 5-3 win. This early suggestion that both teams were rather stronger in attack than defence would prove to be well founded.

The day's outstanding individual performance was Gordon Harris's hat-trick for Burnley against Sheffield United, in front of a crowd of less than 18,000. Southampton's eagerly awaited top-flight debut brought disappointment when the fixtures computer put them up against partners in promotion Manchester City, but even so they would have expected rather more than 19,000 to turn out for such an historic occasion, particularly with expensive new signing Ron Davies on display. Those present at least witnessed the Saints' first ever top-flight goal, fittingly scored by Terry Paine, well on the way to becoming the club's record appearance holder.

Southampton had reacted to the tactical nuances of the World Cup by changing the way the team line-ups were presented in their programme. Manager Ted Bates said: 'We need to check all the propaganda about wingless wonders and the rest. We need to impress on supporters that modern techniques need not be dull or boring. And we need to educate people away from the idea of a goalkeeper, two full-backs, three half-backs and five forwards. That is in the past.' Gone was the 1-2-3-5 presentation of the two teams, replaced by a simple list of one to eleven, plus a substitute.

Other World Cup winners had mixed opening-day fortunes; at Craven Cottage, Alan Ball's debut goal delivered victory for Everton, enabling Ray Wilson to get one over his full-back partner George Cohen's Fulham, whilst Roger Hunt put one past Gordon Banks at Anfield to help Liverpool to a 3-2 win over Leicester. Jack Charlton was forced to sit out Leeds' visit to White Hart Lane, where he witnessed Jimmy Greaves seal Spurs' 3-1 victory.

Greaves was one of few Englishmen – other than certain po-faced journalists – for whom the World Cup Final had been a painful occasion, and many wondered whether his England career was now over. He would never acquire the work ethic so prized by Ramsey – and with his record at club and international level, why should he change? – so all he could do to get back in the side was use sheer weight of goals. Putting one past one of the division's meanest defences was a decent way to start. It was a happy debut for Spurs' new centre-half Mike England and this was also the match which delivered one of the decade's most iconic sporting photographs, with Dave Mackay, biceps bulging like Desperate Dan, literally picking up Billy Bremner by his shirt front and leaving him in no doubt as to what a *real* hard man looked like.

Whilst opening-day live attendances may have disappointed, at least *Match Of The Day* posted record viewing figures, although this was primarily due to the switch to BBC One, opening the programme up to a significantly wider audience in a time slot which it would immediately make its own.

Launched in August 1964, *Match Of The Day* had previously been running for two seasons on BBC 2, a channel to which only a small proportion of the population had access. Viewing figures had gradually improved from the meagre 20,000 who tuned in to the first transmission, but had remained relatively modest. Some ITV regions had also showed highlights of games involving their local teams on Sunday afternoons, but coverage had been intermittent and by no means nationwide.

But the World Cup immediately changed everything. It had been covered to saturation point by television, with the BBC paying £300,000 to deliver a full fifty hours of coverage over the three weeks. ITV provided a further fifteen hours of live action, including the final itself – as with the FA Cup Final, they felt obliged to duplicate coverage even though their share of viewers was small, and surely smaller than would have been achieved if an alternative programme catering for those with little interest in football (plus the Scots) had been offered. England's success had ensured that overall viewing figures were spectacular, further illustrating to the TV companies the potential audience for televised football.

But even this feast of football for the public at large had been greeted with some negativity. The Football League, and many club directors, were concerned that the cultivation of an army of armchair viewers would increase the likelihood of even more televised football, which in turn would simply encourage people to tune into the highlights at home rather than going out to watch the real thing.

So, with the World Cup having broadened the potential audience for football, it was an opportunity for the BBC to build on the enhanced level of interest, and even to cultivate some of the female viewers who had found themselves engulfed by World Cup fever. Although that, according to some, would be as far as it would go. 'Football's new admirers amongst the female fraternity may still enjoy the occasional match on television, but just try to drag them along to your local ground in mid-December with snow on the ground and a bitter wind blowing…' was a typical sentiment. Some clubs were at least prepared to have a go – Brentford and Charlton Athletic offered half-price season tickets for women, with Coventry City offering instruction on the intricacies of the offside rule and other such complicated matters.

Highlights of the first midweek programme saw two goals from the languid and extravagantly talented Peter Osgood prove enough for Chelsea to see off Nottingham Forest, whilst a brace from Denis Law secured a win for United at Goodison Park. Their newly promoted neighbours also made headlines, beating Liverpool with a late goal from the highly promising twenty-year-old, Colin Bell. The press lauded City for a 'magnificent display of fast, attacking football' and noted that even the referee applauded them from the field.

The following Saturday saw the first league tables produced, and Burnley – a side which had punched well above its weight in the decade so far, with a title and four other top-four finishes – led the way, together with Arsenal. Both had begun with three straight wins, although the Highbury attendance of just 26,000 for the visit of Villa suggested that new manager Bertie Mee and coach Dave Sexton had work to do to win over the fans who had drifted away from Highbury following the mediocrity of recent seasons. Billy Wright's three-year tenure had been completely disastrous, both in terms of quality of football and attendances.

Just a week into the new season came the first observations of teams taking tactical note of England's methods, and Sheffield Wednesday were roundly criticised for their stifling display in a goalless draw at Stamford Bridge. Their initial formation was a clear 4-3-3, although as the game progressed and a precious point became ever closer, this was transformed into 4-4-2 and ultimately 5-4-1. Chelsea didn't help themselves by lining up without an orthodox winger, and one reporter noted that 'the flanks at Stamford Bridge were open spaces ready for property development'. Events some forty years later show him to have been only a few yards wide of the mark.

Blackpool's home defeat to newly promoted Southampton, coupled with continuing disgruntlement at the sale of their prize asset, led to the season's first fan demonstration, with protesters gathering outside the ground after the game. Their plight paled in comparison to fourth-division Barnsley, who had also started the season with three straight defeats and were reportedly £43,000 in debt. This prompted a fifteen-year-old schoolboy to visit the club's offices and donate his week's spending money – a two-shilling piece – as a contribution to help his beloved club find a new striker. Rather than thanking the boy and declining his offer the money was gratefully accepted, with the club secretary expressing the wish that there were 20,000 more like him. Only in Yorkshire…

Match Of The Month
27 August 1966, Division One: Leicester City 5 West Ham United 4

Leicester's first home game of the season gave their fans the chance to recognise the contribution made by Gordon Banks to England's triumphant summer and, with the opposition boasting the scorers of all four final goals as well as the team captain, it seemed wholly appropriate that the four heroes should emerge from the tunnel alone to receive the rapturous applause of the crowd.

The match that followed fully lived up to the celebratory mood. Leicester stormed ahead, with Derek Dougan continuing his prolific start to the season, before Jackie Sinclair added a second. The action intensified in the second half with five goals in a fifteen-minute spell, initiated by Peter Brabrook's strike. Sinclair immediately restored Leicester's two-goal lead, but Brabrook took only a few more minutes to reply once more. Two more goals within sixty seconds from Goodfellow and Hurst followed and the game was in the balance until Sinclair completed his hat-trick ten minutes from time.

Hurst's late goal was too late to give West Ham any realistic chance of completing a comeback, and West Ham's World Cup stars had returned from their Wembley euphoria to start their club campaign with three straight defeats. Manager Ron Greenwood was naturally unhappy, but wouldn't be changing his team's approach. 'Our job is to entertain and win points. At the moment, we are only doing half of it.'

Of all the teams in the top flight, West Ham were the least likely to be swayed by the success of 'method' football, and in consequence would endure plenty of humbling defeats to go with the stellar triumphs. Subsequent occasional attempts to change their DNA have generally failed.

Leicester: Banks, Rodrigues, Sjoberg, Cross, Norman, Roberts, Sinclair, Gibson, Goodfellow, Dougan, Gibson.

West Ham: Standen, Burnett, Moore, Charles, Bovington, Peters, Boyce, Brabrook, Hurst, Byrne, Sissons.

Player Of The Month
Alan Ball (Everton)

Ball's outstanding performances in the World Cup, coupled with his burning ambition, made it inevitable that he would move to a bigger club than Blackpool, and just seventeen days after running the Germans ragged at Wembley he signed for Everton for £110,000. At just twenty-one, this was a record transfer fee between British clubs. His impact was immediate as Everton, bidding to regain the title they won two years earlier, began the season in great style. Ball's debut at Craven Cottage saw him score the game's only goal, and he followed it up with an outstanding if ultimately futile display at home to Manchester United, where Law's two goals took the spoils. After just two games, press reporters were marking Ball down as by far his new team's most influential player. 'Ball foraged, harassed and inspired…but he cannot be everywhere nor do everything on his own. Until his colleagues react with equal facility, Everton will suffer frustration…' Three days later, any such frustration was banished as Ball scored twice to condemn Liverpool to defeat in the Merseyside derby and establish himself in Everton folklore within a fortnight of his arrival.

Ball's season continued as it began, with an impressive eighteen goals supplementing his high-energy contribution to the team's efforts. By the time the Mexico World Cup came round, his status as one of the country's outstanding players had been firmly cemented, and received tangible reward with Everton's comprehensive championship win of 1969/70. Over the four seasons, he contributed sixty-eight goals for his club and his performances for England ensured his status as an untouchable member of Ramsey's first XI. He played in all four of England's games in Mexico, but his performances were hampered by the high altitude, and his impact on the tournament was less telling than many had hoped and expected.

A year later, Ball broke the British transfer record for the second time, when double winners Arsenal paid £220,000 for his services. Ball would continue to perform with impressive consistency for his new club, but found himself in an ageing team whose best days were behind them, and his five seasons at Highbury failed to deliver any silverware. Two spells at Southampton bookended a short stint back at Bloomfield Road, this time as player-manager, together with a foray into the North American Soccer League.

Ball turned to management after his playing career was over, but with generally disastrous results. For supporters of the clubs concerned – particularly Manchester City – this has cast a shadow over his name and reputation, but his impact on the game as a player, both for club and country, was immense and he was without question one of the most influential and memorable footballers of the late 1960s and early 1970s. His sheer enthusiasm for the game made him stand out as much as his ginger hair and white boots, and he was much loved not only by supporters of the teams he played for, but also the football public at large.

SEPTEMBER 1966

By the first weekend of September, the celebratory mood surrounding English football had given way to a dose of reality, as the weekend's matches throughout the divisions were tarnished by violence on and off the pitch.

At Burnley, a brutal clash between Burnley and Leeds – a fixture with plenty of previous – was dubbed the 'Battle of Turf Moor', but the five bookings on the pitch were overshadowed by the behaviour off it, as the referee threatened to abandon the match when Burnley fans continued to hurl missiles at Gary Sprake and his fellow defenders. At West Ham, a Liverpool supporter threw a bottle on to the pitch, which smashed close to Jim Standen, the West Ham keeper. There were scuffles reported at lower-league grounds as well, with an inescapable sense that the football hooligan movement, already seen to a limited but increasing extent in previous seasons, was now gathering scale and momentum. But why was it happening?

Reports tended to link the trouble on the terraces to player behaviour on the pitch, in turn leading for calls for stricter refereeing and more stringent punishments for offenders. But whilst there was evidence that on-field flashpoints were mirrored or reacted to by spectators, it was only part of the story. Away fans were arriving early and setting themselves up with the intention of 'taking' the home end, and with no scope for segregation within grounds and all but a handful of games being pay at the gate for standing spectators, police and stewards could do little to prevent the inevitable premeditated trouble.

On a particularly bleak Saturday, the press wasted little time in bemoaning the lack of goals and entertainment, noting that eight of the day's top-flight games had ended in stalemate, seven of them 1-1. The conclusion that cautious defensive football was taking ever more of a grip was easily reached, and with a catalogue of violent incidents both on and off the pitch, it was a chance to put some of the little Englanders in their place. There was an almost smug 'told you so...' tone about some of the reporting, with *The Times* in particular quick to put the boot in. 'The pious mouthings about the Argentines and Rattin at Wembley five weeks ago now find their true perspective.'

Attendances remained disappointing, the reports of trouble on the terraces deterring some of those – especially women – whose interest in football had been stimulated by the World Cup and who were curious as to what the live football experience was like. But another factor was the difficult economic climate, with the country in the middle of a six-month pay freeze. Coventry, with its thousands of car workers, had been particularly affected by the tough conditions and their team's manager, Jimmy Hill, understood that what was offered on the pitch needed to be attractive in order for people to feel it was worth parting with what little spare cash they had. Hill also recognised the role of football as a means of escapism. 'We have got to provide the sort of football that will make people forget that they are broke.'

Back on the pitch, the first Manchester derby for three years saw United secure a relatively untroubled victory, albeit by the only goal. Their new goalkeeper, Alex Stepney, signed for a record £55,000 after just one league game and three months at Chelsea, had few chances to display his credentials but at least could look forward to the regular first-team football denied him by Peter Bonetti's excellent start to the season.

Arsenal and Bertie Mee's unbeaten start came to a shuddering halt at the home of their bitterest rivals, with Jimmy Greaves continuing to exorcise the memory of his World Cup disappointment by bagging two goals. The following week saw Greaves at it again, as he netted a late winner to seal Spurs' come-from-behind win against Manchester United, prompting a pitch invasion at the end of the game. United were always a big scalp, especially for Spurs, who had been involved in several epic encounters with them in recent years. When Spurs next went to Burnley and secured a point in a 2-2 draw, Greaves scored one and made one, and his prolific form led to plenty of speculation that his England career might still have legs. But having achieved ultimate success with his total work ethic, could Ramsey be persuaded to once again embrace Greaves' ethereal qualities?

For now, though, Ramsey's concern was the selection of his Football League XI, traditionally made up of fringe players together with under-23 regulars reckoned to have the potential to make the full squad. Amongst the latter group on this occasion were Tommy Smith of Liverpool, Mike Summerbee of Manchester City and Peter Osgood of Chelsea. Still just nineteen years old, Osgood had produced a string of outstanding performances in his debut season prior to the World Cup, causing the London press to petition for his inclusion in the tournament squad. Whilst Ramsey had predictably ignored such appeals, he could hardly fail to notice Osgood's continuing excellence at the start of the new season and a breakthrough into the senior ranks seemed imminent.

Osgood took a back seat at Villa Park, where a remarkable performance from Bobby Tambling saw him bag five goals in Chelsea's 6-2 victory, yet even that wasn't the day's highest-scoring fixture. At Goodison Park, a Ball-inspired Everton squeezed past West Brom in a nine-goal thriller. The lines about the dominance of defensive tactics, so prevalent in press comment in the season's opening weeks, were quietly put to one side as the day's eleven division one fixtures produced no fewer than forty-four goals.

The Football League XI duly took on the Irish League at Plymouth in front of over 35,000 fans, and a strong side – featuring the back four plus Martin Peters and Geoff Hurst of the World Cup Final team – strolled to a 12-0 win in the most pointless of pointless fixtures. Johnny Byrne scored four times, whilst John Connelly set up six goals as well as scoring a couple himself. Irish goalkeeper Albert Finney said: 'Let me get back to my power station where I work as a steeplejack. I'll be safer 200 feet above ground than I was against these English forwards…'

The Steel City was relishing having both their teams in the top flight, and the season's first derby produced a thrilling 2-2 draw in front of 43,000 fans. United's scorers were Alan Woodward and centre-forward Mick Jones, whilst Jim McCalliog helped to inspire Wednesday's revival. Meanwhile, Burnley's title pretensions were cast into serious question at Old Trafford, where they were on the wrong end of a 4-1 hammering.

Moving along impressively were Leicester City, unbeaten since the opening day of the season and far too good for an Aston Villa side looking set for a relegation struggle. Leicester's 5-0 win included a hat-trick from former Villa striker Derek Dougan, one of the game's genuine mavericks, but one whose ability usually allowed him to get away with some of his eccentric behaviour.

By the end of the month, Chelsea remained unbeaten and stood at the top of the table. This was good news in every way for the Chelsea squad, who received a well-publicised bonus of £55 a man for every week that their team sat on top of the pile. Tommy Docherty had taken up the Ramsey template, telling anyone who would listen that there was no place for wingers in the modern game. His team's playing style was observed as 'high mobility, overlapping with no orthodox wingers,' with Osgood feted as an original, creative artist.

Another original creative artist was making waves in the depths of division three, where Queens Park Rangers looked as though they would be taking the division by storm. Their 7-1 win at Mansfield included a hat-trick from Rodney Marsh, taking his goal tally for the season up to fourteen, clearly suggesting a career destined for a much higher level than this.

Match Of The Month
17 September, 1966, Division One: Burnley 2 Tottenham 2

Spurs, with five wins in their first seven games, arrived at Turf Moor to face a Burnley side that remained unbeaten, even though their previous five games had been drawn. With Spurs struggling to shed their soft-touch travellers' tag and Burnley's crowd making up for in hostility what it lacked in numbers, a home win looked the most likely outcome.

Jimmy Greaves had other ideas. Having come back from his World Cup disappointment in stirring style, most recently with his late winner against Manchester United the previous week, Greaves was at his mesmerising best. Just before the half-hour, he slalomed past three Burnley defenders before dinking the ball across for Frank Saul to head Spurs into the lead.

Burnley had plenty of attacking invention of their own, with Willie Morgan regularly getting the better of Cyril Knowles and Ralph Coates furthering his reputation as an energetic, inventive player of real promise. They had already hit the bar before Morgan crossed for Andy Lochhead to force home an equaliser. Two more goals were shared before half-time, a typically clinical finish from Greaves followed quickly by an equally typical Lochhead header, glanced in at the near post from a corner.

The crowd gave both teams a standing ovation as they left the field at half-time, and although the second half failed to deliver more goals, there was plenty of stylish football to enjoy. Spurs followed up with three straight wins, taking them temporarily to the top of the table; for Burnley, the next game saw them hammered at Old Trafford, but they went on to win seven of their next eight before their season fell away sharply.

Burnley: Blacklaw, Angus, Elder, O'Neil, Miller, Todd, Morgan, Lochhead, Irvine, Harris, Coates.

Tottenham: Jennings, Kinnear, Knowles, Mullery, England, Mackay, Robertson, Greaves, Gilzean, Venables, Saul.

Player Of The Month
Bobby Tambling (Chelsea)

Bobby Tambling made his debut for Chelsea as a seventeen-year-old in 1959, and by the start of the 1966/67 season was homing in on the record as their all-time leading goalscorer. He made significant progress towards this target in September, opening the month with a goal in the 3-0 win at the Dell and tucking away another in a 6-2 hammering of Charlton in the League Cup. The month ended with Chelsea top of the league courtesy of a 3-1 win over Arsenal, with Tambling scoring twice, the second and clinching goal quite superb as he spun off Ian Ure on to Osgood's raking pass, used his pace to hold off two other defenders and smashed the ball high into the net. But his month will be recalled primarily for just one match, away at Villa Park.

A game chosen for the *Match Of The Day* cameras, Kenneth Wolstenholme and some five million viewers saw Tambling break the scoring record for the programme by netting five times in Chelsea's 6-2 win. With their skilful, slick passing Chelsea continually broke away to cut through Villa's defence and Tambling repeatedly found himself on the end of scoring chances. The pick of his goals was the second, latching on to Osgood's clever pass and cutting in from the left to bury a drive past Withers. He had completed his hat-trick by half-time and added another two in the second half as Chelsea coasted their way to an emphatic win. Tambling continued in prolific vein over the next few months, with his final goal of the season, albeit a consolation, coming in the FA Cup Final against Spurs.

Tambling would indeed go on to break Chelsea's scoring record and by the time he moved on to Crystal Palace in 1970 – squeezed out of regular first-team action by the emergence of Ian Hutchinson – he had netted 202 times for the Blues. His record would stand for over forty years until Frank Lampard overtook it, although Tambling's club record of league goals, 164, is still intact.

Tambling's England career was brief. He earned his first cap in November 1962 and scored his only international goal in Alf Ramsey's first game, a 5-2 defeat to France in 1963. His third and final cap came in England's final warm-up game for the 1966 World Cup, at home to Yugoslavia, raising hopes that he might sneak into the final twenty-two, but ultimately he failed to make the cut. A true Chelsea legend, Tambling was voted into the club's all-time best XI in a poll carried out in 2005 to mark the club's centenary.

OCTOBER 1966

England's first full international since the World Cup Final saw them face Ireland in Belfast in the home internationals. This match doubled as a qualifying game for the 1968 European Nations Cup and saw Ramsey select the same XI which had written itself into history just over two months earlier. A routine 2-0 win was greeted with lukewarm press reaction, with journalists continuing their theme of demanding victory with style and flair. A merger of the Brazil '58 team with the Magnificent Magyars of '53 might just have satisfied a press who found it difficult to accept that Ramsey was getting the best from the tools at his disposal. Anyone who had spent the month of July living in a cave would have been hard pushed to believe that the team being written about had just been crowned champions of the world.

With all the home nations in action, as well as Eire, there were only four first division games, as clubs with two or more players selected for national squads could apply to the FA to have their match postponed. Alf selected twenty-two players for his squad, which was bad news financially for clubs forced to postpone games from Saturday to typically less well-attended midweek dates. It was a damning indictment of Arsenal's current status that theirs was one of the few games to be played. Worse still, they fell to a 3-2 home defeat to West Brom, in a match which saw Bob McNab make his Arsenal debut.

In the remaining fixtures, much the most remarkable result was lowly Blackpool's 6-0 rout of Newcastle. After starting the season looking like relegation certainties, Blackpool had suddenly come to vivid life, with this win following an equally remarkable triumph at White Hart Lane. A flash in the pan or proof that there really was life after Alan Ball?

The next full league programme saw an extraordinary fifty goals in the day's top-flight fixtures, with no fewer than seven matches seeing at least one team score four goals. If this was defensive football, please could we have more of it? After cementing their position at the summit with a crushing 4-1 win at Maine Road, Chelsea next travelled to Blackpool for a League Cup tie. Midway through the first half, a crunching tackle between two nineteen-year-olds – Emlyn Hughes and Peter Osgood – left the latter lying on the turf with a badly broken leg.

There was no suggestion of any malicious intent on Hughes' part, but there was consternation from Osgood's team-mates at the fact that his opponent had walked away with not a backward glance nor any sense of concern for the stricken player. Hughes' own career would soon assume an upward trajectory, although based on the memoirs of many of his contemporaries – not least his future team-mates at Anfield – he was a less than universally popular figure. Many years later, Osgood would give his own perspective: 'I bear no grudge against Hughes. My leg got better – he's still got that silly fucking voice…'

In the Football League Cup, there was a highly anticipated tie between the two highest scoring teams in the whole of the league – QPR and Leicester City. A crowd of over 20,000 produced record gate receipts at Loftus Road and a thrilling comeback saw Rangers recover from conceding two goals to Derek Dougan, ultimately prevailing 4-2. With their opponents standing sixth in the first division table, it was a famous victory for Alec Stock's team – and there would soon be more to come.

Another ambitious third division club was Oldham Athletic. Under the chairmanship of a young Ken Bates, they had spent a tidy sum in assembling a team fit to challenge for promotion to the next tier. Bates had been unapologetically forthright about how the funds would need to be recouped – the locals would need to stump up higher admission charges – but the team's success on the pitch meant that plenty of them were willing to do so, with crowds in excess of 10,000 regularly passing through the Boundary Park turnstiles.

One of Bates' innovations was to give away a free programme on admittance to the ground. The programme itself – *The*

Boundary Bulletin – was way ahead of anything produced at most other Football League clubs, packed with information, features and pictures. It was more magazine than programme and also served as a vehicle for the already less than shy and retiring chairman to give both barrels to those foolish enough to provoke him. In the programme for the visit of Torquay United, he flayed the visitors for refusing to accommodate his request for an evening kick-off. Bates no doubt permitted himself a quietly satisfied smile in the boardroom after the game as the Latics battered their Devonian visitors 5-0.

Bates was clearly not a man to be cowed by reputations, as he showed when Burnley's Bob Lord – a bombastic FA bigwig – dared to opine on Oldham's transfer dealings in a less than complimentary fashion. The following week's *Boundary Bulletin* featured a two-page centre spread listing a series of quotes made by Lord over the years, ridiculing his opinions and predictions. It amounted to an extraordinary tirade by Bates, a taste of much more to come as his career assumed a higher profile over the next forty years.

At Maine Road, successive batterings at the hands of Chelsea and West Ham had led City's brash young coach, Malcolm Allison, to conclude that healthy diets alone would be no guarantee of top-flight success, or even survival. The team wasn't short of quality, but was proving too easy to play against. Against his naturally attacking instincts, he persuaded boss Joe Mercer to adopt more cautious tactics. However, rather than adopting the Ramsey template, he instead again turned to Italy for inspiration and introduced a sweeper into his team formation. Tony Book, the team captain plucked from obscurity with non-league Bath, took up the role.

The immediate aftermath of Osgood's injury saw Chelsea give up their unbeaten record in a home defeat to Burnley, and shortly afterwards Docherty called for reinforcements with the signing of Tony Hateley from Aston Villa for £100,000. Villa had previously turned down bids from both Arsenal and Liverpool for the striker, as they held out for their six-figure valuation.

Hateley made his debut at home to Spurs, but it was the man he had replaced in the starting eleven who would make the headlines.

The use of substitutes was now into its second season, although they were only allowed in cases where the referee was satisfied that a player was unable to continue. The very concept of making a substitution for purely tactical reasons wasn't just against the rules but regarded as underhand, almost as cheating. Once a manager had selected his side, he had made his bed and would have to lie on it – why should he get another bite of the cherry if things weren't going as planned?

Tommy Baldwin had been relegated to the bench by Hateley's inclusion, but came out at the start of the second half to replace Peter Houseman. Baldwin duly scored twice in Chelsea's 3-0 win, but a 'Tottenham official' later queried the substitution with the Football League. It was becoming increasingly evident that the 'halfway house' of substitutions only for injury was impractical; how could referees judge whether a player was fit to continue or not? So either allow them for any reason or don't have them at all.

There were advocates of both options, with many still of the view that injuries were just part of the game and that we should go back to the good old days. Those days where games were ruined as a spectacle when a team was reduced to ten men through no fault of their own. Those days when injured players would often struggle on, damaging themselves still further and making their subsequent recovery period even longer. The reluctance of many in the game, particularly its administrators, to embrace change – even when patently for the good – remained deep-rooted.

Houseman, perhaps diplomatically, was left out of Chelsea's next game, at Fulham, which produced Hateley's first contributions of note, his two goals including what it was hoped would become a trademark towering header. Another striker becoming increasingly renowned for aerial feats was Southampton's Ron Davies, who continued his remarkable scoring streak by netting for the ninth consecutive league game. This one was the most important and eye-catching of the lot, securing a shock win for Southampton at Elland Road.

The next striker to move for big money was Ron's unrelated namesake Wyn Davies, signed from Bolton by a desperately struggling Newcastle side. His debut could hardly have gone worse, with Sunderland cruising to a 3-0 win at St James' Park. Things got a little better in their next home game as a poor Manchester City side were beaten 2-0, but a crowd of only 16,000 rattling around the famous old ground showed how disillusioned the Tyneside public had become. So recently regarded as England's hotbed of football, the North East may have given birth to two of the more notable stars of Ramsey's team, but not one of the side – or even the full twenty-two-man squad – played for any of the local clubs. Roker and Ayresome Parks had been used as World Cup venues, hosting the North Koreans, but the turnouts had been much the lowest of the four groups as the tournament almost seemed to pass the region by.

The dark spectre of hooliganism again raised its head. Manchester United fans at the City Ground disgraced themselves, their moods not helped by their team finding itself 4-0 down after an hour, with Chris Crowe netting a hat-trick. Reports of trouble at other grounds went as far down as Southern League Wealdstone, and clubs started to take measures to at least control the epidemic. West Ham responded to trouble at the Liverpool game by banning bottles from the ground and Millwall increased their prices for juveniles. Chelsea would soon follow suit, the increases closing the door to many working-class youngsters whose interest in football had been stimulated by the World Cup. At Turf Moor, where visiting goalkeepers had routinely been pelted by missiles, Burnley fenced off the areas immediately behind the goals.

Down in the fourth division, Barnsley were still deeply in debt and struggling. Having failed to accumulate sufficient contributions from local schoolboys' pocket money, they now went out with a share offer intended to raise £40,000. The offer failed to whet the appetite of the circumspect potential local investors, raising just £1,635. 'What we really need is a millionaire,' said chairman Sir Joseph Richards. It sounded an outlandish sentiment at the time...

Match Of The Month
22 October 1966, Division One: Blackpool 6 Newcastle United 0

With no wins from their first eleven games of the season, Blackpool looked relegation certainties even as early as the middle of October. But they then produced a shock result at White Hart Lane and followed it up with a League Cup win over Chelsea. When a struggling Newcastle side arrived at Bloomfield Road, it was a great chance for Blackpool's season to really gather momentum.

Fans who had seen their team take just one point from the opening six home games received rich compensation as they witnessed a four-goal salvo before half-time. Midfielder Ian Moir set things off with a screaming early goal from a narrow angle, and then doubled the lead with a header. Alan Skirton and Ray Charnley – Blackpool's third highest scorer of all time – doubled the advantage before the interval.

Jimmy Robson added a fifth before Skirton, recently signed from Arsenal and making his home debut, completed the scoring. It was a remarkable all-round team performance from Blackpool, especially considering the absence of long-serving captain Jimmy Armfield, with keeper Tony Waiters playing an important role with two great saves from Bryan Robson before the match was out of Newcastle's reach.

The result raised hopes that Blackpool might be able to get themselves clear of the mire, but it proved to be one of few bright spots in a harrowing season. The devastating defeat set Newcastle on a run of just one win in twelve – including a crushing 3-0 loss at home to Sunderland just a week later – and their first division future would stay in the balance until a late-season surge brought them to safety.

Blackpool: Waiters, Thompson, Hughes, Fisher, McPhee, Rowe, Skirton, Robson, Charnley, Moir, Lea.

Newcastle: Hollins, Craggs, Clark, Moncur, Thompson, Iley, Robson, Bennett, McGarry, Suddick, Knox.

Player Of The Month
Allan Clarke (Fulham)

Signed from Walsall in March 1966, Clarke turned twenty the day after the World Cup Final and although it took him a few months to adapt to the higher level, October saw this tall, lean striker announce himself as a major talent. He drilled home a twenty-yarder to give his team a briefly held lead against Spurs and, four days later, hit two more as Fulham demolished Wolves in a League Cup tie. He then impressed at Anfield by scoring twice in Fulham's creditable 2-2 draw, the second a brilliant individual effort that showed him to be more than just a penalty box predator. Benefitting from the vacancy created by Peter Osgood's broken leg, Clarke was next selected to make his debut for the England under-23 team and helped himself to four goals in the 8-0 rout of Wales. In an outstanding performance, he could have scored even more and was also praised for his unselfishness in setting up opportunities for others.

Just three days later came another two goals, this time what would become trademark tap-ins, as Fulham dispatched West Ham 4-2. Eleven goals in the month cemented Clarke's burgeoning status and he went on to score twenty-four league goals in the season, a particularly impressive total for a struggling team and his best return of his entire career.

Another prolific season followed, but Fulham's relegation saw Clarke immediately seek a move. Indeed, before the Mexico World Cup dawned, Clarke had twice broken the British transfer record, moving to Leicester for £150,000 then, on their own demotion a year later, to Leeds for an additional £15,000. His brief stay at Filbert Street still saw him make a significant impact as, despite the team's difficulties, he helped them to the FA Cup Final, most notably by scoring the winner in the semi-final. At Wembley, unusually for a player on the losing side, he was named man of the match.

Clarke immediately fitted in at Elland Road, forming a formidable strike partnership with Mick Jones, and continued to win representative honours. He was included in the final twenty-two to travel to Mexico and made his full international debut in the game against Czechoslovakia, marking the occasion by coolly slotting home a penalty for the only goal of the game, thereby securing England's progression to the quarter-finals.

Clarke featured regularly for England in the early 1970s, ultimately winning nineteen caps and scoring ten goals. It is, however, his exploits at Leeds for which he will be most remembered, scoring the winning goal in the Centenary Cup Final in 1972 before helping his side win the league championship two years later. Like most Leeds players in the Revie era, Clarke had a darker side to his game and was noted in particular for his tendency to leave his foot in on goalkeepers who dived at his feet. Nevertheless, he was one of the top strikers of his era although, despite all his achievements with Leeds, he would never again enjoy a month of such individual success as in October 1966.

NOVEMBER 1966

Big centre-forwards remained in demand, despite the tactical evolution making them less of a focal point for at least some of the first division teams. The latest to move for a sizeable fee was John Ritchie, with Sheffield Wednesday paying £70,000 to take him away from a Stoke side which had started the season impressively. The move was a surprise, but Stoke manager Tony Waddington had expressed a desire to play a more 'modern' type of football, less reliant on lumping the ball up to the big man up front.

The month began with England's first game at Wembley since their World Cup win, a friendly against Czechoslovakia.

It was an obvious chance to give one or two younger players a taste of full international action, but with the game serving largely as a warm-up for the Nations Cup qualifier against Wales, Ramsey's innate caution, coupled perhaps with a desire to allow the Wembley crowd to pay tribute to the conquering heroes without exception, meant he again fielded exactly the same XI. The 75,000 crowd witnessed a goalless draw, due partly to the visitors' lack of attacking ambition but mainly to England's poor finishing and the brilliant goalkeeping of Ivo Victor. England's thirty-two goal attempts included thirteen on target but despite build-up play later described by Ramsey as 'sheer poetry', they couldn't find a way through. Roger Hunt in particular had a night to forget, with suggestions aplenty that he might prove to be the first of the glorious XI to lose his place in the team.

Hunt cheered himself up by scoring twice in Liverpool's 4-0 rout of a still inconsistent Forest team, but the day's big match was at Stamford Bridge, where Manchester United put on an ominously strong display to come away with a 3-1 win. Young winger John Aston, in for the injured Denis Law not for the first or last time, scored twice.

West Ham were proving as watchable as ever. After crushing Fulham 6-1 and then, two days later, annihilating Leeds 7-0 in the League Cup, they next travelled to White Hart Lane, where 57,000 spectators witnessed yet another seven-goal deluge. This time the Hammers contented themselves with just four of them, still enough for an eye-catching victory with their four forwards – Brabrook, Sissons, Byrne and Hurst – all getting on the scoresheet. It was a magnificent match which even the watching Alf Ramsey – not noted as a man particularly partial to seven-goal thrillers – described as 'tremendous', though what he thought about the defending is not recorded.

The fixture, described by *The Times* as 'a game fit for the Gods', had originally been scheduled for coverage on *Match Of The Day*, a programme whose move to BBC One had already proved to be a resounding success, but the BBC decreed that there were certain events which would be an even greater draw for viewers. One of these was the world heavyweight boxing championship. Cassius Clay was far more popular in the UK than in his homeland and he had already achieved iconic status with his skill and unique charisma. His performance in beating Cleveland Williams on this evening would come to be regarded as his finest of the first phase of his career. But this wasn't what BBC viewers deprived of their football actually saw. Instead, they were treated merely to a preview of the fight together with highlights of Ali's previous bout, against Karl Mildenburger. At least London-based viewers could enjoy the thrilla at White Hart Lane, with ITV stepping in to record the game for their Sunday afternoon slot.

After a slow start to the season, Liverpool were moving into top gear, following up the demolition of Forest by winning at Newcastle and then crushing Leeds 5-0 at Anfield. Leeds' rapid rise under Revie had been secured primarily by defensive organisation, coupled with an extremely physical and uncompromising style of play. Their ruthless approach was as far removed from the beautiful game as had been seen in English club football, and there were plenty who hoped that their second humiliation in two weeks might be the start of a more permanent decline. Revie had openly lamented his failure to land Alan Ball, although the lengths to which he went to lure the player to Elland Road wouldn't become widely known until the publication of Ball's autobiography many years later. Similar tales of mysterious strangers bearing cash-filled brown envelopes would reoccur time and again throughout and after Revie's career.

The month's most reported outbreak of hooliganism occurred at Maine Road, where visiting Everton fans created havoc and bloodshed when the referee disallowed a goal, ironically because he was so busy clearing away the rolls of toilet paper thrown by the fans themselves that he hadn't signalled for the corner to be taken. 'I've never seen so much blood,' said City director Sidney Rose afterwards. 'And I'm a surgeon…' As for the match itself, City won by the only goal, a fine effort from Colin Bell, who was rapidly emerging as a player to watch. It was

Bell's third late winning goal of the season, all absolutely crucial for a side struggling for points. Meanwhile, Alan Ball had been showing the other side of his game, tetchy and spoiling for a fight throughout, and lucky to stay on the field.

The month ended with two more notable individual scoring efforts. At Turf Moor, the prolific Andy Lochhead scored all four in Burnley's 4-2 win over an Aston Villa side looking increasingly like relegation fodder, whilst at Old Trafford David Herd also helped himself to four goals in the 5-0 rout of Sunderland. Herd's haul was particularly notable for the fact that his goals were scored against three different keepers. Jim Montgomery had already been beaten by the Scotsman when he was carried off with concussion in the first half. Herd then put one past Charlie Hurley before Hurley was replaced by John Parke for the second half. Herd showed no mercy, putting another two past the reluctant keeper to seal United's emphatic victory. It would be another twenty years before the achievement of scoring a hat-trick against three different keepers would be repeated, with Alvin Martin achieving the feat against Newcastle, his third goal coming against the formidable obstacle of Peter Beardsley.

England returned to Wembley two weeks after the Czech stalemate for the visit of Wales, and produced an impressive performance even if the eventual 5-1 scoreline was slightly flattering. *The Times* praised England's 'highly scientific teamwork', noting that 'they can now do things almost blindfold with an instinctive knowledge of one another's intentions and movements.' Wales boss Dave Bowen put it more graphically. 'It was like playing against twenty-two men,' he said. The performance was a great testament to what Ramsey had achieved – the players had had very little preparation time yet were able to slot into their roles almost without thinking.

Hurst netted twice in the first half, but Wales made a spirited response before Bobby Charlton's drive slipped through Tony Millington's fingers to restore a two-goal advantage. Brother Jack nodded home the final goal after Hennessey's unfortunate own goal had put the game out of Wales' reach, and it was a highly satisfactory evening for Ramsey and his men. The crowd of 76,000 was some 35,000 more than had attended the same fixture two years earlier, emphasising the upsurge in interest in the national team.

Match Of The Month

7 November 1966, League Cup Fourth Round:
West Ham United 7 Leeds United 0

Having ground out a 1-0 win at Highbury, Leeds travelled across to Upton Park two days later for a League Cup tie against a West Ham side who had warmed up for the occasion by putting six past Fulham. The competition was by now finding its feet with most clubs putting out full-strength sides and, as usual with West Ham, no one knew quite what to expect. But what no one could possibly have anticipated was the actual outcome, as Leeds succumbed to their heaviest defeat of the entire Revie era.

West Ham took only two minutes to break through, with a goal from John Sissons, by which time David Harvey had already made two fine saves. By half-time, Sissons had completed his hat-trick as the Hammers came off four goals to the good. Tormentor-in-chief was Johnny Byrne, who time and again outwitted Jack Charlton to deftly play in his team-mates. Geoff Hurst also bagged a hat-trick to make it seven goals in just three days following his four-goal burst against Fulham, with Martin Peters also finding the net. Apart from one superb individual effort from Hurst, the goals all came from well-constructed team moves as West Ham demonstrated once again that they were capable of hitting heights beyond the reach of almost all others.

This was an incredible result, given that Leeds' only absentees of note were Gary Sprake – for whom a young David Harvey deputised and made several outstanding saves – and Peter Lorimer. West Ham were eulogised even by their opponents for their phenomenal performance, with Norman Hunter conceding that the speedy Brabrook had run him off the park and the watching Lorimer describing the Hammers as 'simply awesome'.

West Ham: Standen, Bovington, Charles, Peters, Brown, Moore, Brabrook, Boyce, Byrne, Hurst, Sissons.

Leeds United: Harvey, Reaney, Bell, Bremner, Charlton, Hunter, Madeley, Belfitt, Greenhoff (Bates), Giles, O'Grady.

Player Of The Month
Geoff Hurst (West Ham)

In the course of just 120 minutes, Geoff Hurst had catapulted himself to the status of all-time national legend, but he didn't let his new-found fame distract him from the day job. Already a prolific striker for his club, and a key player in the sides that had won the FA and Cup Winners' cups, he began the new season in outstanding form and November saw him embark on the most extraordinary scoring sequence of his career.

It began with a four-goal haul at home to Fulham, two of them searing drives which reminded some of his *coup de grace* in the World Cup Final. Just two days later, Hurst hammered home another three in the 7-0 League Cup demolition of Leeds, one of which was another 'they think it's all over' replica. These were not goals scored by accident. He had to be satisfied with just one the following Saturday, but it was the decisive goal in the Hammers' 4-3 win at White Hart Lane and the best of the lot, coming after a length-of-the-pitch move started by Bobby Moore close to his own goal.

Another strike followed in a comfortable win over Newcastle, before Hurst rounded off the month by scoring at Elland Road, albeit in a narrow 2-1 defeat. As if ten goals for his club weren't enough, Hurst also bagged a couple for England in their 5-1 thrashing of the Welsh at Wembley.

His twenty-nine league goals was a personal best for a season, and after making his international debut only five months before the World Cup began, Hurst had now established himself as England's premier striker. He had undoubtedly benefitted from having club team-mates Moore and Peters in the side, not just as familiar friendly faces but also as players with whom he had developed a special on-field understanding. His near-post run to glance home Peters' cross against Argentina was a classic West Ham move, and a similar run saw him meet Moore's free kick for his first goal in the final.

The subsequent three seasons saw him continue to score frequently – including a six-goal haul against Sunderland in 1968 – but West Ham's innate inconsistency meant that his side never again made a serious challenge for honours. Ironically, in 1970, he was joined at Upton Park by Jimmy Greaves – the man whose injury had given him his World Cup chance – and they marked their first club game together by both scoring twice at Manchester City.

The Mexico World Cup saw Hurst strike to win a tight game against Romania, but it proved to be his only goal of the tournament. He continued to lead England's attack for the next couple of seasons, but having turned thirty his powers began to wane and his England career ended with twenty-four goals in forty-nine appearances. Hurst was transferred to Stoke in 1972 and was a regular there for the next three seasons, but will forever be associated with West Ham – as well as a late July afternoon in Swinging London.

DECEMBER 1966

By now, *Match Of The Day* had become staple viewing, although there had been little evolution since the start of the season. In particular, the action replay – hugely popular during the World Cup, even if it only repeated the original footage from the same angle and at the same speed – hadn't yet been made available for bread-and-butter matches. It was a case of 'blink and you'll miss it', with the only chance to see goals again being to hope for a showing on Sam Leitch's Saturday lunchtime football preview show.

With just one league fixture being shown each week, it was vital for the BBC to choose well. There was a natural tendency to select well-supported clubs with star players, with Manchester

United and Chelsea both featuring four times in the first nine weeks of the season, but no guarantee that the game chosen would feature thrills, spills and, most importantly, goals. Matches were chosen six weeks ahead, during which time what originally looked likely to be a tightly contested top-of-the-table clash could easily have descended into a routine encounter between two out-of-form sides. Even so, with so little televised football available, the burgeoning viewing figures suggested that the majority of viewers weren't particularly discerning, happily tuning in irrespective of the fare on offer.

There were still clubs opposed to the filming of games, fearing that the effect on live attendances would be detrimental, even though the match to be shown that evening wasn't revealed until after the half-time whistles had blown around the country. The only people in the know before that were the fans at the chosen game itself, where the sight of the BBC camera vans outside the ground would create an additional buzz of excitement and the even more fervent hope that the team could turn on the style. Predictably, Bob Lord was one of the objectors, banning TV cameras from Turf Moor, a stance he continued to take for another five seasons. There were, however, many clubs who recognised that allowing a wider audience to embrace the excitement would – particularly among younger viewers – lead to a desire to see the real thing.

Most ITV regions by now also showed a match each week, featuring one of their local clubs. This would be screened on Sunday afternoon, and was again a no-frills production, even allowing for the additional time available to put the programme together. Brief opening credits, straight into the action, adverts at half-time, more action, closing credits. And that was it. Pure unadulterated football. There's a lot to be said for it…

Liverpool were highly fancied in the European Cup, where they and their fans were still smarting from their deeply suspicious exit to AC Milan two years earlier, and their second-round tie against little-known Ajax of Amsterdam didn't look too forbidding. However, their trip to a fog-enshrouded Olympic stadium produced one of the competition's most startling results to date, with the Dutch side securing a 5-1 lead to bring to Anfield. It would be a few more years before the flexibility and fluidity of 'total football' would come to characterise the Dutch game. Nevertheless, Liverpool and Shankly were shocked by the quality and movement of their opponents, featuring a nineteen-year-old Johan Cruyff, as they roared into a 4-0 half-time lead.

Shankly remained typically defiant after the match, attributing the result to the conditions, and maintained that his team were well capable of turning the tie round in the second leg. The Liverpool public believed him, turning out in force at Anfield a week later to create an atmosphere which their visitors can never have experienced. The crush in the Kop was so great that the first half was played out against a backdrop of stretcher bearers carrying spectators around the perimeter of the pitch.

Distracting as this must have been, and despite an early flurry of Liverpool pressure in front of a baying crowd, Ajax retained their discipline. Their passage through to the quarter-finals was never in doubt. Two slick counter-attacks were coolly finished by Cruyff to render Roger Hunt's brace irrelevant, and Ajax's impressively composed performance caused many journalists to reappraise their 'fluke result' verdicts on the first leg. Some, indeed, were moved to predict that Ajax could be serious contenders for the cup. They would be proved right eventually, but for now the suggestion that Liverpool had been brushed aside by a new footballing force would soon be given the lie, as Ajax were well beaten in the quarter-finals by Dukla Prague. Nevertheless, they had already demonstrated a new style of football, even if not too many seemed to have noticed.

Back on the domestic front, there were further signs of a revival at Highbury, where Arsenal won their fifth successive game. Bertie Mee was given much credit, having recruited several new players and, as one journalist put it, reversing the club's recent practice of selling good players and buying bad ones. Their newest victims were a Chelsea side still clearly missing Osgood's x-factor, with Tony Hateley struggling to make any worthwhile contribution.

On the weekend before Christmas, attendances at most grounds were well below average, with Christmas shopping taking priority. But parents looking for gifts for their football-mad offspring weren't exactly spoilt for choice, as there had been little attempt to build on World Cup fever. Much the most popular football game was Subbuteo, whose manufacturers had recently made the significant technical and aesthetically pleasing advance of replacing the cardboard slot-in figures with moulded plastic ones. This was great news for Britain's glue manufacturers, opening the door for swathes of plastic footballers up and down the land to suffer multiple fractures after being trampled underfoot by clumsy parents.

There were surprisingly few competitors, with the special World Cup-themed 'Willie Football' little more than a glorified game of shove ha'penny, with a couple of sticks wedged at each end of the table acting as goalposts. Compared with the skill and tactical variations of Subbuteo, it seemed not so much last year's thing as the plaything of a different generation.

Many fans who had felt obliged to traipse round the busy markets rather than take their regular spots on the terraces will have been doubly disappointed when they discovered what they had missed, as the day produced some of the season's most thrilling games. At Stamford Bridge, Chelsea and West Ham shared ten goals, while *Match Of The Day* viewers were treated to Manchester United's game at West Brom, which produced an extraordinary first half featuring seven goals. David Herd hit three of them for United, this time all past the same keeper, with Jeff Astle contributing two for the Baggies. Albion hit post and bar in the second half but couldn't find an equaliser, with the result that United finished the day at the top of the table and looking increasingly like title favourites.

Another thrilling encounter took place at Elland Road, where fewer than 30,000 turned out for the visit of Spurs, although when Leeds raced into a 3-0 lead by half-time a routine home win looked inevitable. The excellent Jimmy Greenhoff had scored two of them, and after the interval Leeds squandered several opportunities to make the game absolutely safe. They were so nearly made to pay for it, as Greaves' sublime strike prompted a spirited revival, with Spurs pressing spiritedly and stylishly for the remainder of the game. Substitute Keith Weller made a telling impact, crossing for Gilzean to bring Spurs within striking distance, but the equaliser they ultimately deserved just eluded them. The Christmas spirit had certainly permeated Elland Road, as the relieved crowd applauded both teams off the field at the end of the game, with Dave Mackay making a point of shaking the hand of every Leeds player – even Billy Bremner.

New Year's Eve brought a couple of blockbuster fixtures, but both of them – the Merseyside derby and Leeds' visit to Old Trafford – ended disappointingly goalless. More fittingly, England's year of glory was signed off by stellar displays from two of the team's heroes, Geoff Hurst and Gordon Banks, as their teams met at Upton Park. Hurst, forty-two goals in the calendar year, was in towering form and a hat-trick was the minimum his efforts deserved. Banks, however, was having one of those days, and repelled everything that came his way in a performance which had fans, journalists and players shaking their heads in wonderment. It wasn't the first time, and wouldn't be the last.

Match Of The Month
17 December, 1966, Division One: Chelsea 5 West Ham 5

West Ham continued to be the team to watch in the months immediately following the World Cup. Spectators not only had the chance to see the three main men from the final in the flesh, but a disproportionately high number of their games had produced a feast of goals. Nine at Leicester, three sevens in a week and now, surpassing them all, this astonishing match at Stamford Bridge.

Chelsea's early-season promise had dissipated somewhat, with the loss of Osgood still being keenly felt, and his replacement

Tony Hateley struggling to fit into the team's style of play. But Docherty's men boasted plenty of quality, with Tambling up front together with the guile of the recently acquired Charlie Cooke.

West Ham were dominant in the early stages, forcing three spectacular saves from Bonetti and having Byrne's goal chalked off for a hair-breadth offside decision. By the half-hour mark, they had seemingly taken a grip on the game with goals from Brabrook and Peters. Baldwin pulled one back before the interval, and the early part of the second half produced a scarcely credible five goals in the space of eleven minutes. A rare goal from Hateley, assisted by Standen's almost comical slip, brought the hosts level before a crisp volley from Charlie Cooke put them ahead. Far from being deterred by having their comfortable advantage overturned, West Ham simply went down the other end and banged in three quick goals. Sissons bagged two of them, one via a deflection and the other through a Bonetti howler, before the keeper almost redeemed himself by touching Byrne's penalty on to a post only to see the striker put away the rebound.

Two down with ten minutes to go, Chelsea pushed West Ham back and were rewarded by Tambling's successful penalty and then, with just seconds remaining, the same player hit a shinner which bobbled into the corner of the net. It was a goal of significance not just for its impact on the day's result, but also because it established Tambling as the club's all-time leading goalscorer, overtaking Roy Bentley. For him, and the 50,000 inside the ground, it had been a day to remember.

Chelsea: Bonetti, Kirkup, McCreadie, Hollins, Hinton, Harris R, Boyle, Baldwin, Hateley, Cooke, Tambling.

West Ham: Standen, Bovington, Charles (Burnett), Peters, Brown, Moore, Brabrook, Boyce, Byrne, Hurst, Sissons.

Player Of The Month
Rodney Marsh (QPR)

Rodney Marsh was perhaps the most charismatic and well known third-division player of all time. Having started out with Fulham, he was transferred to Rangers in March 1966 and instantly became a crowd favourite at Loftus Road. The season had already seen him score three hat-tricks by the end of November, and his stellar form continued throughout the month.

Rangers were making strong progress in the League Cup and the quarter-finals saw them drawn at home to second-division Carlisle United. By half-time, two slick finishes from Marsh had put Rangers 2-0 ahead and on a sticky pitch they held on despite Willie Carlin's reply. Marsh continued to score freely in the league programme as Rangers built up a commanding lead at the top of the table. Goals in a 3-1 win at Colchester and a Boxing Day win over Brighton were followed by a brace in a 4-1 hammering of Watford on New Year's Eve. The latter game was graced by the presence of Alf Ramsey, making a rare venture into the third division to see what all the fuss was about.

Marsh ended the season with over forty goals in all competitions as Rangers romped away with the third division title, as well as famously taking the League Cup. Despite overtures from several clubs and a firm bid from Tottenham, Marsh remained at Loftus Road, adamant that Rangers were themselves good enough to get into the first division. He was proved right, as they were promoted from the second division at the first attempt despite their star man being absent through injury for much of the campaign.

On his return to the top flight, Marsh again suffered long-term injury as Rangers seldom showed the form needed to give them a chance of staying up, and they were relegated well before the end of the season. He continued to shine in the second division, and eventually Malcolm Allison was persuaded to pay £200,000 to bring him to Manchester City in April 1972. Allison's inclusion of a clearly unfit player disrupted a side which were hot favourites to take the title, and despite some memorable moments in his four years at City, the abiding memory will always be his role in the title that got away.

A self-indulgent maverick, Marsh hardly fitted the Ramsey template but he nevertheless won nine caps, his one goal coming with a cracking volley against Wales. His international career is most remembered for his oft-quoted alleged exchange with Alf Ramsey:

> 'If you don't work harder, I'll pull you off at half-time.'
> 'Blimey, Alf, all we get at Man City is a cup of tea and an orange.'

Marsh claimed that this incident signalled the end of his England career, although whether Ramsey would have selected him again – and whether the conversation took place at all – is questionable.

Ramsey's immediate successors were Joe Mercer – who had vocally opposed Marsh's signing at City – and Don Revie, a man hardly likely to find the player's self-centredness appealing. Despite sporadic bursts of brilliance for City, and suggestions that being made team captain indicated a new maturity, there was little chance of further international recognition. Marsh left to play in the USA in 1976, briefly returning to Fulham to partake in a spot of cabaret with George Best.

Marsh never added to the club honours he won as a lower-league player but is remembered as one of the era's true mavericks, a wonderfully skilful and entertaining player who produced moments at all of his clubs which their fans will remember forever.

JANUARY 1967

The year began with the not terribly surprising news that Alf Ramsey had been knighted, and there was also an OBE for Bobby Moore. The awards were widely welcomed, though there was disappointment in some quarters about the lack of recognition for the rest of the squad.

Liverpool and Manchester United remained favourites for the title, although Leeds, Tottenham and, unexpectedly, Nottingham Forest were all still in contention. Tottenham's weakness in recent seasons had been their away form, but the acquisition of Mike England seemed to have made them a more resilient proposition. Their fixture at Old Trafford saw key players absent from both sides – Law for United, Mackay and Gilzean for Spurs – but the quality of the play suffered little. Jennings was in imperious form for Spurs, making no fewer than five outstanding saves, whilst Stepney also excelled, in particular with one crucial save from the otherwise well-policed Jimmy Greaves. As the game neared its conclusion, United at last broke through from a set piece, forced home by David Herd, and held on for an important victory. Spurs, however, had put up an impressive fight, suggesting that the flaky travellers of recent seasons may have been consigned to history.

Also consigned to history that evening, at least by the BBC, were the Jimi Hendrix Experience. In one of the most incongruous pairings ever seen on television, they somehow found themselves booked on the Saturday teatime *Happening For Lulu* show. Their blistering feedback-drenched performance failed to keep to the script and they were promptly banned from appearing on the channel again.

A man well used to bans of his own was Nobby Stiles, who had returned for the Spurs game after a twenty-one-day suspension imposed after receiving his third caution of the season. Despite his World Cup heroics, Nobby wasn't the most popular figure on opposition grounds, with his uncompromising tackling and frequently assigned brief to eliminate whoever the home team's flair player might be. However, at Maine Road the following week, he came off the pitch to an unlikely standing ovation after his last-minute own goal salvaged a point for City in the Manchester derby.

The FA Cup third round took place on the final Saturday of the month, drawing season's best crowds at many grounds, even for fixtures which didn't look particularly attractive. 63,500 fans packed into Old Trafford for the visit of Stoke City, a crowd higher than that recorded for the visit of champions Liverpool or for the Manchester derby.

At the other end of the scale, non-league Nuneaton drew an incredible 17,000 for the visit of second division Rotherham, and the home team responded with a tremendous display, eventually settling for a 1-1 draw after leading for a long period of the game. Bedford drew almost 15,000 for the visit of Peterborough, but didn't fare quite so well on the pitch, shipping six goals to the third division side.

Attendance figures around the country reaffirmed the cup's unrivalled popularity with the public, but the one thing the day lacked was a genuine giant-killing. Struggling fourth division side Barrow came closest, holding Southampton to a 2-2 draw, whilst at Upton Park, Geoff Hurst's hat-trick still wasn't enough to see off Swindon Town, for whom Don Rogers – along with Rodney Marsh, the third division's outstanding and most high-profile performer – netted twice to further fuel speculation about an imminent move to bigger and better things.

In the second division, Plymouth Argyle made the trip to the Den to face a Millwall side whose unbeaten home record had extended to an extraordinary fifty-nine games. However, Plymouth, without an away win all season, went in at half-time with a 2-0 lead and, despite severe intimidation from the home fans – clearly an important factor in establishing the record in the first place – held on to record a famous victory. It was nevertheless a harrowing day for the visitors on and off the pitch. The Plymouth keeper was subjected to a second-half barrage of missiles, later confirming that '…there were bottles flying, tin cans, stones, matchboxes filled with grit, coins…' After the game, their team coach received similar treatment, with bottles being hurled at and then through the windows.

Elsewhere in the capital, Tony Hateley continued to struggle at Stamford Bridge, his performance against Villa described by *The Times* as being that of a 'passenger', and highlighting his inept shooting and ball control. Despite this, Chelsea still managed a come-from-behind win to remain in the top five. Spurs' defeat of Burnley was notable for an astonishing goal by Greaves, who slalomed through a swathe of tackles in a run from the halfway line before burying a precise low shot to give his side the lead. Many of those present reckoned this to be an even better goal than his similar televised effort against Manchester

United the previous season, but sadly there were no cameras present to enable anyone else to form a view.

Liverpool's narrow win over Southampton, for whom Ron Davies yet again scored to continue his spectacular debut season in the top flight, meant that they returned to the summit, albeit having played a game more than their Manchester rivals. Leeds were also looking strong, with black South African winger Albert Johanneson having a particularly fine month, scoring in three matches. Despite increasing racial tensions within the country, there was no sense of antipathy towards Johanneson – instead, he was regarded affectionately by Leeds fans and even by many opposition supporters. There was a novelty and curiosity value about him, and in the eyes of the man on the terraces he was far removed from the swathes of immigrants who had been greeted with antagonism and worse in their newly adopted surroundings.

QPR's spectacular progress continued with a crushing 4-1 win away to second-division Birmingham in the first leg of their League Cup semi-final. They soon made even bigger headlines when proposals were announced for them to take over neighbours Brentford at the end of the season. They would sell their Loftus Road ground, move to Griffin Park, and Brentford FC would cease to exist. Brentford's general manager claimed that the club needed gates of 11,000 to break even and were losing £500 a week. The abolition of the minimum wage was a key factor in their financial struggles, as it was proving to be for so many of their counterparts, with more than half of the league clubs running at a loss. It didn't take long for local businessmen to respond to Brentford's plight, eventually buying out the chairman's shares to rescue the club.

Brentford's narrow escape from extinction was greeted with universal relief, but with so many clubs facing a potentially similar scenario, the Football League was adamant that a trip back to the future was what was needed. 'We shall have to put a stop to these tremendous wages being paid to footballers,' they declared via their *Football League Review* mouthpiece, noting that clubs large and small were living beyond their means and surviving only by fan input into development associations and directors dipping into their own pockets.

Match Of The Month
14 January 1967, Division One: Southampton 4
Leicester City 4

Ron Davies had proved to be an instant success on his arrival from Norwich, leading the league's scoring charts after hitting the target in ten consecutive games. Although Martin Chivers had struggled to maintain the scoring touch he had revealed in the Saints' promotion season, the two of them formed one of the division's most potent strike pairings. Leicester remained one of the division's most entertaining teams, with Derek Dougan in particular profiting from the supply line provided by Mike Stringfellow and Jackie Sinclair.

Davies was off the mark within five minutes, before David Webb's blunder presented Tom Sweenie with a quick equaliser. Webb redeemed himself by crossing for Davies to restore Southampton's lead, before some vintage trickery from Terry Paine saw him deliver a perfect cross for the striker to complete his second hat-trick of the season with a simple header.

David Gibson's header cut the arrears and, just a minute later, Leicester were awarded a penalty and a perfect chance to equalise. Gerry Gurr made an acrobatic save, tipping Sinclair's fiercely struck shot on to the bar, and when some more great play from Paine set up Chivers to head home Southampton's fourth, it looked as though Sinclair's miss would be terminal.

Leicester threw increasing numbers forward as they sought to recover and, whilst indebted to Banks for two brilliant saves to thwart Southampton counter-attacks, were rewarded by two quick goals. Sweenie grabbed his second with a classy volley before John Roberts blasted home a late equaliser.

Whilst the match produced an eye-catching scoreline, the outcome could hardly be called a surprise, with both teams already having been involved in several high-scoring games this season. For Southampton, it meant nineteen goals conceded in their last five league games, but with Davies so prolific up front their defensive frailties never threatened to endanger their newly won status. Banks, meanwhile, must have wished for some better defenders, but at least was being given plenty of opportunities to hone his craft.

Southampton: Gurr, Jones, Hollywood, Webb, Knapp, Walker, Paine, Chivers, Davies, Melia, Thompson.

Leicester: Banks, Rodrigues, Norman, Roberts, Sjoberg, Cross, Sinclair, Sweeney, Dougan, Gibson, Stringfellow.

Player Of The Month
Ian Storey-Moore (Nottingham Forest)

Storey-Moore, a twenty-one-year-old winger who had made his Forest debut at just seventeen, was proving to be a crucial part of the team. Fast and skilful, he was equally comfortable going outside his man to cross for the likes of Joe Baker, or cutting in to go for goal himself.

Forest had made a decent start to the season but, after being hammered 4-0 at Anfield in early November, sat in mid-table. From then, however, they embarked on an extraordinary run, losing just once in twenty-eight games, as they put together an unlikely bid for a cup and league double. Storey-Moore was central to their challenge, scoring and creating goals, and January saw him come into his own. A vital winning goal away at West Brom kept Forest just a point from the summit and the following week Storey-Moore excelled in a 1-0 win over Leeds as his team recorded their sixth straight win. The month ended with Forest squeezing past Plymouth in the FA Cup, with Storey-Moore again on target.

Storey-Moore's form continued, and the most famous performance of his career came in the cup quarter-final against Everton two months later, when he completed his hat-trick with a last-minute goal which took four attempts to score, his successive efforts striking defender, goalkeeper, crossbar and netting.

This proved to be by far Storey-Moore and Forest's finest season, as they declined rapidly from double aspirants to a mid-table and ultimately relegation-threatened side. Eventually, in one of the most bizarre transfer episodes ever seen in the English game, he moved to Manchester United only a day after being paraded at the Baseball Ground as a new signing for Derby County. It was hoped he would provide a tonic for the fast fading United, but his impact at Old Trafford was negligible.

Storey-Moore won two under-23 caps and then, back in prime form in the 1969/70 season, Ramsey selected him for the full side, in the game against Holland in Amsterdam. By now insisting that the 'Storey' be dropped from his name, Moore was reported as one of England's best performers on the night, and it was widely expected that further caps would follow, possibly even in Mexico. However, this would prove to be his only England appearance, as his career tailed off in disappointing fashion. For a brief period, though, he was one of English football's brightest young things.

FEBRUARY 1967

West Ham, so thrilling and flamboyant in the first four months of the season, had suffered a depressingly familiar reversal in fortunes. Jeff Astle's hat-trick had condemned them to a 4-0 defeat in the first leg of the League Cup semi-final, a bitter disappointment after seeing off Leeds and Spurs. Worse still, their FA Cup replay produced a belated third-round shock, as Don Rogers inspired Swindon to a 3-1 victory. A dismayed Ron Greenwood lamented the lack of application of his men. 'Some of them didn't feel as ashamed as they should...' It wasn't the first or last time that the 'soft Southerners' tag would be levelled at his team.

The Hammers' return to the league programme then saw them humiliated at the Dell, going 4-0 down after 30 minutes as Southampton cruised to a crushing 6-2 victory. 'The final disintegration of a once-magnificent side,' mourned *The Times*. For Bobby Moore, there was at least the not inconsiderable consolation of being named in the list of the top ten tie men of the year by the British Tie Manufacturers Association. 'Obviously he puts the same enthusiasm into choosing his ties as leading his club or country on the football field,' said association chairman Sidney Davis.

The FA Cup fourth round attracted another full house to Old Trafford, despite the lowly nature of the opposition – Norwich City, fourth from bottom in the second division. But, for the second time in seven years, United suffered a shock defeat to the East Anglians, whose healthy contingent of followers once again regaled their heroes with repeated renditions of 'On The Ball, City...' United had evidently thought the result would be a foregone conclusion, and their lack of spirit after going behind surprised their opponents. 'Some United players just packed it in without putting up a fight.'

At Molineux, Wolves faced holders Everton and more than 53,000 strong-minded souls managed to resist the competing attraction at the nearby Civic Hall, where Ted Heath, esteemed Leader of the Opposition, was addressing the assembled throng on the subject of housing policy. Those who had opted for a little more excitement on their Saturday afternoon saw Wolves almost make the most of their escape at Boundary Park in the previous round by leading until a late and controversially awarded penalty was converted by Alan Ball to secure a fortunate replay for his side. More than anyone, Everton had Gordon West to thank for their continuing survival, a series of spectacular saves preventing Wolves from going two up and then safeguarding parity after the equaliser.

Teams who had made an early cup exit had been left with a blank Saturday on fourth-round day. Ironically, given the number who had objected to the introduction of the League Cup a few years earlier on the grounds of the additional burden it would place on the players, few took the opportunity to give them a week's rest. Instead, a number of short-notice friendlies were set up, most eye-catchingly at Leicester City, who welcomed Glasgow Rangers – recent victims of their greatest ever humiliation, the cup defeat at Berwick Rangers – for a fixture which attracted over 24,000 to Filbert Street. Revenue evidently remained a far greater priority than player welfare. The afternoon could have gone better: John Sjoberg fractured his jaw in an accidental collision and police were bombarded with bottles as fighting broke out on the terraces.

While plenty of journalists bemoaned the quality of some of the footballing fare on offer – and in particular the violence both on and off the pitch – at least many of them did it with some considerable style. The master of them all, Geoffrey Green, was still delivering his peerless prose to *Times* readers, and Eric Todd of *The Guardian* wasn't far behind him when it came to bringing colour, warmth and an idiosyncratic touch to his reporting. Eric would find something to smile about from even the most dreary and disappointing encounters and possessed the unfailing ability to make his readers smile as well.

At the more pompous and lecturing end of the spectrum of serious football journalists were Brian Glanville and Hugh McIlvanney, both of whom often preferred to accentuate the negative aspects of the game to such an extent that readers must have wondered whether they actually enjoyed watching football at all. They were nevertheless both outstanding writers, even if Glanville's love of the Italian language would occasionally bring bemusement to some of his readers. In addition, *Observer* readers would sometimes be treated to reports by the great John Arlott, already well on his way to becoming one of the most revered cricket broadcasters of all time. Arlott's would become a very familiar voice over the years and, reading his reports, it's easy to imagine him actually speaking the words, always written with such care and precision, in that wonderful Hampshire burr.

The Guardian's David Lacey was another accomplished wordsmith, though his powers were put to the test by a turgid goalless encounter between Chelsea and Manchester City. Chelsea had continued to struggle without the still-stricken Osgood, unable as yet to integrate Hateley into their style of play, whilst City were continuing with their cautious approach as they sought to eke out sufficient points to ensure survival. As they would demonstrate repeatedly over the years, these Kings Road aristocrats had a rather more unsavoury side to their game and their frustration at being unable to penetrate the stubborn City rearguard brought this to the fore. 'Chelsea kicked out in all directions and it was hardly worth the Manchester City trainer sitting down,' Lacey wrote. The facts bear this out, with the recorded actual playing time for the match extending to 106 minutes.

At Old Trafford, surprise title challengers Nottingham Forest showed their credentials, playing a full part in an enthralling match which curiously remained goalless until a few minutes from the end. Then Denis Law, the game's outstanding performer, fired home the winner to send the home fans into ecstasy and Eric Todd into poetic rapture as he ruminated on Law's possible future in retirement. 'He would have made a splendid highwayman, a second Scarlet Pimpernel, he could be another Raffles. Maybe some police force will invite him to give lectures on breaking and entering or on loitering with intent. He is a master of both...' The result gave United a clear edge in the title race, but Forest's excellent performance had served notice that they were genuine contenders.

Tottenham's game at home to Fulham attracted a number of American journalists, eager to get a flavour of the live experience in 'the country that gave the game to the world'. The World Cup Final had attracted as many as ten million viewers in the USA and the formation of the North American Soccer League was imminent, with several major sponsors convinced that there was money to be made.

They picked an eventful enough game, Spurs winning 4-2 in a contest punctuated by the dismissals of Terry Venables and Fred Callaghan for fighting. For the visitors, as no doubt for many of the regular attendees, this was the highlight of the day. 'Not until this week have some of us appreciated the physical character of it...It was great, man...especially that punch-up! Our people back here will lap it up.' Time would tell whether this bullish outlook would be justified, but what was for sure was that the global reach of television had the power to influence and convert.

Match Of The Month

*11 February 1967, Division One: Manchester United 1
Nottingham Forest 0*

Unbeaten for over two months, Forest came to Old Trafford in third place, attracting close to a full house eager to discover whether they could stand up to the toughest of tests against the title favourites. An early foray which saw Hindley produce a great save from Stepney gave due notice of Forest's ambition and confidence, and from then on two evenly matched sides delivered a magnificent spectacle.

A match filled with near misses and great saves looked set to become one of the best goalless draws in living memory before the game's outstanding performer, Denis Law, finally made a decisive contribution. After forcing a superb acrobatic save from Peter Grummitt, Law reacted quickest to the resulting corner and, with his customary athleticism, contorted himself to fire a waist-high volley into the net.

Despite the defeat, Forest earned rich praise and respect for their performance, with their desire to attack and use of two wingers providing a refreshing contrast with the approach adopted by most of United's visitors. They were undeterred by the narrow defeat, setting off on another unbeaten run which would span a further thirteen games and see them mount a serious challenge in both league and cup. United, meanwhile, with Best, Law and Charlton all in their pomp, looked perfectly placed to resume their acquaintance with silverware, moving to within a point of champions Liverpool with a game in hand.

Manchester United: Stepney, Dunne, Noble, Crerand, Foulkes (Ryan), Stiles, Best, Law, Sadler, Herd, Charlton.

Nottingham Forest: Grummitt, Hindley, Winfield, Hennessey, McKinlay, Newton, Lyons, Barnwell, Baker (Hinton), Wignall, Storey-Moore.

Player Of The Month
Ray Wilson (Everton)

Wilson came to Everton relatively late in his career, having spent twelve years at Huddersfield after being spotted by Bill Shankly. He quickly made up for lost time, being part of the side that won the 1966 FA Cup and picking up his first domestic honour.

Having signed Alan Ball, Everton were widely expected to challenge again for honours but some poor results around the turn of the year had seen them drop out of the title race. They recovered well in February, however, recording three successive league wins without conceding a goal, as well as progressing in the FA Cup over two ties with Wolves. Their most notable result was their 2-0 win over Leeds in which Wilson excelled, and he performed impeccably throughout a month in which any threats to Everton's goal came almost exclusively down the other flank.

Wilson was a classy left-back capable of excellent and sometimes penetrative passing, and also comfortable making the overlapping runs essential to Ramsey's tactical gameplan. He was, however, first and foremost a defender and these qualities earned him sixty-five full caps. The vogue for more attacking full-backs led to his replacement by Terry Cooper, although by then Wilson was thirty-three and wear and tear were beginning to show.

Despite being a 'proper' defensive full-back, Wilson seldom resorted to overly physical means to deal with opponents and also possessed an outstanding temperament. This was never better demonstrated than in the World Cup Final itself, when his badly misplaced header set up Haller to give West Germany the lead. Far from being distracted by such a costly error, he scarcely put a foot wrong in the remainder of the game.

Wilson famously set up an undertaking business after retiring from the game and remains one of England's finest ever full-backs. With the increasing emphasis on attacking attributes, it is unlikely that players of his defensive excellence will ever be seen again.

MARCH 1967

The upgrade of the Football League Cup brought its first Wembley final, and the match lived up to its newly enhanced status, with third-division QPR coming back from 2-0 down to defeat West Bromwich Albion. The match clearly captured the public imagination – whether or not it was the romance of Rangers playing at Wembley rather than the status of the competition itself – with a record ten million tuning in to watch *Match Of The Day* later that evening. Rangers, however, would be denied the further prize of European football, with UEFA's small print stating that eligibility was restricted to first division teams. The Football League, perhaps not envisaging such an outcome now that the prize was so great, promised to take up the cudgels on Rangers' behalf.

Arsenal had also taken heed of the pulling power of the final, switching their match against Manchester United to the previous night and being rewarded with a 63,000 full house. United recognised the inconvenience that the Friday night fixture would cause for their supporters – this being an era where most of them still came from Manchester – and took the decision to show the match at Old Trafford on closed-circuit TV, attracting over 28,000 to witness the 1-1 draw.

United's next game was at Newcastle but, despite being by far the game's biggest draw and used to playing in front of full houses up and down the land, they could attract only 37,000 to St James' Park. Admittedly, the match came just a week after Newcastle suffered a 3-0 pasting in the Tyne–Wear derby, but it emphasised again how tough things were in the North East, with even the supposedly fanatical Geordies turning away from their team.

By far the most anticipated tie of the FA Cup fifth round was the Merseyside derby at Goodison Park. With both teams in easily the most successful phases of their history, demand for tickets was such that Liverpool decided to provide a live closed-circuit screening at Anfield. The experiment was an overwhelming success, with over 40,000 fans paying to watch the action unfold on four huge screens inside the centre circle, and would prompt similar transmissions of major matches, particularly European ties, over the next few years.

The Goodison crowd of over 64,000 meant that more than 100,000 people were watching the Saturday-night action unfold in real time but, on a windswept evening, they witnessed a match which, at least in the first half, was little more than a brawl. The referee, described in one report as extravagantly tolerant, allowed numerous assaults to go unpunished and the general consensus was that at least two players should have been dismissed. Ian St John, himself the victim of some brutal tackling, was one of them, his vicious retaliatory punch on Alan Ball going unnoticed by the referee but not by Everton keeper Gordon West. During a subsequent injury break, West ran upfield to attack St John and had to be forcibly led back to his goal by his team-mates. Ball it was, though, who would have the last word, firing home the winner just before half-time. Still only six months into his Everton career, he had already assumed legendary status with the Goodison crowd.

Ball had been not so much unfazed by his record transfer fee as inspired by it, but the same could not be said of Tony Hateley. With just one league goal since Christmas, he was struggling to win the fans over but at least found the net to seal Chelsea's cup progress against Sheffield United. In the other ties, Norwich had high hopes of creating another upset after their stunning win at Old Trafford but Sheffield Wednesday, forewarned and forearmed, coasted to a routine 3-1 victory. Norwich were left to focus on the battle to avoid demotion to the third division, but could forever console themselves with memories of one of the greatest of all cup upsets. The day's only surprise result came as second- division Birmingham at last prised open the Arsenal defence to score a late winner at St Andrew's. But with Arsenal having been so mediocre in recent years and still in the early stages of Bertie Mee's rebuilding programme, this was hardly a shock of seismic proportions.

Sheffield Wednesday built on their cup progress with a league win at Fulham to move well away from the danger zone. Their star man, as at Norwich, was John Fantham, who struck both goals in a 2-1 victory. The watching John Arlott, however, was left bemused by the two teams' formations, observing that 'the Ramsey tactic had reached absurdity'.

'Neither side employed an orthodox wing player, and both were at pains to maintain a majority defence…' lamented Arlott, who one sensed was already thinking wistfully ahead to a nice lazy day at Arundel, an early sight of the Indian tourists, the sound of willow on leather and a soothing bottle of decent claret.

Liverpool's hopes of retaining their title were dealt a severe blow with defeat at Burnley, whilst Manchester United, despite losing David Herd with a broken leg, cruised past Leicester City. United's 5-2 win was the sixth occasion that Gordon Banks had conceded four or more goals in the season; not for manager Matt Gillies the adoption of negative defensive tactics – or, if so, his players weren't very good at carrying them out. After West Ham, Leicester were the division's leading scorers, but transfer deadline day saw their striking resources diminished with the surprise departure of Derek Dougan to second-division promotion favourites Wolves. Dougan wasted little time in establishing himself, drawing an extra 5,000 to Molineux for his home debut against Hull and marking a flamboyant performance with a hat-trick.

Liverpool soon had the perfect chance to make up ground in the title race, as Easter Saturday saw them host United in a crucial encounter. The weight of the occasion and the windy conditions got to both teams, as a game of few chances petered out into a goalless draw. Although the game was fiercely contested, with Tommy Smith and Nobby Stiles amongst its most conspicuous performers, most of the day's violence occurred behind the goal at the Anfield Road End, where a series of vicious fights broke out. To the extent that the participants cared about football at all, it would be those returning home down the East Lancs Road who derived more satisfaction from the result, their team maintaining a two-point lead over their rivals and having crossed their most difficult remaining fixture off their schedule.

Forest, however, remained determined to have their say, a comfortable 2-0 win at Hillsborough seeing them close the gap on United and extend their outstanding record to just one defeat in their last twenty-four games. With a cup quarter-final to look forward to as well, there were quiet murmurings of the most unlikely double.

The remaining Easter programme – embracing a full set of fixtures on both Monday and Tuesday – comprised a series of double-headers. United's were against Fulham and saw them accrue three points from two tight games, largely thanks to Nobby Stiles, who scored in both. Liverpool fell further adrift, twice being held by Arsenal, but Forest reaffirmed their credentials by completing a comfortable double over Burnley. With two goals in each game, Joe Baker was leading their front line with aplomb and clearly central to their challenge, which was now very real.

The success of *Match Of The Day*, pulling in regular viewing figures of around five million, had whetted further the appetite of TV executives towards increasing the amount of televised football on offer. The prime proposal came from the BBC, who offered almost £800,000 for the right to show thirty-five live games during the following season. It was proposed that these games would take place on Thursday evenings, so as not to clash with any other live football. Given that a few clubs still found even recorded highlights unpalatable, this was always an offer unlikely to be accepted.

League chairmen voted overwhelmingly against all the proposals, despite the efforts of a minority group, led by Manchester United. There was still a deep suspicion about the effect of television on live attendances, with many clubs reportedly turning down the proposals on principle rather than because the offer wasn't sufficient. It was obvious that the debate wouldn't end there, although it would be almost twenty years before clubs could finally be persuaded to allow live coverage of league games. In the end, agreement was reached for the BBC to pay £66,000 for the rights to continue to cover games on *Match Of The Day*, doubling the previous season's outlay.

Match Of The Month
4 March 1967, League Cup Final: QPR 3 West Bromwich Albion 2

This had been a breakthrough season for the Football League Cup. Initially derided on its introduction in 1960, Alan Hardaker's brainchild had struggled to gain any sort of traction over the succeeding six years, with many of the country's top teams declining to enter. However, the double incentive of a Wembley final, plus qualification for the Inter-Cities Fairs Cup for the winners, instantly changed the way that clubs and their fans viewed the competition. Crowds for the earlier rounds of the tournament had increased significantly, and the big teams generally put out their strongest sides. Even so, there were still plenty of shocks, with runaway third-division leaders QPR making it all the way to Wembley to face holders and hot favourites West Bromwich Albion.

The first half took the path that most had anticipated, with Albion almost routinely finding themselves two goals to the good, both courtesy of simple finishes by Clive Clark, and squandering several further opportunities to make the game completely safe. However, expectations of a straightforward victory were put on hold when a flashing header from Roger Morgan brought Rangers back into contention after an hour or so. With fifteen minutes remaining, Rodney Marsh, cult hero of the Loftus Road crowd, brought himself into broader national consciousness with a magnificent equaliser, weaving between three Albion defenders before firing a precise low twenty-yard shot into the bottom corner.

West Brom's spirit and energy levels now sagged noticeably, and there was almost a sense of inevitability about the eventual outcome, confirmed when thirty-six-year-old Mark Lazarus prodded home a loose ball with eight minutes left, although the stud marks later revealed on Sheppard's chest supported his side's vehement claims that the goal should have been disallowed.

This dramatic final, watched by a full house and enjoyed later by *Match Of The Day*'s record audience to date, was the day when the League Cup truly came of age.

QPR: Springett, Hazell, Langley, Keen, Hunt, Sibley, Lazarus, Sanderson, Allen, Marsh, Morgan R.

West Brom: Sheppard, Cram, Williams, Collard, Clarke, Fraser, Brown, Astle, Kaye, Hope, Clark.

Player Of The Month
Nobby Stiles (Manchester United)

Nobby Stiles had been a central part of Ramsey's World Cup-winning team, stamping his authority, if occasionally too belligerently for some, on several games throughout the tournament. His most notable performance came in the semi-final, in which he generally managed to subdue the hitherto unstoppable Eusebio. Like so many players of his kind, he was loved by his own club's fans but a source of contempt and derision to those of their opponents. However, his comical toothless victory jig with the World Cup warmed the heart of every Englishman and softened attitudes towards him, and thereafter he became more of a pantomime villain.

Stiles' ball-winning capacity was crucial to United's style of play, allowing their more creative players the freedom to do their thing, and was especially important in difficult away games. This was seldom better illustrated than in the Easter Saturday game at Anfield, in which he, more than anyone, ensured that United's defence remained protected and unbreached as they secured a crucial point to retain breathing space between themselves and the champions.

Stiles then revealed another side to his game, with two vital goals over the remainder of the Easter programme. At Craven Cottage, he salvaged a point with a perfectly timed surge into the box to get on the end of Charlton's cross. In the return fixture at Old Trafford a day later, playing in a slightly more advanced role, he gave United the lead with a rare header and then, with seconds remaining, tirelessly put in the cross from which Bill Foulkes headed United's priceless winner. For all the column inches given to his more flamboyant colleagues, his contribution over this crucial period of the season can be seen as a decisive factor in ensuring that the big prize returned to Old Trafford. It also served as a reminder that he was capable of adding an attacking flair to his more familiar characteristics.

Stiles played only seven more times for England after the World Cup, primarily due to the emergence of Alan Mullery, but also as a result of a series of injuries. He completed a memorable double by winning the European Cup with United in 1968, once again facing Eusebio at Wembley and having the better of the duel, even if unable to keep him under quite such close restraint.

He travelled to Mexico as part of the 1970 squad but spent the whole tournament on the sidelines. Although still only twenty-eight at the time, his England career was over, and so too was his time at United. He moved on to Middlesbrough for a couple of seasons before a couple of short and unsuccessful managerial stints brought his career in the game to a close. Immortalised much later in 1996's anthem 'Three Lions', he will always remain a legendary figure in English football history.

APRIL 1967

Liverpool's faltering grip on their title was loosened further still at White Hart Lane, where Jimmy Greaves added two more goals to his tally, leaving the title as a two-horse race between United and Forest. Just two points behind the leaders with six games remaining, Forest's attentions then turned to the FA Cup quarter-finals.

In a thrilling match, Ian Storey-Moore made a name for himself by scoring a hat-trick as Forest beat Everton 3-2 in a game televised by the *Match Of The Day* cameras. The programme rounded off an epic day for TV viewers: whilst Storey-Moore was doing his stuff in real time, they had been treated to coverage of the most dramatic of all Grand Nationals, with 100-1 shot Foinavon cantering through the carnage to register a famous victory. After seeing John Steed and Emma Peel ward off another sinister threat in a gloriously bonkers *Avengers* plotline featuring such luminaries as Charlotte Rampling, Brian Blessed and Donald Sutherland, they then settled down in their millions to watch the Eurovision Song Contest, witnessing a barefoot Sandie Shaw register the UK's first ever victory with her charmingly nervous rendition of *Puppet On A String*. It meant that *MOTD* didn't hit the screens until almost midnight, but Storey-Moore's exploits meant that those who stuck with it were handsomely rewarded.

The BBC's deal with the FA actually allowed them to screen two cup games in each round up to the quarter-finals, but their other selection failed to deliver goals for the viewers, as second-division Birmingham were held by Spurs. Unsurprisingly, the BBC had decided against showing the Leeds–Manchester City tie. City had become arguably the most dour and negative side in the division as they battled to retain their newly won status, and Leeds were hardly synonymous with flowing, entertaining football. The two sides' recent league meeting at Elland Road had been a desperately dull goalless draw, and few pundits expected City to do anything other than once again employ their stifling sweeper system in a bid to achieve a similar result.

Once the final scores came through, Leeds' 1-0 win might have led casual observers to conclude that they had just about managed to penetrate City's obdurate defence, but the reality was anything but. Before the game, Malcolm Allison had canvassed his players and received overwhelming support for the suggestion that they should throw off the shackles and take the game to their opponents. In Bell, Summerbee and Crossan, they certainly had the talent to make such an approach pay off, and it so nearly did. City dominated from the outset but poor finishing, bad luck and an inspired performance from Gary Sprake denied them the victory they deserved. A scruffy set-piece goal from Jack Charlton saw a relieved Leeds through, and they were fulsome in their praise of their opponents afterwards. Whilst defeat was hard for City to take, this match provided the template for a more enterprising approach which would catapult them to great things over the next few years.

The remaining tie saw Chelsea score an injury-time winner to edge past Sheffield Wednesday in what a less-than-entranced *Observer* correspondent described as a 'dull, unimaginative slog', and attention then turned to England's most eagerly awaited international since the World Cup Final – Scotland's visit to Wembley.

The eagerness, as ever, was mainly on the part of the Scots. Always the game they wanted to win more than any other, the one consolation they could take from having had to endure England's day of glory was that it would give them the chance to beat the world champions on their own patch. It was a prospect they had craved almost from the moment that Bobby Moore had lifted the trophy. The bitterness and jealousy felt by the Scots was epitomised by Denis Law, who openly described that day as the worst of his life. Their supporters, many of them ticketless, most of them kilted and all of them inebriated, duly descended on London in their thousands.

With Greaves brought in to replace Roger Hunt, this was the first change to an England side since the Argentina quarter-final seven games ago. However, the shape and mobility of the team would soon be altered dramatically. Jackie Charlton suffered a bad injury after just ten minutes and with no substitutes permitted he was moved out of harm's way, with Martin Peters redeployed as centre-back. The patched-up and clearly immobilised Charlton rematerialised as a nuisance centre-forward, but the Scots had players of sufficient skill to exploit the situation, and when Law put them ahead they dominated proceedings, aided further by an injury to Ray Wilson, which left England's defence almost unrecognisable. Four goals were shared in a frantic last ten minutes, but Scotland were not to be denied. Their joyous supporters swarmed all over the pitch afterwards to celebrate a famous victory, wasting no time in proclaiming themselves as unofficial world champions.

As the unwashed, reeking hordes eventually made their way back northwards, England were left to reflect on the reality of the situation – that they had had only nine fit men for most of the game and still come close to salvaging something. So it certainly wasn't time for Sir Alf to reconsider tactics or personnel, although Greaves' much-anticipated return had been a disappointment. The real damage was that England were now second favourites to qualify for next year's European Nations Cup.

Gordon Banks had been powerless to prevent any of the Scottish goals, and indeed had produced one of the greatest saves of his or anyone else's career, acrobatically arching backwards to claw Law's chip over the bar. But his form for Leicester had been inconsistent, and with a young and impatient Peter Shilton making it clear that he had had enough of reserve-team football, manager Matt Gillies had a decision to make. Ultimately, feeling that, at 29, Banks' best days might now be behind him, he decided to give Shilton his head and allowed the England keeper to leave.

There was plenty of interest: Bill Shankly couldn't persuade his board to shell out such a sum for a mere goalkeeper; Ron Greenwood had already shaken hands on a deal to buy Bobby Ferguson for £13,000 more than would have been needed to secure England's No 1; Joe Mercer had tried unsuccessfully to barter the price down and, in the end, it was Stoke City who came up with the requisite £52,000.

Jim Baxter, feted by Scottish fans for his highly skilful and at times contemptuously arrogant display at Wembley, returned to Nottingham for Forest's next game at Sunderland, and was quickly brought back down to earth. Forest suffered a surprise defeat, their first in fourteen games, and when they could only draw at Arsenal it gave United a three-point cushion with just three games remaining. Hugh McIlvanney had enjoyed his fellow countrymen's victory at Wembley, betraying his partisanship by saying that the Scots would 'undoubtedly' have won even if

England had had eleven rather than nine fit men, but the trip to Highbury saw him back to his customary curmudgeonly self. 'This match was dominated by Arsenal in the first half, Forest in the second, and dullness in both.'

Forest's more realistic hope of silverware was now the FA Cup, and there was widespread anticipation that their semi-final against Spurs would see both teams rise above the recent trend of fear-fuelled caution. They duly did so in an entrancing match, with Forest having the better of the overall play but unable to match Spurs' clinical finishing. Once again Greaves was to the fore, a magnificent twenty-yard volley giving Spurs the lead, before a mistake from the otherwise impeccable Hennessey allowed Frank Saul to hit a second. Hennessey made partial amends by pulling a goal back, but Forest couldn't quite get the equaliser they deserved.

The other semi-final, between Chelsea and Leeds, wasn't quite such an aesthetically pleasing affair and descended into an increasingly bitter and violent struggle. Tommy Docherty's decision to sign Tony Hateley, hitherto a conspicuous failure, suddenly bore the most precious fruit as his majestic header from Charlie Cooke's cross proved to be the game's only goal – or at least the only one which was allowed to stand. In the last minute, Peter Lorimer lashed home a twenty-five-yard drive following a quick free kick, only for the Leeds fans' and players' celebrations to be cut short after the referee spotted what to everyone else seemed an indiscernible infringement.

Confusion still reigned as the final whistle blew seconds later, and it ultimately transpired that the kick had been taken before the referee's whistle had blown, as the Chelsea wall was less than ten yards away from the ball. Quite why Chelsea should be the ones to benefit from their own reluctance to obey the rules was never explained, but the upshot was that they had made it through, meaning that Wembley would stage its first ever all-London final.

Meanwhile, the touchpaper for the stormiest rivalry of the era had been well and truly lit.

On the same day that the cup had generated all the headlines, Manchester United all but sealed the first division title with a comfortable win over relegation-threatened Aston Villa. This vital game at Old Trafford attracted a crowd of 55,000, an impressive figure but still some 8,000 shy of the number who had turned up for United's fourth-round cup tie against apparent no-hopers Norwich City. Even the most crucial of league games couldn't compete with the magic of the cup.

Match Of The Month

8 April 1967, FA Cup Sixth Round: Nottingham Forest 3 Everton 2

Forest's stellar form – one defeat in 27 games and five straight wins – saw them come into the cup quarter-final with a real chance of carrying off the double. To continue their unlikely quest, they would next have to see off cup holders Everton in a tie that was much the most anticipated and difficult to call of the four.

Other than the injured Gordon West, both teams were at full strength, although Forest's resources were depleted as early as the second minute when Joe Baker, in scintillating form of late, fell victim to a heavy challenge from Brian Labone. Baker hobbled on for half an hour or so before finally giving up the ghost to be replaced by Alan Hinton, a change which saw Ian Storey-Moore moved to a more central attacking position.

Shortly after the change, a glorious pass from Alan Ball released Jimmy Husband to race through and fire past Grummitt, and as the match moved well into the second half it appeared as though that might be enough. But then the game exploded. Storey-Moore equalised with a simple tap-in and, within a minute, latched on to Frank Wignall's pass to crash a searing twenty-yarder past Rankin to turn the tie on its head. Prompted and inspired by Harvey and Ball, Everton redoubled their efforts and were duly rewarded ten minutes from time when Husband drilled home his second to complete a superb flowing move.

Neither side showed the remotest inclination to settle for a replay, and there were close shaves and great saves at both ends. But then, with seconds remaining, came one of the most extraordinary goals in FA Cup history. Latching on to Wignall's knockdown, Storey-Moore's shot was blocked by the desperate lunge of John Hurst. The ball rebounded back to the winger-cum-striker, whose next attempt was parried into the air by the diving Rankin. Storey-Moore leapt to head the ball goalwards, saw it crash against the bar and come back out for him to nod over the prostrate keeper and, at the fourth time of asking, find the back of the net.

Forest thus progressed to within one game of Wembley in the most dramatic fashion, but their victory came at a heavy price. They would be shorn of their leading striker for the rest of the season and with even the slightest slip-up likely to be terminal to their hopes of creating history, it was a blow they could ill afford. But the presence of the *Match Of The Day* cameras at least ensured that this glorious encounter, and Ian Storey-Moore's most famous day, would be preserved forever.

Nottingham Forest: Grummitt, Hindley, Winfield, Hennessey, McKinlay, Newton, Lyons, Barnwell, Baker (Hinton), Wignall, Storey-Moore.

Everton: Rankin, Wright, Wilson, Hurst, Labone, Harvey, Young, Ball, Brown, Husband, Morrissey.

Player Of The Month
Jimmy Greaves (Tottenham Hotspur)

Jimmy Greaves is more famous for not playing in the World Cup Final than are some of those who actually did so. By far the finest English striker of his generation, Greaves' career began as a seventeen-year-old at Chelsea, for whom he netted 124 goals in just 157 appearances. He was first capped for England at just nineteen and adapted immediately to international football. After a brief spell in Italy, he returned to London with Spurs and carried on scoring at a prodigious rate. Prior to the World

Cup, Greaves was seen as England's greatest hope of making significant progress. However, injury, the emergence of Geoff Hurst and Ramsey's preference for hard-working team men meant that Greaves' place in World Cup history turned out to be rather less prominent than he had hoped and imagined.

Greaves rebounded from his bitter disappointment by returning immediately to peak scoring form. As the season progressed, littered with brilliant individual goals and predatory strikes, clamour for a return to the England side intensified, especially in light of Roger Hunt's loss of form. April was the clinching month for Greaves. He began it by scoring two eye-catching goals against Liverpool, the first direct from a corner which he claimed to be absolutely deliberate and the second a delicate chip over Tommy Lawrence. He finished it with a magnificent opener in the cup semi-final against Forest, a perfectly placed volley from outside the box. In between, he found time to slot a couple past Birmingham to put Spurs on easy street in their quarter-final replay, and also was welcomed back into the fold for England's game against Scotland. Sadly, he couldn't recapture his club form in a disappointing display, although his cause can't have been helped by the succession of injuries suffered by his team-mates and the consequent reorganisations.

Greaves would play just twice more for England, scoring one further goal, before the curtain came down on his international career, despite continuing to plunder goals galore at club level for the next couple of seasons. His record of forty-four goals in fifty-seven games represents by far the most impressive strike rate of post-war forwards with significant international careers. His club figures are just as remarkable, with a total of 366 goals, all in the top flight.

But for all the compelling statistics, the essence of Greaves was the manner of his goals. Along with Denis Law, he was the greatest instinctive striker of his era and arguably any other. Although TV coverage has allowed some of his finest goals to be preserved for posterity, he was a player who had to be seen in the flesh to appreciate how special he was, succeeding by speed of thought as much as movement and with a unique elegance and calmness about his finishing. He didn't do ugly goals; he didn't do many long-distance thunderbolts, either. The vast majority were passed gently into the net, some after brilliant dribbles, others after anticipating the path of the ball a fraction more quickly than those around him. No player in English football history has – nor probably ever will – merited the description 'natural goalscorer' more than Jimmy Greaves.

MAY 1967

Manchester United travelled to Upton Park needing just a point to secure the title, but were in no mood to limp over the line. Within ten minutes, they were three goals to the good and their ultimate 6-1 victory saw them cement their triumph in the most emphatic style. The following week saw them presented with the trophy at Old Trafford, the crowd caring little that the match itself, against Stoke City, had petered out into a goalless draw. Matt Busby, acknowledging that the Norwich cup defeat had turned out to be a good thing, emphasised the way the game was going. 'Ability is no longer enough, although there is no substitute for it. You have to have a combination of ability and workrate.' A relatively new expression, 'workrate' would rapidly become one of the game's most over-used terms.

Another expression gaining credence in football-speak was 'professionalism'. Rather than having its usual positive connotation, the term was instead being used to imply something underhand or ruthless. Nowadays, the term has become such common parlance that one almost forgets that it essentially means to break the rules in order to win. A professional foul is one committed by way of premeditated deliberate cheating as opposed to a slight mistiming of a tackle by a player genuinely attempting to win the ball fairly. At least there was little chance of United's march to the title being hindered by any such 'professionalism', as West Ham's reluctance to become immersed in the more physical aspects of the game was quite remarkable.

Their cumulative disciplinary record over almost five seasons read cautions three, sending-offs nil.

With both relegation places already having been decided, there was little meaningful action on the first division's final Saturday, although the two teams bidding their farewells had sharply contrasting fortunes. Blackpool, long since doomed, went to Anfield and came away with a 3-1 victory, whilst Villa, relegated the previous week, were hammered 6-2 at Southampton, for whom Ron Davies bagged another four goals to take his league total to thirty-seven for the season. No top-flight player has matched this total since.

Led by the inventive, often ground-breaking manager Jimmy Hill, Coventry City could look forward to a debut season in the first division with the added kudos of being promoted as champions. It completed an extraordinary transformation; Hill's first season at the club, just five years previously, had seen the side narrowly escape relegation to the fourth division. The Coventry public had shown that they could support a top-flight side, celebrating their promotion by beating previous leaders Wolves in front of over 51,000 people – over 6,000 more than their previous record attendance.

With Wolves also being promoted, the Midlands would still boast a strong representation in next season's first division, despite Villa's demotion.

With QPR having enjoyed by far the best season in their history – runaway division three champions and League Cup winners – there was already speculation that they might be good enough to power straight through division two as well. Their one disappointment came with the confirmation that they wouldn't be permitted to play in Europe, with the Fairs Cup secretary showing little sympathy in turning down the league's request to allow their participation. 'If the top English clubs are foolish enough to allow a third division team to win the League Cup, then that is their problem...' QPR would be joined in the second division by Middlesbrough, who clinched their place with a 4-1 win over Oxford in front of almost 40,000 fans.

Lower down the second division, Derby County's dismal season, which saw them finish seventeenth, ended with manager Tim Ward resigning. The board's choice as his replacement was thirty-one-year-old Brian Clough, who along with his assistant Peter Taylor had impressed in transforming fourth-division Hartlepools' fortunes. Ward offered a word of warning about the mentality of the club's directors: 'I told a director that we had a player out with jaundice and he asked me whether we had to pay him first-team wages…' But Clough had already established a reputation as a man not to be messed with and he set out his stall right from the outset. 'I'm not here to be popular. If that's what they wanted, they should have gone for Bruce Forsyth.'

The mild winter meant that the cup final, as was always intended but seldom accomplished, could take place after all league issues had been decided. The final's traditional curtain-raiser was a game between England and Young England, but only 13,000 turned out at Highbury to watch a strong-on-paper but limp-in-practice England side easily beaten by their more eager young opponents. Rodney Marsh capped his outstanding season with two goals in a 5-0 win, but the lack of interest shown both by the public and the senior side was enough to convince the FA to discontinue the fixture.

And so to the final itself. Some feared that the parochial rivalry between the two teams might produce a rather unsavoury spectacle, but the game was played out in a sporting and often entertaining fashion. Wembley still carried with it a cathedral-like aura, enhanced further still on cup final day by the pomp, ceremony and presence of royalty, and tended to bring out the best behaviour in the participants.

Spurs, on a run of twenty-three unbeaten games, lived up to their favourites tag by generally having the better of play and were rewarded just before half-time when Jimmy Robertson struck home a low shot from the edge of the area. When Frank Saul swivelled to put away a smart finish from Robertson's flick-on midway through the second half, the argument had been settled. Tambling's headed consolation was too little, too late and, at twenty-two years old, skipper Ron Harris had been denied the distinction of becoming the youngest captain to lift the cup.

Instead the honour of receiving the trophy went to the redoubtable Dave Mackay, whose season had been bookended by firm grips. Firstly Billy Bremner's throat and now the FA Cup. It was Spurs' third cup win of the decade so far and, coupled with QPR's triumph in the League Cup, at least signalled an element of resistance to the northern dominance seen in recent seasons. Spurs' victory was well received, it being noted with considerable pleasure by some critics that their two orthodox wingers had played a vital part in stretching the Chelsea defence, as well as scoring the two goals.

Immediately after the cup final, Wembley welcomed Spain for a shoot-out between the world and European champions. England's side, largely through injury but partly due to many clubs being away on their post-season tours, was much changed, with only five World Cup winners on duty. Amongst those taking their places was Chelsea's John Hollins, winning what would prove to be his only full cap. Greaves retained his place in the side and, as so often in the past, emerged from a quiet performance with a goal to his name. Roger Hunt was also on target as England registered an ultimately comfortable victory. Given that Spain were potential opponents in the European Nations Cup quarter-finals, the result was a particularly satisfying and encouraging one.

On the same night, almost beneath the radar, Leeds United reached the final of the Inter Cities Fairs Cup by eliminating Kilmarnock. After so many near misses since their promotion three years previously, the final – to be played at the start of the following season – would give them another chance to bring home the first piece of silverware in the club's history.

The following evening brought Celtic's momentous victory in the European Cup Final, as their relentlessly energetic attacks finally overcame the stifling cynicism of Inter Milan. At last a British side had triumphed in Europe's premier competition and, not that Manchester United would want for incentive, proved that these much-hyped continental sides could be beaten.

England then went on tour to Vienna, where they registered a fine win over Austria. Alan Ball, indefatigable to the last, scored the winner in a game marked by another fine display by Alan Mullery, whose extra mobility and qualities, both in attack and defence, suggested that the absent Stiles' restoration to the side was now under serious question. However, a three-pronged strike force of Hunt, Hurst and Greaves failed to gel and the game would signal the end of Greaves' international career.

Match Of The Month
6 May 1967, Division One: West Ham United 1
Manchester United 6

United arrived at Upton Park for their penultimate fixture needing a win to seal their second title in three years. They could hardly have hand-picked more accommodating opposition: West Ham's form since the turn of the year had been a shadow of what they had produced in those heady autumn months. There had still been entertainment aplenty, but most of it had been at the wrong end of the pitch from their own supporters' perspective.

The doors were closed long before kick-off on Upton Park's biggest crowd since the war and United wasted little time in delivering what many of them wanted to see. They had come into the game on the back of eight successive away draws but now, with the finishing line in sight, they showed their true capabilities. Within just ten minutes, Charlton, Crerand and Foulkes had already put them three up, as West Ham were swamped by a whirlwind of attacking football. From then on United were able to coast, intermittently adding to their tally through Best and a couple from Law, as West Ham's fans slowly drifted away from the ground.

Their capitulation, albeit to the champions, had been typical of their recent performances, and there was a touch of irony in the fact that their final home game had produced seven goals.

In their November pomp, they had featured in three seven-goal thrillers in eight days, coming out ahead in all of them. Here, however, they had been second best by several streets.

It was an emphatic and exhilarating way for United to clinch the title and for all his quiet satisfaction afterwards, Matt Busby left no one in any doubt where his ultimate ambition lay. The dark shadow of Munich still lingered heavily over Old Trafford and Busby felt he owed it to the victims to lift the trophy in whose pursuit so many had perished. With a team of genuine talent, and the added incentive of a 'home' final at Wembley, the next season would bring a real chance of success.

West Ham: Mackleworth, Burkett, Charles, Peters, Heffer, Moore, Redknapp, Bennett, Boyce, Hurst, Sissons.

Manchester United: Stepney, Brennan, Dunne, Crerand, Foulkes, Stiles, Best, Law, Sadler, Charlton, Aston.

Player Of The Month
Alan Mullery (Tottenham Hotspur)

Mullery signed for Spurs from Fulham in 1964, quickly establishing himself in a side struggling to recapture the glories of the early 1960s. The 1966/67 season saw them produce a level of consistency not seen since their double win in 1961. After losing narrowly at Old Trafford in January, Spurs went unbeaten for the rest of the season, a total of twenty-four games, and Mullery featured in every single one of them.

His energy and defensive discipline were important factors in Spurs losing the soft-touch tag which had dogged them for several years, and May saw them play four league games without conceding a single goal. Mullery in particular excelled against a vibrant West Ham at Upton Park, where his calm and authoritative display set the foundation for Spurs' 2-0 win, a result which guaranteed European football irrespective of the outcome of the forthcoming cup final. This achievement soon proved irrelevant, as Spurs duly beat Chelsea at Wembley, with Mullery outstanding. In a widely praised display of mobility and ultimately stamina, he helped to subdue Charlie Cooke as well as launch numerous Tottenham attacks, and it was Mullery's surging run and shot which set up Jimmy Robertson to score the opening goal.

Mullery had won his first full England cap in 1964, but initially failed to impress and was left out of the World Cup squad. But now, his increasingly influential displays for Spurs, together with Nobby Stiles' injury problems, brought him back into England contention. Mullery firmly established himself in the England side in 1967/68, even though Stiles was by then fully fit, and remained a regular despite famously becoming the first Englshman to be sent off in a full international, in the European Nations Cup semi-final against Yugoslavia. Indeed, in a representative match against Mexico a year later, Mullery was dismissed again.

Mullery started all four games in Mexico, much to the chagrin of Malcolm Allison on the ITV panel, who repeatedly denigrated his abilities as a footballer and was piqued that his own player, Colin Bell, hadn't been picked in his stead. In reality, they were different types of player, with Mullery's more defensive role crucial to the team's balance, and Allison's ire might have been better directed at the selection of the visibly ageing Bobby Charlton ahead of Bell. Mullery silenced Allison with an outstanding display against West Germany, scoring England's first goal before they went on to suffer a cruel defeat.

Mullery won the last of his thirty-five caps in 1971 and moved to second-division Fulham a year later where, with Bobby Moore alongside him, he helped the team to an unlikely cup final appearance in 1975. He also scored BBC's goal of the season with a screaming volley against Leicester City in 1974. Mullery then turned to management although, like most of his era to go down this route, he was generally unsuccessful.

Summer 1967

There was no question of clubs having had enough football, as many teams embarked on post-season jaunts, often to distant lands. Chelsea went to Bermuda for a three-match tour, but it didn't prove to be quite as relaxing as they might have expected. Two of the games saw Chelsea players dismissed, and in one of them Docherty threatened to take his team off the pitch in response to their treatment from both opposition and officials. In a move which would have unexpectedly severe repercussions, the Bermudan FA saw fit to write to Lancaster Gate complaining about Chelsea's general conduct.

For Wolves, Stoke and Sunderland, the summer meant masquerading as US teams in the newly formed United States Association. Stoke played out a 0-0 draw with Wolves in a match billed as Cleveland v Los Angeles. The Sunderland side turned out under the guise of Vancouver in the ten-team league, which also featured sides freighted in from Scotland, Ireland, Holland, Italy and Brazil.

England had a tour of their own to undertake, as they had agreed to participate in the Expo 67 tournament in Montreal. The team fielded went under the guise of 'The FA XI' and went on to win the four-team competition, beating Borussia Dortmund 3-2 in the final, with two goals from Frank Wignall. Although several regulars were away on club duty, the team still featured Banks, Cohen, Wilson, Ball, Hunter and Bell.

Attendance figures for the season just gone had revealed an increase – an aggregate of 28.9 million compared with 27.2 million in the previous season – but it was impossible to determine how much, if any, was attributable to the impact of the World Cup. The early-season fixtures had produced disappointing attendances, but things had improved after Christmas. There was wide debate as to the impact of television, with both sides using the arguments to suit themselves. Had TV whetted the appetite of the public by showing a range of exciting games, persuading more of them to go out and get a taste of the real thing? Or was it simply the milder weather, meaning that there were hardly any postponements, together with a closely fought title race, which had generated the increase? What was for sure was that the BBC were well pleased with their viewing figures, with an average of seven million tuning into *Match Of The Day* each week.

One of the noticeable features of the attendance statistics was the wide variation in attendances experienced by the vast majority of clubs. The form of the home team, the nature of the opposition, the importance of the game and the weather were all major factors in determining the size of the crowd on any given day. Season tickets were relatively uncommon, restricted to seated areas and often only to the main stand, and accounted for less than 25 per cent of clubs' average attendances. Liverpool sought to change this by offering tickets for the Kop and Paddock for the forthcoming season, and the response was highly encouraging. A guaranteed place in the famous Kop for just £4 4s was a bargain which many happily snapped up.

Analysing attendance figures – and indeed any other statistics associated with the game – was the stock in trade of the Football League's statistician, Walter Pilkington, who had a weekly column in the *Football League Review*. This official mouthpiece of the Football League was incorporated within the programmes of over seventy league clubs, and was an incredibly self-righteous vehicle for Football League propaganda, an unmistakeable tone of 'We know best' permeating its every page.

Some of Walter's facts and figures were interesting and pertinent, but with a column to fill every week he would inevitably be forced into more esoteric areas, producing lists and tables which were of little relevance or consequence – unless, of course, you had a mind like Walter's. Walter's accompanying commentary seldom threw much light on exactly what point this week's torrent of statistics were trying to make, but did occasionally provide a glimpse of the man behind the numbers.

He deplored the increasingly extravagant goal celebrations which were creeping into the game. 'I would like to ask what is "professional" about players hugging and kissing the scorer of a goal…I can understand the desire to express it in some form but to me, and many others, I am sure, this girlish mobbing of a manly athlete who has done his job well is nauseating. Frankly, I cringe at the sight of it.'

One senses that Walter would also have disapproved of the counterculture emerging throughout pockets of a country which otherwise remained in economic crisis. The Summer Of Love created a feelgood factor – indeed a feel *very* good factor – for much of the nation's youth as the groovy, psychedelic music, with mind-altering substances to match, took a hold. The Beatles' *Sergeant Pepper* formed the soundtrack to the summer, and on long, lazy Sunday afternoons its iconic songs could be heard flooding out through open bedroom windows all around the country.

1967/68:

Manchester: A City United in Glory

AUGUST 1967

The Charity Shield brought United and Spurs together at Old Trafford to produce an encounter which would live long in the memory, not only of those present but also the millions who tuned in to *Match Of The Day*, desperate for their football fix after the summer hiatus. The game, a 3-3 draw, saw two explosive goals from Bobby Charlton, both ripping past Jennings from outside the area, but it was the Spurs keeper himself who made most of the headlines. Late in the first half, his prodigious clearance bounced just outside Stepney's penalty area before looping over the keeper to nestle snugly in the back of the net. Stepney glanced sheepishly at the referee in the hope that such a goal was somehow illegal, only to be disappointed. It was reckoned to be the first time this had ever occurred in a game between English clubs.

Spurs' performance was highly impressive and, on the back of their twenty-five-game unbeaten run from the previous season, there were plenty tipping them to put in a serious title bid. And when the real action began a week later, they started impressively, with a comprehensive 3-0 win at Leicester City.

The opening day's biggest crowds were predictably to be found at the two Merseyside–Manchester tussles. At Goodison Park, Everton saw off the champions with relative ease, Alan Ball netting a brace in a 3-1 victory, whilst Liverpool's visit to Maine Road produced no goals but plenty of incident, with Tony Book's late penalty miss denying City victory. Both games featured dozens of arrests following bouts of violence instigated by travelling supporters who had infiltrated home ends. The Summer Of Love evidently hadn't quite extended to the terraces.

Newly promoted Wolves made a flying start with an easy win at Fulham, but their counterparts from Coventry already seemed in disarray. Having masterminded their ascent into the first division and completely transformed the club, Jimmy Hill had announced his decision to retire in order to focus on other footballing activities, widely assumed to mean a career in broadcasting. Hill would remain at the helm until a successor could be found, but was unable to prevent his club's first ever top-flight appearance ending in defeat at Turf Moor.

Leeds, starting the season with the imminent prospect of the Fairs Cup Final to look forward to, began in disappointing fashion, being held to a 1-1 draw by Sunderland, for whom the young Colin Suggett was a constant threat. Leeds ultimately dealt with him in what was becoming a time-honoured tradition, the second of two brutal tackles by Hunter seeing the youngster carried from the field. One of the features of the match was the strange performance of Sunderland keeper Jim Montgomery, apparently living in constant fear of the newly introduced four-step rule. To be on the safe side, he generally chose to make his clearances from a static position having taken no steps at all. It created a bizarre spectacle and contributed to an unusually nervous performance from the keeper.

It soon transpired that Montgomery wasn't alone in his confusion, as referees' interpretations of what was and wasn't allowed were quickly found to vary. If a goalkeeper collected the ball from a backpass, could he carry it for four steps, pick it up again and clear it? Should the steps taken in each phase of holding the ball be added up and a free kick awarded if the sum exceeded four? It soon became evident that different interpretations were being applied, but it took some time for the position to be resolved. With so few games being televised, it was impossible to assess definitively how each referee was dealing with the new ruling.

Things got little better for Leeds four days later, as they came away from Old Trafford empty-handed. Brian Kidd impressed for United and showed he wouldn't be intimidated by the robust attentions of his opponents, most notably when squaring up to Billy Bremner. Bobby Charlton's goal secured the points for the champions, for whom Law was outstanding.

Liverpool, criticised for an overly physical approach in their opening fixture, again showed plenty of appetite for a scrap in their home game with Arsenal. An uncompromising encounter was settled by two goals from Roger Hunt, starting the journey towards his third century of Liverpool goals. Hunt now had a new attacking partner, with Shankly's long-standing pursuit of Tony Hateley having been undeterred by the player's largely underwhelming season with Chelsea.

Last season's top league scorer, Ron Davies, opened his account for Southampton with a brace in a 3-2 win over Manchester City and his partnership with Martin Chivers, also on target, again promised to produce more than enough goals for the Saints to survive, or even prosper. They both found the net again in the return match a week later and, 2-1 down at half-time, it looked as though City's wait for a first win of the season would continue. However, a stirring second-half revival, spearheaded by Bell and Young, saw City take the points and revive optimism that their fine finish to the previous season might be a taste of things to come.

At White Hart Lane, Everton threatened to continue where they had left off against United, only to be hamstrung by an injury to Alan Ball, who was carried from the field after just fifteen minutes. Spurs immediately went ahead, but their resilient opponents came back to share the spoils in a result which satisfied both sides, extending Spurs' unbeaten run to thirty games. Thirty-one was marked up a few days later, with West Ham easily seen off at White Hart Lane. Once more, however, the afternoon was marred by terrace violence before and during the game. Hooliganism was becoming an ever-increasing problem on the terraces and a staple subject for the headlines, but constructive ideas on how to deal with it were few and far between. Amidst the cries to reintroduce national service and bring back the birch, there were suggestions that the cages seen at continental grounds were the only realistic way to restrain and control the troublemakers. It would take the deaths of ninety-six people over twenty years later for the authorities to recognise that this too was a flawed solution.

Tony Hateley's Liverpool scoring duck was broken in emphatic style at home to Newcastle, his hat-trick the centrepiece of a 6-0 win, and he was on the scoresheet again when Liverpool travelled to Highbury. Alas, his spectacular towering header flew past his own keeper to put Arsenal on the way to a 2-0 win, but at least he managed to keep his temper as several Arsenal players gave him congratulatory pats on the back. The fun and games were watched by a crowd in which those in the posh seats had paid £1 for a ticket, meaning that Arsenal boasted the most expensive admission charges anywhere in the division, a tradition the club has proudly maintained to this day.

West Ham remained true to their principles, their trip to Burnley producing a third successive six-goal feast for spectators. This time, the goals were evenly shared, with Hurst and Peters among the scorers, but West Ham's defence, thirteen conceded in just four games, was as much a cause for concern as ever. Expensive new keeper Bobby Ferguson had thus far failed to make the desired impact, with several mishaps causing fans to think that Jim Standen, let alone Gordon Banks, would have made a better fist of things.

As well as unrest on the terraces, there were increasing incidences of player dissatisfaction being made public, as journalists encouraged players to spill the beans. So many stories emanated from Chelsea that Tommy Docherty ordered his players not to talk to the press. Stoke City had given Peter Dobing his cards after he rejected the terms he was being offered and Mike Summerbee had asked for a transfer from Manchester City after refusing to sign his contract.

Joe Mercer acted decisively over Summerbee's behaviour, stating unequivocally that he would have to honour the remaining year of his contract and under no circumstances would he be sold before then. Ever since the abolition of the minimum wage, an increasing number of players were attempting to call the shots, but the vast majority of them were quickly put back into their places.

Slowly, however, an insidious new development was having an impact – the agent. Despite the fact that league clubs could only deal directly with the players in negotiations, agents were beginning to recognise the rich pickings available from linking up with the game's biggest stars. Much of their initial work was in areas outside the game – securing and negotiating terms for endorsements, appearance fees and so on – but there was an inevitability that this would be the tip of the iceberg. 'If the day ever dawns when one agent controls a dozen players from a dozen different clubs – and is allowed to direct that control within the game itself – then the only result will be anarchy.' For once, the *Football League Review* was on the money.

Match Of The Month
19 August 1967, Division One: Everton 3
Manchester United 1

United's first match as defending champions was a tough assignment at Goodison Park. Although Everton's recent record in this fixture was dismal, United's reputation as slow starters would have given their fans encouragement, as would the restoration of Alex Young to the attack to partner eighteen-year-old Joe Royle.

It was, however, the midfield where Everton really held sway. Kendall, Harvey and Ball, all under twenty-three years of age, possessed contrasting but complementary qualities and the three of them gelled beautifully. Ball in particular had much the better of his family argument with Nobby Stiles, his energy and enthusiasm rubbing off on his team-mates, who harassed United out of their stride.

Ball gave Everton an early lead and his team dominated the first half. The second period saw them step up to an even higher level, and they laid siege to United's goal for a full twenty minutes. After a series of narrow escapes, Ball finally broke through again with a close-range finish, before Alex Young smashed home the goal of the day with a flashing drive. Charlton's late reply for United was almost an irrelevance, giving the final scoreline a misleadingly close look.

Everton had been outstanding throughout and with such a youthful side, their fans' optimism seemed well justified. After just this one match, *The Guardian*'s Eric Todd was moved to write, 'Everton are on the threshold of greatness', adding that they might not cross it this or even next season, but cross it they definitely would. And indeed they did, even if it took them another couple of seasons.

Everton: West, Wright, Wilson, Kendall, Labone, Harvey, Young, Ball, Royle, Hurst, Morrissey.

Manchester United: Stepney, Brennan, Dunne, Crerand, Foulkes, Stiles, Best, Law, Charlton, Kidd, Aston. Sub: Sadler.

Player Of The Month
Roger Hunt (Liverpool)

Hunt made his Liverpool debut in 1959, survived the clear-out after Bill Shankly arrived at the club, and immediately rewarded the new boss by scoring forty-one goals as Liverpool were promoted back to the first division. His exploits were recognised by Walter Winterbottom, who capped Hunt in 1962, and when Alf Ramsey took over Hunt became an England regular, playing every minute of their World Cup campaign.

Hunt had endured a difficult first season after the World Cup, his fourteen Liverpool goals being his lowest haul in his eight years at the club. After a sequence of fruitless international performances he had been dropped in favour of Jimmy Greaves, but came back after the summer break determined to win back his England place.

Liverpool's first home game was against Arsenal and Hunt showed that his goalscoring instincts had returned by scoring twice from just three opportunities offered by a notoriously miserly defence. The first was a searing drive which left Jim Furnell helpless, the second a predatory follow-up after Furnell had parried Ron Yeats's shot. Hunt followed up with another double in the 6-0 drubbing of Newcastle four days later, as well as playing a prominent role in helping new strike partner Tony Hateley to hit a hat-trick.

Hunt's improved form continued through the season as he netted twenty-five league goals and won back his England place. Hunt was a classic Ramsey player, full of unselfish running to create space for others but also a prolific goalscorer himself, although his unflashy style of play meant that in phases where the goals dried up he was often the man whose credentials were questioned. His eighteen goals in thirty-four England appearances was a ratio comparable with the very best, and he remains Liverpool's all-time leading scorer of league goals. When one considers the strikers who have graced Anfield since then, this is testament to the calibre of this often unsung hero.

Even though Hunt scored three goals in the final stages, he is seldom recalled as being one of the key players in England's triumphant campaign. Recollections of his role in the final are often restricted to Geoff Hurst's much-quoted contribution to the 'was it over the line?' debate. 'Roger was following up and was so sure the ball had crossed the line that he turned away to celebrate rather than just nodding in the rebound...' The fact that Wolfgang Weber was perfectly positioned to nod the ball clear before Hunt could get anywhere near it seems to have escaped Geoff's notice. Still, never let the facts get in the way of a good story.

SEPTEMBER 1967

Thirty-three games unbeaten, and fresh off the back of a most un-Spurs-like smash and grab win at Everton, Tottenham arrived at Turf Moor with every expectation of extending their sequence. A couple of hours later, they were back in the dressing room picking the bones out of a 5-1 pasting. Their main tormentors were centre-forward Andy Lochhead, who gave Mike England a torrid afternoon, and winger Ralph Coates, newly restored to the side after a bout of appendicitis. It was another illustration of what this young but wildly inconsistent Burnley side was capable of.

Tottenham's only consolation was that their drubbing still wasn't the afternoon's most eye-catching result. At Stamford Bridge, a hapless Chelsea – thrashed 5-1 at Newcastle just four days previously – were now put to the sword by Southampton and their ruthless strike force of Martin Chivers and Ron Davies. Davies helped himself to four, Chivers to two, and Chelsea's only cause for satisfaction was the return to form of Peter Osgood. Still easing his way back after his broken leg, Osgood scored a goal so sublime – beating six men in a run from the halfway line before sliding the ball home – that the crowd's continued applause rang out for over a minute. On a dismal day for London clubs, West Ham's 3-1 defeat at Manchester United almost seemed like a good result.

Whatever the thrills provided on the pitch, week after week the headlines continued to centre on the hooliganism occurring off it. When Billy Bremner was sent off at Fulham, it sparked an instant fracas on the terraces, prompting observations once again that player behaviour, or misbehaviour, was often the catalyst for trouble. Whilst there was some truth in this – many fans took particular delight in revelling in and sometimes mimicking the violent antics of their team's hard man – it didn't explain the fact that much of the trouble occurred before kick-off. One suggestion increasingly being put forward was for player suspensions to be far more severe, so as to discourage on-field violence and dissent, in turn reducing the risk of flare-ups amongst the fans. Bremner's punishment was awaited with keener anticipation than usual.

West Ham's Bobby Ferguson – the world's most expensive goalkeeper – had hardly lived up to his billing, and was dropped by Ron Greenwood after shipping eighteen goals in just six appearances. Even the gentlemanly Greenwood must have wished he had reneged on his verbal agreement, pulled out of the Ferguson deal and gone for Banks instead. Coincidence or not, the Hammers next went to Sunderland and, with Ferguson watching from the stands, came away with a 5-1 victory featuring the statistical quirk of all three World Cup winners on the scoresheet. The most spectacular goal was scored by Bobby Moore, his twenty-yard volley being greeted by a sheepish grin. Hopes that West Ham could be about to embark on one of their purple patches were swiftly quashed, however – the following week, Dougan's two goals gave Wolves the spoils at Upton Park, despite the crowd's feverish support for the reinstated Jim Standen in goal.

Chelsea's visit to Anfield gave Tony Hateley the chance to deliver another demonstration of Brian Glanville's much-loved *immutable law of the ex*, and he did so with authority, scoring two goals within ninety seconds at the start of the second half to send Liverpool top of the league. One of the sides closely behind them was Manchester City, whose 5-2 hammering of Sheffield United was their fifth win in succession. They were earning rave reviews for their attacking football and their next game, at Arsenal, was eagerly anticipated. With four goals in each of their last two games the hosts, for the first time in many years, were laying claim to be the best team in London.

Arsenal won a tight game 1-0, with the watching Hugh McIlvanney clearly wishing he had stayed at home. Describing the game as 'an anaesthetising succession of brutal collisions, a contest as subtle and edifying as an infantry engagement on the Somme', he bemoaned the lack of entertainment, criticising the Arsenal fans for showing enthusiasm for winning irrespective of the quality of the spectacle. Surely Arsenal should have dealt more convincingly with such moderate opposition, he mused. As for that moderate opposition, only Bell and Summerbee were exempted from criticism. Winger Paul Hince, possibly the only professional footballer to have his performance described in the press as 'spectacularly fatuous', was likened to a ballboy who had inadvertently strayed on to the pitch.

After their long unbeaten run, Spurs appeared to be reverting to their old flouncing ways away from White Hart Lane. Their 5-1 drubbing at Burnley had been followed by an even more painful 4-0 reverse at Highbury and now they were well beaten at Old Trafford. United's 3-1 win was sealed only in the final few minutes, but Spurs were under the cosh throughout as United, for the first time this season, rediscovered their championship form.

Their next engagement was the Maine Road derby, where younger fans had started their day with an extra dose of excitement. BBC's launch of Radio One had given them their own mainstream radio channel, and the voice of Tony Blackburn and his upbeat, funtastic jingle-filled show would soon become part of their daily lives. City kicked off in the unaccustomed position of looking down on their neighbours in the league table, but ninety minutes later the old order had been restored, as two goals from Bobby Charlton overturned Bell's early strike for City. When City rather unluckily lost at Sunderland the following week, hitting the woodwork three times, most concluded that their earlier winning streak had been nothing more than a flash in the pan.

Leeds' slow start to the season had been a surprise, and they suffered further disappointment as Dynamo Zagreb held out for a goalless draw at Elland Road to claim the Fairs Cup. Goals had been in short supply, and Revie turned to the transfer market to bring in Sheffield United centre-forward Mick Jones for £100,000. The critics were generally unimpressed, with many sensing a touch of desperation in the signing – how else could a player widely regarded as little more than a journeyman striker have commanded a six-figure fee?

Wolves were making a decent fist of their return to the top flight, and their strike force of the cavalier Dougan and the silky Peter Knowles was now augmented by eighteen-year-old Alun Evans. Evans had made an impressive debut at West Ham and his first home game, against Burnley, saw him steal the headlines with a late winner. Knowles, an England under-23 regular, had earlier scored twice for Wolves, responding to the fans' cries of 'Give it to Knowles – we want goals!' Wolves then went to a Sheffield Wednesday side riding high in the table, where Knowles and Evans both scored again to earn their side a point. Their enterprising play had made Wolves a welcome addition to the first division, suggesting ambitions which extended beyond mere survival.

Liverpool narrowly won the Merseyside derby with a superb goal from Roger Hunt, leaving their neighbours closer to the foot of the table than the top. Everton's midfield of Harvey, Kendall and Ball was generally acknowledged to be the finest in the country, but the team were struggling to turn their creative play into an end product. Ernie Hunt, an £80,000 signing from Wolves, had now made four appearances without a sniff of a goal and with Alex Young seeming to have lost some of his earlier sharpness, Evertonians were eager for the return of the young prodigy Joe Royle.

Match Of The Month
2 September 1967, Division One: Chelsea 2 Southampton 6

Southampton's first season back in the top flight had seen them achieve their basic target of survival, but now they hoped for something rather better. With the experience and craft of Terry Paine and Jimmy Melia, the prodigious goalscoring prowess of Ron Davies and the increasing influence of his strike partner Martin Chivers, they certainly had the tools to achieve it.

Against a Chelsea side in poor form generally and stung by a midweek thrashing at Newcastle, the Saints enjoyed their finest first division moment so far, as Ron Davies created havoc amongst a defence in complete disarray. With just half an hour gone, Davies had helped himself to a hat-trick with three clean finishes and seemingly put the game beyond the hosts. Chelsea's teenage centre-half Colin Waldron endured a grim afternoon, although Tommy Docherty afterwards reiterated his claim that the boy was destined to become a truly great player.

The start of the second half saw Chelsea hint at an unlikely revival with some concerted pressure. The home fans were delighted to see their young idol, Peter Osgood, back in the fold after finally recovering from his broken leg, but so far this season he had still been easing his way back in, with only sporadic signs of the brilliance which had been so commonplace a year ago. But now he surpassed even those heights with a goal of sheer majesty. Collecting the ball in his own half, he slalomed his way gracefully past five Southampton players before gliding past keeper Forsyth and stroking the ball into the net.

Hopes of a comeback were soon quashed, as two goals from Chivers put the Saints in the safety zone, before a more prosaic effort from Osgood brought modest consolation. Davies completed the scoring with his fourth of the game, prompting an outbreak of terrace violence and sealing a stunning result for his team. But for most in the crowd, the day would be remembered for Osgood's moment of genius.

Chelsea: Bonetti, Hinton, McCreadie, Hollins, Waldron, Harris, Cooke, Baldwin, Osgood, McMillan, Tambling.

Southampton: Forsyth, Webb, Hollywood, Fisher, Gabriel, Walker, Paine, Chivers, Davies, Melia, Sydenham.

Player Of The Month
Stan Bowles (Manchester City)

With City 1-0 up against Leicester in a League Cup tie, manager Joe Mercer brought on eighteen-year-old Stan Bowles for his first team debut. Forty-five minutes later, Bowles left the pitch with two goals to his name and with the Maine Road crowd wondering whether a new star had been born. Bowles scored with a calm fifteen-yard shot to put City 2-0 up, won the penalty from which Tony Book increased the lead and completed the scoring with a fierce first-time drive. He was rewarded with a start in the next game, in the league at home to Sheffield United, and just before half-time he got himself on the scoresheet again with a close-range header. Dovetailing well with City's more established stars, he then latched on to Neil Young's through ball to fire home a beautiful shot for the final goal in City's 5-2 win.

Two weeks later, Bowles started in the Manchester derby at Maine Road, and was in no way fazed by the occasion. He almost made headlines of a different kind, after a fracas with United's own eighteen-year-old, Brian Kidd, and it took the intervention of both sides' senior players to dissuade the referee from sending them both off. These were different days indeed.

Sadly, this month was as good as Bowles' career at City got, as his off-field activities frequently incurred the wrath of Mercer and Allison. As Mercer memorably said: 'If he could pass a betting shop like he can pass a football, he would be one hell of a player.' Allison from time to time paid off Bowles' gambling debts but ultimately became exasperated with the player's lifestyle – which unwisely included late-night sorties to the same nightclubs as Big Mal himself frequented – and in 1970 he was released to join third-division Bury.

Spells at Crewe and Carlisle followed and it looked as though Bowles' immense promise would not be fulfilled. However, in 1972, he was transferred to Queens Park Rangers to replace Rodney Marsh – who ironically had moved to Manchester City – and over the next few years his career finally blossomed. He helped Rangers to promotion and was then an integral part of the side which came thrillingly close to taking the first division title in 1976.

By then, Bowles had become a full international, making his debut in Ramsey's final game at the helm. Things then came full circle when Bowles was reunited with Joe Mercer during the latter's caretaker spell as England manager, but after featuring in Mercer's first two selections – and scoring his only England goal – he reacted badly to being substituted and sought solace at the White City dog track rather than staying at the team hotel. Mercer didn't select him again after this incident, but Bowles won two further caps under Don Revie.

Bowles had a brief spell at Brian Clough's revitalised Forest before drifting back into the lower leagues. A player of immense skill, and also loved by fans for his off-field exploits, he was voted QPR's greatest ever player in an online poll amongst their supporters in 2004.

OCTOBER 1967

A year ago, Chelsea were sitting at the top of the first division table, looking set fair to establish themselves as one of England's premier club sides. The injury to Peter Osgood knocked them out of their stride, although they recovered well enough to reach the FA Cup Final. Now, however, they were a club in crisis. Battered 5-1 at Newcastle, then 6-2 at home by Southampton, their manager Tommy Docherty was handed a twenty-eight-day FA ban for his misdemeanours on the club's pre-season Bermudan tour and almost immediately resigned from his post.

Docherty's departure left Chelsea managerless for the trip to Elland Road, where they suffered a 7-0 beating from a Leeds side which had mustered only ten goals in its previous nine league games. Leeds would shortly have a high-profile absentee of their own, with Billy Bremner about to start a twenty-eight-day suspension imposed for his dismissal at Fulham. At least he signed off in style. Leeds were three up after quarter of an hour and never looked back. Having created four goals, Bremner completed the rout with a spectacular overhead kick, and was given a standing ovation as he left the field to begin his period of exile. The fact that he only had himself to blame for damaging his side's title challenge had been totally ignored, in an illustration of the blind loyalty which was increasingly becoming a characteristic of fans throughout the country. Jim Baxter had also recently received a similar ban, further indicating that the Scottish contingent in English football needed to learn how to behave themselves.

Right on cue, that impression was enhanced by events at Old Trafford, where Denis Law and Ian Ure spent most of the afternoon spoiling for a fight and eventually succumbed to the urge, promptly finding themselves dispatched to the dressing rooms to continue their feud in private. It was a witless performance from two such experienced players, especially in view of the recent sentences handed down, and there were pleas for the FA to get even tougher on Law and Ure to encourage professional footballers everywhere to recognise their responsibilities.

Law's performance in United's next game was subdued and almost sheepish, as if he was embarrassed by his antics the previous week. Despite this, United were way too strong for Sheffield United, a team already looking like prime relegation candidates. The action at Bramall Lane was marred by the behaviour of the travelling supporters who, well before the game started, uprooted the corner flags before being ejected by the police. Their actions were almost comedic in comparison with events at the Den, where referee Norman Burtenshaw was knocked to the ground semi-conscious by Millwall thugs after disallowing what would have been a late equaliser for their side. Trouble at the Den was hardly merely a modern phenomenon – the ground had been closed four times in its history, dating as far back as 1920 – but taken in conjunction with commonplace violence at grounds all over the country, this latest outbreak brought genuine fears for the safety of players and officials.

West Ham were quickly back to their old ways, taking part in a seven-goal thriller at home to Stoke. It wasn't a thriller in the conventional 'swinging to and fro' sense, though – Stoke's four all came within eight minutes of each other, after they had found themselves 3-0 down well into the second half. In typical style, West Ham then went to Stamford Bridge the following week and saw off the hosts with a polished performance. New Chelsea manager Dave Sexton could at least take some encouragement from the attacking flair shown by his team – notably Osgood, who scored another magnificent if ultimately futile solo goal – but he had clearly inherited a defence which required major surgery. West Ham fans celebrated their 3-1 win by destroying tube trains on the way home, smashing windows and ripping out fittings, leaving fellow passengers to wonder what would have happened had they lost.

The latest in the series of players to become disgruntled about their personal terms was Francis Lee of second-division Bolton Wanderers, a player desperate for first division football. Unlike most of the other malcontents, quickly put back in their box by their clubs, Lee took the argument a step further by going on strike. Despite his evidently feisty nature, he had shown enough quality over the previous couple of seasons to attract a number of suitors, and eventually Manchester City rescued him from his self-imposed exile for a fee of £65,000. Lee's first game saw City end their run of three straight defeats with a 2-0 win over Wolves.

With so much turbulence on and off the pitch, it was a relief to many to get back to international action, where spectators and players, at least thus far, had been rather more sedately behaved. England's next engagement as they attempted to reach the knockout stages of the European Nations Cup was in Cardiff. Mullery's form in the post-season internationals saw him retain his place ahead of Nobby Stiles, while Keith Newton of second-division Blackburn Rovers came in for the injured Ray Wilson. The remaining nine positions were filled by World Cup winners.

With Wales missing their first-choice strike force of Wyn and Ron Davies, a comfortable afternoon was expected. England's 3-0 win suggests that this was duly accomplished, but the scoreline was given gloss by two very late goals and Wales on several occasions came close to equalising Peters' first-half opener. Banks, described by Ramsey as 'magnificent', made three excellent saves as Wales created far more chances than anyone could have imagined. Critics were generally unimpressed, observing that Wales seemed by far the more motivated team and that England seemed almost casual once they had taken the lead. But they had got the job done, as Ramsey's team usually did, and were given an added lift by the result from Belfast, where Scotland's defeat allowed England to return to the top of the qualifying group.

The day's only top-flight league match was a significant one, as Manchester City's 4-2 win at Fulham featured a first goal for Francis Lee and signalled Fulham's fifth successive defeat. Fulham remained rooted to the foot of the table whilst City nudged their way back into the top five. When City won their next game, at home to a dogged, defensive Leeds, several critics were impressed enough to suggest that this was a team that could put in a surprise challenge for honours.

Last season's surprise package, Nottingham Forest, had struggled to make the same impact this time round, but ended the month with their two best results of the season so far. After dismantling a Spurs side whose season seemed to be disintegrating, Forest then faced Manchester United in front of a record attendance at the City Ground. United were without the injured Stiles, and it showed as Forest dominated midfield and were twice able to release Joe Baker to beat Stepney. Frank Wignall added a third, rendering Best's late goal irrelevant, as United suffered their first reverse since the season's opening day.

A further factor in United's defeat had been the ineffectual performance of Denis Law, who took the field under the heavy cloud of knowing that this would be his last appearance for some considerable time. He and Ian Ure had both received six-week bans from the FA for their altercation at Old Trafford, severe sentences which reflected the fact that this was hardly a first offence for either, as well as the FA's desire to clamp down even further on behaviour likely to inflame the crowd.

Hopes that the FA's increasingly hard line would serve as a deterrent to others quickly received another blow, and this time the offenders weren't even Scottish. In a violent encounter between Newcastle and Everton, the referee saw fit to bring the two captains together at half-time to get their teams to cool it. It didn't work. Early in the second half, Newcastle's Ollie Burton was dismissed after a contretemps with Alex Young, but the day's real drama was reserved for its final minutes. Everton keeper Gordon West, a man prone to occasional bouts of violent temper, lashed out at and floored a Newcastle forward after clearing the ball. The referee had followed the ball's path, but his linesman had seen the incident and the officials' subsequent conversation resulted in West being ordered off and a penalty awarded. Stand-in keeper Sandy Brown couldn't deliver any heroics, and Newcastle duly took the points. But the headlines once more were all about player misbehaviour; it was a rare day indeed when football headlines focused purely on football.

Match Of The Month
7 October 1967, Division One: West Ham United 3 Stoke City 4

West Ham's reputation as the team to watch if you wanted goals – as long as you weren't bothered at which end they went in – had not diminished. The season's first two months had brought brilliance and incompetence in equal measure as Bobby Moore fought valiantly to prevent his side conceding more goals than their prolific forwards banged in at the other end. Moore's efforts hadn't been helped by the uncertain start made by the world's most expensive goalkeeper, Bobby Ferguson, who after a nervous error-strewn start to life south of the border had been rested for a couple of games, as Ron Greenwood sought to take the pressure off him.

Ferguson was restored to the side for the visit of Stoke, allowing comparisons to be drawn with the man at the other end, England's finest, Gordon Banks. Banks was much the busier man in the first half as West Ham were at their irresistible best. He had no chance with any of their three goals, two from Hurst and the other an acrobatic volley from Martin Peters, and West Ham would have been even more out of sight had it not been for a couple of spectacular saves. Harry Redknapp had created two of the goals and, with his eye-catching pace and crossing ability, looked destined for big things.

Stoke had scarcely threatened and, despite showing more signs of life in the second half, they were still three down with less than half an hour to go. Eight minutes later, they were 4-3 up as the Hammers completely imploded. Central to Stoke's revival were the crafty pair of George Eastham and Peter Dobing, whose clever promptings were aided and abetted by some hapless defending. Dobing and Burrows each scored as Moore's centre-back partner Cushley went walkabout, with the Stoke attackers striding unchallenged into the area, and Ferguson's ghastly fumble allowed Burrows to level the scores. Just two minutes later, Dobing raced away, again totally unchallenged, to fire past Ferguson. West Ham were too stunned to mount any kind of response and, hardly for the first time, their fans were left to exit the stadium shaking their heads in disbelief.

West Ham: Ferguson, Bonds, Charles, Peters, Cushley, Moore, Redknapp, Bovington, Brabrook, Hurst, Sissons.

Stoke: Banks, Skeels, Bentley, Palmer, Bloor (Bernard), Allen, Bridgwood, Eastham, Dobing, Vernon, Burrows.

Player Of The Month
Mike Summerbee (Manchester City)

Signed by Joe Mercer shortly after arriving at the club, Summerbee made an instant impression as a right-winger, playing an important part in City's promotion in his first season. After a year of consolidation in the first division, Summerbee had been switched to centre-forward in an experiment initiated by Malcolm Allison, and put in some outstanding early-season performances as City found themselves amongst the leaders.

After three successive defeats had threatened to undo much of their good work, Mercer and Allison responded by signing Francis Lee from Bolton. Lee and Summerbee quickly formed a productive partnership on the field, as well as a close and long-standing friendship off it. After a comfortable win at home to Wolves, City travelled to Craven Cottage, where Summerbee scored twice to help City to a 4-2 win, the first a fine header which illustrated his attributes as leader of the line. The following week, a tight game against Leeds was settled when Summerbee's superb cross was headed home by Bell for a late winner.

In between times, City had two League Cup games with Blackpool, Summerbee equalising with a ferocious shot in the 1-1 draw at Maine Road before netting the clinching goal in a 2-0 replay win at Bloomfield Road. The goal demonstrated Summerbee's capacity for improvisation, for after slipping he was still able to manipulate the ball over the line from a seated position.

Never previously a prolific marksman, Summerbee continued to revel in his new role, scoring regularly as City maintained their surprise title challenge, and was called up by Alf Ramsey for England's crucial European Championship game against Scotland at Hampden Park. Summerbee's appetite for a battle meant that he would hardly be fazed by such a hostile environment, and although he didn't make a major impression on the game, England still came away with the draw they needed.

Summerbee kept his place for the first leg of the quarter-final against Spain, but again struggled to make an impact, and after another quiet game in Hanover was then discarded by Ramsey. It was evident that, successful as he had been for City in the role, centre-forward wasn't Summerbee's natural position. Nevertheless, he continued to lead the line for City all the way to the end of the season, opening the scoring in the game at St James' Park which saw City take the title.

The following season saw Summerbee move back to right-wing and he thrived once more, helping City to more glory by setting up Neil Young's cup final winner. Summerbee also featured strongly in City's cup successes the following season, scoring the goal which sent City to the League Cup Final. Despite this, he failed to make Ramsey's twenty-two for Mexico but his outstanding form for City won him a recall to the England side in

1971. He won five further caps before defeat by West Germany in the European Championships brought his international career to an end.

Summerbee was a rarity for a winger as he thrived on physical contact and relished his battles against the game's renowned hard men, often being noted for 'retaliating first'. He is regarded as one of City's finest ever players and still works at the club in an ambassadorial role.

NOVEMBER 1967

The World Cup had created an enhanced interest in football amongst schoolboys – and, due in no small part to the 'pop-star' appeal of George Best, an increasing number of schoolgirls – but there was still very little reading material for them to get their teeth into. The only weekly football magazine in circulation was *Soccer Star*, a rather drab and po-faced publication aimed predominantly at adults. Editorial pieces often adopted a lecturing, supercilious tone, frequently expounding the view that newspaper journalists knew next to nothing about football and that subscribing to the magazine was the only way to get a real insight into the game and its tactics.

One of the magazine's leading contributors was Eric Batty, an eccentric and wilfully contrarian pseudo-intellectual who had long been convinced that English football needed a root-and-branch overhaul if it was ever to prosper. He was a leading proponent of the view that Ramsey's tactical approach would send English football back into the dark ages, and England's triumph had done nothing to convince him otherwise. Indeed, he openly proclaimed his disappointment that England had prevailed. Eric's ideal team would have consisted of a goalkeeper and ten crafty ball-players, each of whom would take turns to waltz through the opposition defence and score without breaking sweat. All-out effort was the desperate recourse of those without the requisite skill to play the game properly, and to win by such means was almost vulgar. Eric was undoubtedly the prototype for what Alan Partridge would go on to refer to as 'a mentalist'.

A year or so after the World Cup, *Soccer Star* belatedly realised that there was a younger market to be tapped into, introducing more pictures of star players and launching the *Soccer Star Club,* which for a mere two shillings entitled its members to a natty badge and not much else. A number of youngsters mistakenly sent their applications to join this elite group to the address for the magazine's *Bart and Mart* section and were reprimanded in the magazine for this lack of attention to detail. So if these pesky kids weren't exactly to be welcomed with open arms into the *Soccer Star* fold, then where could they get their weekly football fix?

Step forward Jimmy Hill. Having stunned the football world by resigning as Coventry manager, just weeks after masterminding their first ever sortie into the first division, Hill had decided to move into football broadcasting. However, he had also recognised that there was more than enough room for another football magazine on newsagents' shelves and, in November 1967, the first issue of *Jimmy Hill's Football Weekly* was released. Colourful and more upbeat and user-friendly than *Soccer Star*, it was well written enough for adults but also contained features specifically aimed at the younger reader, notably a double-page 'play better football' feature with tips to help them improve their games. Jimmy's role was to act as consultant editor, which in practice meant penning a short editorial piece and leaving everything else to the staff, but by lending his name to the magazine he gave it a cachet sufficient for a successful launch.

Hill's former club, Coventry, continued to find their first foray into the topflight a daunting experience, with just two wins from their first fifteen games. When fellow strugglers Fulham arrived at Highfield Road and comprehensively took the points with a 3-0 win, there were few who gave what was now Noel Cantwell's team any realistic chance of survival.

Fulham themselves had been rooted to the foot of the table, but this would be the first of three consecutive victories without conceding a goal. With Johnny Haynes briefly recalling the glories of yesteryear, Allan Clarke back amongst the goals and captain George Cohen at his inspiring best, there was now real hope that this popular club would pull away from trouble. Their win against Forest was particularly impressive, although the mood of viewers who stayed up to watch it on *Match Of The Day* had been darkened an hour or so earlier, as programmes were interrupted to bring the sombre news that the pound had been devalued, plunging in value from $2.80 to $2.40. Perhaps the broader implications may have been lost on some of the viewers, but the tone of the announcement left an unmistakeable sense that, world champions or not, our international standing had somehow been diminished.

Billy Bremner returned from suspension in time for the visit of Manchester United, helping his team to a 1-0 win which was comfortably their best result of the season. A week later they were brought back down to earth at lowly Sheffield United, who played all but nine minutes of the game with the unlikely figure of Alan Woodward in goal after Alan Hodgkinson dislocated a finger. Woodward made some outstanding saves, and Mick Hill's goal from one of his team's few attacks delivered a memorable and ecstatically received victory, with Woodward applauded off the field not just by the crowd but also by his team-mates. The consistency which had so characterised Leeds' performances in the previous few seasons was still proving elusive.

Their defeat at Elland Road may have denied Manchester United the chance to top the table, but they had another chance to reach the summit when they visited the existing incumbents, Liverpool, a couple of weeks later. This time United made no mistake, two goals from Best ruining Liverpool's hitherto perfect home record. To achieve such a result without the talismanic Law made a major statement and established United as firm favourites to retain their title.

Their neighbours were still impressing however, this time with a ruthless 6-0 battering of Leicester City. This match saw Maine Road witness the acceptable face of football hooliganism, as many of the cast of *Coronation Street* were amongst the crowd.

The storyline saw Annie Walker, the snooty, condescending landlady of The Rovers, become so provoked by rowdy behaviour on the way back from the game that she threw her rattle at the miscreants, only for it to miss its target and instead smash a window. When police found a toilet roll planted in her handbag, the stunned Mrs Walker, so beautifully portrayed by Doris Speed, was escorted away and taken to the cells in one of her most humiliating screen sequences. By the next episode, she was safely back pulling pints and turning her nose up at Elsie Tanner's latest love interest.

Tommy Docherty's abruptly truncated reign at Chelsea had generally been highly successful, and most people assumed that another high-profile role would quickly fall into his lap. It was, therefore, a little surprising to see him swap the bright lights of the Kings Road for the slightly less obvious attractions of downtown Rotherham. The Doc was clearly a man who needed to work and wasn't too concerned where. 'I cannot sit around and wait for people to be sacked,' he said, before embarking on his new £6,000-a-year job – a twenty per cent increase on his pay at Chelsea – in charge of a team which he admitted he had never even seen play. It was certainly a coup for the Yorkshire club's directors, and Rotherham's first home game under their new manager almost doubled their average gate. Hull City rather spoiled the occasion by winning 3-1.

Docherty's old club were showing little evidence of improvement under Dave Sexton, although there were more promising signs from Osgood as his superb performance inspired his team to victory over Sheffield Wednesday. They nonetheless finished the month fifth from bottom, but there was still room for two London sides to slot beneath them as the table made grim reading for the capital's clubs. At least Fulham were showing signs of a revival, but West Ham, above the relegation zone only on goal average, were too often easy pickings. They were scoring plenty but usually contriving to concede one or two more, with their home game with Manchester City typifying their season. City left East London with a 3-2 win, highlighted by two superb goals from Lee, who had adjusted to the higher level instantly and wouldn't have been too upset to find that Alf Ramsey had been in the crowd.

Lee looked as though he might be one for England's future, but England's present concerned the game against Northern Ireland as their European Nations Cup qualification programme continued at Wembley. With the Irish shorn of the injured Best, this was expected to be a straightforward assignment for Ramsey's men, but they again made heavy weather of it, labouring to a 2-0 win. Mullery once more took the place of the injured Stiles, and another accomplished performance suggested that he was in the process of making the position his own. David Sadler deputised for Jack Charlton and did well in the face of a rare substandard performance from Bobby Moore, but England's forwards were far from their best. Still, goals from Hurst and Charlton got the job done, and meant that England 'only' had to draw at Hampden Park in February to book their passage. A baying 137,000 crowd would make that task far from a formality.

Match Of The Month
11 November 1967, Division One: West Brom 8 Burnley 1

Burnley arrived at West Brom for a mid-table clash between two talented but erratic sides, and attracted a crowd of less than 20,000. There were at least as many stay-at-home Albion fans who later wished they had made the effort. When the final score came through on the *Grandstand* teleprinter, West Brom's total needed to be spelled out as EIGHT to ensure that viewers didn't think it was a typographical error.

The Baggies boasted the attacking talents of Jeff Astle, Tony Brown, Bobby Hope and Clive Clark and all four were influential in the outcome. After Hope buried a spectacular twenty-yarder, Clark dived bravely to head a second with just twenty minutes gone. Three more goals followed before the interval, from Brown, John Kaye and Eddie Colquhoun, who ventured forward to bury the goal of the game from long distance.

Damage limitation was Burnley's only objective in the second half, but they still conceded another three, Clark and Hope each getting their second before Astle finally got himself on the scoresheet with Albion's eighth. West Brom also had two clear penalty shouts turned away and Harry Thomson, largely blameless for the goals, made several great saves. Burnley achieved some meagre consolation near the end with a goal from Arthur Bellamy, but returned to Turf Moor having suffered their heaviest defeat since the war.

Although the opposition on the night was feeble, this was another illustration that, when the mood took them, West Brom had the ability to hit heights that few teams could live with. They would go on to prove it several more times before the season ended.

West Brom: Osborne, Colquhoun, Williams, Brown, Talbut, Fraser, Stephens, Kaye, Astle, Hope, Clark.

Burnley: Thomson, Angus, Latcham, O'Neill, Waldron, Harris, Morgan, Lochhead, Irvine, Bellamy, Thomas.

Player Of The Month
George Cohen (Fulham)

Cohen made his Fulham debut in 1956 at just seventeen and, after winning a succession of under-23 caps, made his full England debut in 1964. He immediately became an England regular, and played in every match of the World Cup finals. A strong but skilful full-back, his play was also characterised by the attacking, overlapping runs so essential to Ramsey's team formation.

Fulham had been perennial flirters with relegation over recent years, but had always managed to extricate themselves from the mess. This season, the escape act looked set to be a particularly testing challenge after a dreadful start left them rooted to the foot of the table as November began. From nowhere, they then put together three straight wins, and while Allan Clarke's goalscoring exploits took the headlines, the real foundation for the team's success was the three clean sheets they achieved.

Coventry, Forest and Stoke may not have been the most formidable of opponents but, for a team in Fulham's predicament, this was a notable achievement, especially given that they had conceded in every one of the season's fourteen preceding matches. Cohen's performances in all three games, as defender, captain and leader, were exemplary, inspiring his team-mates and quelling the threat down the left flank, notably from Forest's emerging star Ian Storey-Moore. The Forest game marked Cohen's 400th appearance for the club, and saw him – and all of his team-mates – pocket a £20 win bonus as a result of the club's '£10 a point' incentive scheme. He also played a crucial role in Fulham's League Cup win over Manchester City, helping to repel City's momentum after they threatened to overturn a 2-0 deficit.

To complete a highly successful month, he played for England against Northern Ireland and, whilst no doubt relieved not to have to contend with George Best, produced a typically solid and composed display. Best later revealed that he regarded Cohen as the finest full-back he ever played against. Just when it seemed that things had taken a turn for the better for this enormously popular player, he was carried off after just fifteen minutes of Fulham's next game, against Liverpool. He returned briefly to the team after a few weeks' absence, but soon broke down again and the injury ultimately forced him to retire at just twenty-nine years old. He retired with thirty-seven caps to his name.

Cohen spent his whole club career with Fulham, making over 450 appearances, and his contribution will be recognised by a statue to be unveiled outside Craven Cottage late in 2016. Revered not just by Fulham fans, he is widely regarded as one of England's greatest ever full-backs and his engaging personality has only served to enhance his popularity. Blessed with a dry wit, one of his most memorable lines is a reflection on the frustration of being incarcerated in the team hotel before and during the

1966 World Cup. 'After six weeks, even Nobby Stiles started to look attractive...'

DECEMBER 1967

Times were tough for Prime Minister Harold Wilson, with he and his Cabinet getting untold grief over the pound's devaluation and with railwaymen causing nationwide disruption with their work to rule. Wilson was now monstrously unpopular and there was a sense that he was hanging grimly on to power even though the next election was well over two years away. He decided to seek some respite by visiting Old Trafford and, bravely attending without recourse to disguise, witnessed United just about overcome a fine West Brom side which deserved at least a point. Undeterred by the setback, the Baggies went to Stamford Bridge for their next game and duly secured an impressive 3-0 win.

Chelsea remained wildly inconsistent, but they were hardly alone. Burnley's capacity for extreme off-days, illustrated by their 8-1 pasting at West Brom a few weeks earlier, quickly came to the fore again at Highfield Road, where Bobby Gould scored a hat-trick in Coventry's 5-1 rout. It was an extraordinary result, their first win for eleven games and reminiscent of Blackpool last season, where long sequences of poor results were interrupted by occasional spectacular victories. Coventry could only hope to avoid meeting the same fate as the seasiders, as they sought to prise themselves away from the bottom of the table.

Fulham's resurgence almost continued in their next game, at home to Liverpool. Clarke, in a rich vein of form, gave them the lead, prompting a one-man pitch invasion from a Liverpool supporter who broke from the terraces and ran sixty yards to attack Fulham winger Les Barratt in a case of mistaken identity. The miscreant was duly carted off by police eager to deliver their traditional 'back of a Black Maria' treatment, and so missed Hateley's late equaliser, Fulham's first concession for five games. More damaging to their cause was the knee injury which had forced George Cohen off early in the game, a blow from which he would never fully recover.

Cohen was forced to miss England's game with Russia four days later, and Cyril Knowles stepped up from the under-23s to earn his first senior cap at a snowbound Wembley. An enthralling, full-blooded, high-quality game saw England give their finest performance since the World Cup Final, and the final 2-2 scoreline was shaped primarily by the brilliance of Russian keeper Psenitchnikov and some errant finishing from Hunt in particular. England were widely praised for the fluidity of their attacking play, it belatedly being recognised in some quarters that the lack of orthodox wingers didn't necessarily equate to a lack of width. The movement of Ball and Peters, together with the overlapping sorties of the two full-backs, ensured plenty of crosses for Hurst and Hunt to feed on.

Ramsey, perhaps irritated by the scoreline but at least happy that some journalists were starting to acknowledge the quality of his team, was in extraordinarily bullish mood afterwards, claiming that his side 'can be the greatest that football has ever had, the greatest football will ever know'. Even his most fervent supporters would have thought this a little optimistic but, at the time, Ramsey's assertion that England *would* win the World Cup had seemed even more outlandish. Could he be proved right again?

Further praise was given for the sporting spirit in which the match had been played, again illustrating the wide disparity in player behaviour between international and club games. The FA's aspirations that the severe punishments meted out to Denis Law and their own Ian Ure would have encouraged players to behave themselves hadn't quite percolated around Highbury's marble halls. Their 1-0 defeat at Burnley saw both Frank McLintock and Peter Storey ordered off as Arsenal totally lost their discipline; perhaps there had been a few residual feuds to settle after their League Cup tie three days earlier, when Bob McNab had also enjoyed an early bath. Arsenal's improvement in results under Bertie Mee had been clear for all to see, but their often uncompromising and physical approach had made them difficult to love and they were frequently referred to as

London's equivalent of Leeds United. This wasn't intended as a compliment.

The original Leeds had started to see their results pick up, giving them cause for optimism as they travelled to Anfield. Frosty, snowbound conditions around the country had seen several games postponed and how Leeds' keeper Gary Sprake must have wished this was one of them. Defending the Kop end, he had already been beaten by Roger Hunt when, just before half-time, he collected a backpass and, under no pressure, shaped to throw the ball out to Terry Cooper. The slippery ball didn't quite take leave of his glove in the direction he had intended, and he was left in shivering, isolated embarrassment as the ball went straight into the net behind him, producing one of the most bizarre own goals in football history.

Sprake had excelled in many games for Leeds and would continue to do so, but his capacity for inexplicable, high-profile blunders would come to define him. As the half-time whistle blew just a couple of minutes after Sprake's howler, Liverpool's PA announcer wasted little time in spinning local boys The Scaffold's 'Thank You Very Much', followed by Des O'Connor's hit of the day, 'Careless Hands'. The Koppites needed little encouragement to join in, continuing to serenade the keeper throughout the second half.

The look on Jack Charlton's face when he realised what had happened was a picture, and though all at Leeds rallied to the keeper's defence in public, their private thoughts were in time revealed to have been rather different. The relationship between Sprake and his former team-mates deteriorated further still many years later, when the keeper spilled the beans first to the *Daily Mirror* and then in his autobiography about Revie's attempts to bribe opponents and his other underhand dealings. Nothing was ever proved one way or the other, but the rest of the players remained thick as thieves behind Revie and Sprake found himself ostracised from the group.

Liverpool's next home game saw them host title pretenders Manchester City, who were fresh from a magnificent performance in beating Spurs 4-1 on a Maine Road skating rink. The Anfield crowd were treated to a thrilling match on a more conventional December surface, as City showed no inhibitions and took the game to their hosts. It looked as though they would pay for failing to take any of a host of chances when Roger Hunt put Liverpool ahead, but they continued undaunted and Lee's brilliant equaliser was well deserved.

Cyril Knowles' promotion to the senior team had given hope to his under-23 colleagues that they too could be in line for full caps, and it was a strong junior team which took on Italy in Nottingham under Ramsey's watchful eye. Cyril's brother Peter featured in the side, as well as Emlyn Hughes, Brian Kidd, John Hollins, Tommy Smith and Howard Kendall. Southampton's Martin Chivers, who had recently asked for a transfer and had a £125,000 valuation placed on his head, did his cause no harm by heading the winner in a fine display. Coming after his recent hat-trick for the Football League, it was a further indication of Chivers' form and potential as he awaited his chance at a 'bigger' club.

Back in the league, Manchester City's momentum continued with a 4-2 win over Stoke, and they went into the holiday period in the highest of spirits, with the praise of opposition managers, critics and supporters ringing in their ears. City's players, like the rest of the population, were then faced with an almost impossible choice on Christmas night: *Ken Dodd's Christmas Show* or Cliff Richard starring in *Aladdin*? It was surely this sort of programme clash which hastened the development of the video recorder.

At least the previous evening's dubious televisual delights were soon forgotten as City made a Boxing Day trip to the Hawthorns, where another cracking match saw them fight back from two down, only for West Brom to hit a last-minute winner. It was a game which would have graced *Match Of The Day*, but the BBC's agreement with the Football League didn't cater for league football to be shown on any day other than on a Saturday – not even on this, the most sports-filled day of the year. At least those who weren't able to get out to a game were catered for by ITV, enabling them to get their sporting fix in the form of wrestling from Watford, before switching channels and settling down to be totally bemused by the BBC screening of The Beatles' *Magical Mystery Tour*.

Three days later, Albion completed a memorable double at Maine Road, with an ultimately comfortable 2-0 win. It was a huge blow to City's title hopes but another illustration that Albion had the wherewithal to beat anyone on their day. Meanwhile, United had completed a double over Wolves, cementing their position at the top at the turn of the year, with Liverpool three points behind and City a further two adrift.

Match Of The Month
9 December 1967, Division One: Manchester City 4 Tottenham Hotspur 1

On a day when heavy snow had forced several postponements, as well as abandonments of games in progress, it was a relief to the 32,000 who had braved the appalling conditions at Maine Road that the pitch was deemed playable. It was an even greater relief to the *Match Of The Day* producers, who otherwise would have been bereft of football to show to their burgeoning Saturday-night audience. As it turned out, the game was to become one of the most famous ever screened on the programme, as City turned in a quite stunning performance, fondly remembered as 'The Ballet On Ice'.

On a snow-white pitch, the players at first moved tentatively but, as they became more familiar with the surface, the action became ever more compelling. A calm finish from Jimmy Greaves gave Spurs an early lead, but after that they barely registered as an attacking force. Driven forward by Alan Oakes and Mike Doyle, City belied the conditions to produce attacking football of a quality seldom seen even on the perfect playing surfaces of mid-August.

After a series of great saves from Pat Jennings, Colin Bell lashed home City's equaliser. Jennings continued to defy City until midway through the second half, when Summerbee's superb header left him helpless to give City a richly deserved lead. Summerbee had revelled in the switch to centre-forward this season, with the recruitment of Franny Lee giving City pace and aggression down the right. On the left, Young and Coleman were equally menacing, as Spurs were attacked on all fronts. Both of them added further goals as Spurs took a dreadful battering, with Jennings by far their star man and the woodwork being struck several times, on one occasion from consecutive shots by Lee and Young.

It was a demonstration to the nation at large that this City side, at the very least, were well worth watching and, at best, might even prove to be genuine contenders for the league title.

Manchester City: Mulhearn, Book, Pardoe, Doyle, Heslop, Oakes, Lee, Bell, Summerbee, Young, Coleman.

Tottenham Hotspur: Jennings, Kinnear, Knowles, Mullery, Hoy, Mackay, Saul, Greaves, Gilzean, Venables, Jones.

Player Of The Month
Tony Brown (West Brom)

Tony Brown had joined West Brom from school, and made his debut in 1963 at just seventeen. It took some time before he became a regular starter and at one stage he submitted a transfer request in a bid to secure first-team football. One of Jimmy Hagan's most valuable contributions as West Brom manager was to turn the request down. Brown was soon restored to the first team, quickly becoming a fan favourite, and this season saw him find his best form as part of West Brom's strongest team for many years.

December saw Brown and his team fully demonstrate their qualities. At Old Trafford, he was the game's outstanding player, scoring West Brom's goal in an unlucky 2-1 defeat. Brown then produced typically energetic performances to help his team to impressive away wins at West Ham and Chelsea. To finish the month, he played a starring role in West Brom's two matches against Manchester City, which saw them record a double over the title challengers. In the game at the Hawthorns, Brown scored West Brom's second goal with an unstoppable volley before setting up Jeff Astle to net the late winner. Four days later at Maine Road, he put in another man-of-the-match performance, crossing for Krzywicki to put West Brom ahead before scoring a typical goal to seal the victory. Making a surging run from midfield, he latched on to Astle's pass, rounded Pardoe and slotted the ball calmly past Mulhearn. Brown was very much the modern midfielder, always in the game, full of energy, with an eye for goal which saw him score more frequently than many out-and-out strikers.

The season saw Albion go on to lift the FA Cup, with Brown making vital contributions en route, even if his tally for the season of fifteen goals was slightly below par. His capacity for scoring goals from midfield reached its zenith in 1970/71, when he was the league's leading scorer with twenty-eight goals. Belatedly in the eyes of many, Brown was called up by Ramsey for the 1971 home international against Wales. It proved to be his only cap, perhaps reflecting the fact that England were particularly strong in midfield throughout his era, but it can certainly be argued that many less effective players were given more opportunities.

Brown holds the West Brom record both for appearances and goals scored, the latter a remarkable achievement given his role as a midfield player. Many of his 218 goals for the club were spectacular efforts, often the result of him latching on to the ball outside the area, and he was also renowned for his ability to strike balls on the volley. Brown's status with West Brom fans was given tangible recognition in 2014 when a statue of him was unveiled outside the Hawthorns.

JANUARY 1968

The new year began with the economy still in dire straits, and a novel idea for improving matters came from five secretaries at a heating and ventilation firm in Surbiton. In response to a company memo saying that the country's balance of payments deficit would vanish if everyone worked a five-and-a-half-day week, the women volunteered to work an extra half-hour each day without pay. The publicity they received saw a short-lived campaign gather momentum, under the banner 'I'm Backing Britain', with official endorsement coming from beleaguered Prime Minister Harold Wilson.

Certain newspapers backed the campaign enthusiastically, but the unions naturally were strongly opposed to the concept of any of their members doing something for nothing and the movement gradually petered out. Supporters of the campaign surely missed a trick by not citing England's World Cup team as prime examples of what could be achieved by working an extra half-hour for free.

If any team had the determination to put in extra effort in order to prevail, it was Don Revie's Leeds. They had struggled to find any kind of momentum in the first half of the season, but the new year saw them slip ominously into gear. Fulham's November resurgence had been halted by George Cohen's long-term injury, and they put in an insipid performance as Leeds crushed them 5-0 at Craven Cottage. Mick Jones had endured a difficult time since joining the club, struggling to prove his worth and then being out injured, but here he showed what he was capable of, a fifty-yard run seeing him power through and past four defenders before rounding Macedo to roll the ball home. Jimmy Greenhoff completed a hat-trick to put the seal on a mismatch which Geoffrey Green described as 'like taking pennies from a blind man's tin'.

Revie's men then dealt out a similar thrashing to Southampton at Elland Road. Jack Charlton, said against Fulham to have 'commanded the centre with the crushing authority of a schoolmaster controlling backward pupils', was absent injured, but the deputising Madeley was as usual a more-than-competent deputy, augmenting a solid defensive display by scoring two goals. Leeds didn't even miss new captain Bremner, who had previously revealed his surprise at being given the role ahead of Jack Charlton, ostensibly the more obvious and experienced choice. The reason Big Jack had turned down the position was his intense superstition, a trait which permeated the whole club; he had always insisted on being last out of the tunnel.

Fulham's partners in distress, Coventry City, were also recipients of a heavy beating, 4-1 at home to Newcastle. There was plenty of sympathy for their plight, with the ground-breaking work led by Jimmy Hill having earned much admiration. Hill's innovations had included a revamped stadium with two cantilever stands, a 'Sky Blue Club' where fans could socialise before and after games, a private radio station and a recorded telephone service enabling supporters to phone up and hear team news, ticket information, injury updates etc. This was evidently a man seriously ahead of his time.

The unusually comfortable and welcoming matchday environment at Highfield Road contributed to the fact that, despite being entrenched in the relegation zone, Coventry games were attracting an average of over 33,000 fans, the seventh highest in the division. If only their team could respond to it. Their 'after you, Claude' defending reached its nadir with Newcastle's second goal by Jackie Sinclair, allowed to meander unchallenged from the left touchline to the penalty spot before firing home. Cue Geoffrey Green again. 'He might have been General de Gaulle on some unchallenged triumphal procession down the Champs Elysees.'

Hugh McIlvanney seldom seemed to enjoy his football. Maybe his employers at *The Observer* took pleasure in repeatedly sending him to Highbury to watch what was still by far the least interesting of the London teams. Finally, on a day when snow and frost had caused most other games to be called off, poor Hugh cracked. 'If this game fairly represents the benefits to be brought to us by Highbury's underground heating system, it is time to start cutting through a few cables. The ground conditions were atrocious and the football slightly worse.' And he was only warming up. 'Arsenal should have issued portable gas stoves at the turnstiles: then those that did not have matches could at least have committed suicide.'

Marvelling at the fact that 27,000 hardy frozen souls had stayed to the end, despite being lashed by snow and icy rain, McIlvanney observed: 'Faced with such a demonstration of mass masochism, any anthropologist would have fled to the nearest licensed premises. He would have found that one or two journalists had beaten him to it.' Only one or two? The rest of the report did suggest that he had stayed through to the bitter end, but it seemed obvious that here was a man who needed to relocate to Manchester, where his beloved United would never dare inflict such tortures.

Other journalists had a rather different agenda, and the man from the *Sunday People* struck gold in persuading Bobby Thomson of Stockport County, no less, to reveal a few salacious titbits about his life of debauchery in his days at Aston Villa and Birmingham. Dubbing him 'the Errol Flynn of football', *The People* ran headlines such as 'Orgy XI…and the BEAST' and 'Vice captain? That was me…' as Thomson described in not particularly explicit terms his life of wine, women, song and the occasional game of football.

The Football League took serious umbrage not with Thomson but with the *Sunday People*, leading to a quite marvellous spat. The league management committee claimed that the articles 'offended normal decencies, and we have been asked by several clubs to register their disgust at this type of journalism.' They asked clubs to withhold facilities at their grounds to representatives of *The People*, which basically meant that the hacks would need to pay to get in and, worse still, would have to buy their own refreshments. That would clearly never do, and *The People*'s sports editor described the League's action as 'a shocking, outrageous interference with the freedom of the press'. *The People* laughably defended the publication of the tale by hoping that the articles would serve as a warning to younger players with more money than sense. One suspects that most would have regarded them as more encouragement than warning.

And so these parties at polar opposites of the moral compass continued to hurl insults at each other. Alan Hardaker's 'Not for the first time this newspaper has sullied the public reputation of league football by publicising the braggings of an insignificant minority of people connected with it' was met with a splendid riposte, with *The People* describing the Football League Management Committee as toy-town tyrants, before claiming that 'the Football League does not like it revealed that some players come off the field with monumental hangovers, half-sloshed or utterly fatigued after a roistering night'.

The month's fixtures, diminished in number by the poor weather, came to a close with the third round of the FA Cup. Fulham, under new manager Bobby Robson, had warmed up for it with a miserable home defeat to Leicester, their lifeless display prompting one long-suffering fan to observe 'they must be saving themselves for Macclesfield...' Either that or they had been out on a roistering night. When the non-leaguers duly arrived at the Cottage a week later, they looked set to create the story of the round by reaching the interval 2-1 ahead. Fitness eventually told as the part-timers succumbed to two late goals, leaving the day's headlines to second-division Carlisle United, who made the short journey to St James' Park and pulled off a stunning 1-0 victory. It was Newcastle's first home defeat of the season.

Carlisle's win was the day's only definitive shock, but there were many more inspired performances from the underdogs, notably third division Reading's goalless draw at Manchester City and Bournemouth holding Liverpool. Liverpool fans were making a habit of solo exhibitionism; this time, a fan ran on to the pitch to argue with the referee and it needed six policemen to cart him away. On a day filled with 'if onlys', the nearest of the near things was Colchester's game with West Brom, in which the referee's controversial intervention denied the hosts what would have been a last-minute winner. It was a decision which would ultimately assume enormous significance for the visitors.

The heavyweight clash of the round brought the champions and cup holders together at Old Trafford. Spurs earned a replay when new signing Martin Chivers scored his second goal two minutes from the end of yet another enthralling match between the two sides, duly whetting appetites for what was to come at White Hart Lane.

What actually came was a little disappointing, as the tension of the occasion took hold and rendered the first hour a fraught, physical battle with few chances at either end. The culmination of this increasingly tetchy period came when Kinnear and Kidd clashed violently enough to cause referee Jack Taylor to banish them both to the dressing room. It was as if a pressure valve had been released, as both teams immediately sought to exploit the extra space. The decisive moment came well into extra time, as Jimmy Robertson bundled home the scruffiest of goals to keep the holders on track to retain their trophy. Disappointing as the result was for United, they still had the twin goals of European glory and retention of the league title to aim for. Would this setback prove to be a blessing in disguise?

As usual, all the lower-league teams who heroically forced replays were undone second time around, most emphatically Reading, who suffered a 7-0 mauling at Elm Park at the hands of a rampant Manchester City. Such was the majesty of City's display that the PA announcer was moved to observe: 'Ladies and gentlemen, you have just witnessed the finest team this country has produced in a long, long time.' Time would tell.

Match Of The Month
27 January 1968, FA Cup Third Round:
Manchester United 2 Tottenham Hotspur 2

The tie of the round brought together the league champions and the cup holders at Old Trafford in front of the usual 63,500 FA Cup full house. Other than for the missing Stiles, United were at full strength, while Spurs had strengthened their attack with the purchase of Martin Chivers from Southampton for a British record £125,000. But could the newcomer compensate for the absence of Jimmy Greaves?

The first instalment of his answer to that came within four minutes of the start, when his powerful strike put the visitors ahead. Spurs had little time to consolidate as a mistake from Pat Jennings, coupled with the remarkable anticipation and reaction speed of George Best, saw United get back on terms. Best charged Jennings' clearance down and followed up to slide the ball home.

The match then settled into a pattern which saw Spurs look the more coherent team, and they created enough chances to be well ahead, only to find Alex Stepney in superb form. United relied more on flashes of individual brilliance and eventually, with just ten minutes left, found themselves ahead through Charlton's drive through a ruck of players.

Spurs, however, showed enormous spirit and belief and with just a minute remaining, Chivers latched on to Gilzean's flick to lash an angled drive past Stepney. There was an agonising wait for both sides as the referee went to consult his linesman, who had raised his flag at the point Chivers struck the ball, but after protracted discussions Mr Finney pointed to the centre circle. It was later revealed that the discussion had centred on a handball by United's John Fitzpatrick. Spurs made the most of their late reprieve by squeezing through in a tightly contested replay, leaving United free to focus on their other commitments.

Manchester United: Stepney, Dunne, Burns, Crerand, Sadler, Fitzpatrick, Best, Kidd, Charlton, Law, Aston.

Tottenham Hotspur: Jennings, Kinnear, Knowles, Mullery, England, Mackay, Robertson, Gilzean, Chivers, Venables (Jones), Beal.

Player Of The Month
Mick Channon (Southampton)

Channon made his Southampton debut in 1966, but appeared in the first team only intermittently until the sale of Martin Chivers in January 1968 created a vacancy to partner Ron Davies up front. Channon seized his chance immediately, with a series of impressive displays which established him as a regular starter.

He began the month by scoring against Chelsea in what proved to be Chivers' last game at the Dell, although

Southampton lost a thrilling match 5-3. After taking a pasting at Elland Road, Southampton performed much more creditably at Anfield the following week, with Channon's performance meriting a number of favourable mentions in the match reports. His strong and enthusiastic running repeatedly stretched the Liverpool defence and he was unlucky not to score. He finished the month by scoring the winning goal in the FA Cup replay at Newport, after his team had laboured throughout.

Channon struggled for goals through the remainder of the season, but Ted Bates' perseverance with him slowly began to reap rewards, and by 1969/70 he was becoming a regular marksman. Improving noticeably year by year, his goal output continued to increase and after winning four under-23 caps, he was called up to the full squad, winning his first cap against Yugoslavia in 1972.

Channon established himself as a regular in the England side for the next five years, despite Southampton's relegation in 1974. In all, he won forty-six full caps, scoring twenty-one goals, was one of the most prominent players of his era and by far England's most reliable striker. Although by then a second-division side, Southampton won the FA Cup in 1976, with Channon a key player throughout their run.

Channon was transferred to Manchester City in 1977 but achieved only modest success, and returned to the Dell two years later. He stayed for another three years, lifting his total appearances for the club above the 600-mark, and his tally of 227 goals remains a club record.

Channon's innate fitness was illustrated by his move to Norwich in 1982. He held down a regular place throughout his three years at Carrow Road, and won a League Cup winner's medal in 1985 at the age of thirty-six. Even then, he enjoyed a further full season at Portsmouth before retiring from the game in 1986.

Channon was as well known for his interest in horse racing as for his football prowess, having reportedly told many of his managers that 'football was just a hobby' for him. With a career goal tally which exceeded 300, he made a pretty decent fist of it.

FEBRUARY 1968

Spurs and United met again at White Hart Lane just three days after their 120 minutes of intense cup combat at the same venue. The quality of the game reflected the recent exertions of its participants but, after Chivers capitalised on United's defensive lethargy to put Spurs ahead, two moments of brilliance turned the game United's way. Best's weaving run and explosive shot brought them level before Charlton, having missed an earlier penalty, blazed home a typical twenty-yarder three minutes from time to deliver a crucial win for his team. Greaves, restored to the Tottenham side after being excluded from both cup ties, was so hesitant in front of goal that some wondered whether an inexorable decline had begun for English football's golden boy. Greaves was again relegated to the bench for Spurs' next game, a narrow victory at struggling Sunderland, and seemed further away from an England recall than ever.

With newspapers full of stories about the world's first successful heart transplant, it was inevitable that some reference would soon be worked into a match report. *The Observer* was quickest off the mark, observing that West Ham had 'dissected a disjointed defence with the surgical precision of a Barnard'. That defence belonged to poor old Fulham, on the wrong end of a 7-2 battering at Upton Park and in danger of being cut adrift at the foot of the table. The golden trio of Moore, Hurst and Peters all featured on the scoresheet in a match thoroughly enjoyed by Warren Mitchell's Alf Garnett, who paraded in claret and blue around the ground before kick-off to a rousing reception.

The League Cup had reached the semi-final stage, and the draw set up the first managerial meeting between Messrs Clough and Revie. Clough's Derby had shown signs of improvement but were still languishing in the lower reaches of the second division when they welcomed Leeds to the Baseball Ground. Leeds won 1-0 to make the second leg seem a formality but Derby, with

Hector, O'Hare and Hinton all impressing, showed defiance and self-belief at Elland Road before succumbing on a 4-2 aggregate. Once again, Leeds were one match away from silverware; their opponents this time, in a final not necessarily guaranteed to have connoisseurs of the beautiful game licking their lips, would be Arsenal.

Leeds continued their four-fronted trophy assault by seeing off Forest in the FA Cup with a narrow win at Elland Road. Forest's season was declining rapidly, their sustained challenge for last season's double becoming a distant memory. Joe Baker scored at Elland Road, but his influence was diminishing as injuries and advancing years took their toll. Their main goal threat remained Storey-Moore, but the supporting cast hadn't offered anywhere near enough, and their dizzying recent ascent to the cusp of the double was beginning to look like a flash in the pan.

The round passed almost shock-free, the nearest thing to a surprise being Rotherham's win at Aston Villa as Tommy Docherty's golden touch with his new club continued. The day's most newsworthy items yet again involved spectators, but this time had little to do with hooliganism. The games at Walsall and Carlisle, against Liverpool and Everton respectively, were both held up as walls unaccustomed to containing capacity crowds collapsed under seldom experienced strain. Although no one was seriously hurt, stretcher bearers were needed at both venues, as masonry patently unfit for purpose was exposed.

Many lower-league grounds saw a whole year's fixtures played out in front of sparse attendances, with crash barriers and walls never put under even slight duress. The Football League and the clubs themselves insisted that barriers and containing walls had to be and indeed were tested regularly, but it was obviously difficult to simulate the structural stress caused by overcrowded swaying hordes of people. And at cash-strapped clubs, would directors have given priority to making repairs which might never be needed?

The cup replays produced two classic encounters, the first at Filbert Street, where Leicester followed up their goalless draw at Maine Road by producing a superb comeback from 2-0 down to edge City out 4-3. West Brom's replay at Southampton was similarly dramatic, the tie being decided by Albion's last-minute winner, denying the Saints the possibility of a tasty local derby against Portsmouth.

Now it was time for international football to take centre stage for what, in terms of its overall significance, was the most important match ever staged between England and Scotland. Always a more meaningful game for the Scots, this one had the locals cranked up to a frenzy even weeks before the day of destiny. Newspaper propaganda portrayed the English as, amongst other things, 'ruthless physical boneshakers', and there were fears that the antagonism would spill over into crowd behaviour. But if anyone could prepare England for a siege, it was Ramsey. Greeted by a Scottish journalist on arriving Glasgow airport with 'Welcome to Scotland, Sir Alf', he famously responded: 'You must be fucking joking!'

Faced with the absence of Jack Charlton, Ramsey went for experience in the shape of Everton's Brian Labone, but he had a difficult choice to make up front, where Roger Hunt's prodigious work ethic struggled to compensate for a continuing lack of goals. Into the squad came Mike Summerbee, a winger converted to centre-forward with great success this season. It was a daunting stage for anyone to make an England debut, but Summerbee's form, confident nature and appetite for a physical battle persuaded Ramsey to give him the nod. Blackburn's Keith Newton deputised for the injured Cohen, with Mullery's place ahead of Stiles now apparently firmly cemented.

In a ferocious and expectant atmosphere, England got through the opening phase with few scares, before a beautiful twenty-yarder from the ever-improving Martin Peters put them ahead and reduced the din to manageable proportions. But on a treacherous pitch, costly mishaps were always likely and when Banks slipped in the goalmouth whilst attempting to save John Hughes' shot, the ball slithered home to restore Scottish voices to full throttle. With an inspired Charlie Cooke at his most inventive and dangerous, England suffered in the remainder of the half, but hung on to parity.

Ramsey's words at the interval ensured that greater attention was given to Cooke as the second half began. As his contributions became less penetrative, England took a grip of the game with a superbly organised performance and until a final desperate flurry were never again in danger. When the chips were down, Ramsey's men had delivered again. It hadn't always been pretty, but away from home against desperate opponents, on a diabolical surface in a seething cauldron of noise, what more could anyone reasonably expect?

Better finishing, for one. Most reporters observed that England had squandered several good openings after taking the lead and could have spared themselves considerable angst. But through they were, to face reigning champions Spain in a two-legged quarter-final. And whilst the Scots' win at Wembley a year earlier would forever be etched in their followers' memories, Ramsey and his men could now dismiss that result as being of no consequence whatsoever.

Match Of The Month
19 February, 1968, FA Cup Fourth Round Replay:
Leicester City 4 Manchester City 3

Two days after holding Manchester City to a goalless draw at Maine Road, Leicester took the field at Filbert Street in front of a capacity crowd of almost 40,000. Joe Mercer's men had been similarly held by Reading in the previous round, only to recover their scoring form quite emphatically with a 7-0 replay win. Midway through the first half, it looked as though Leicester were en route to a similar fate, as Lee and Summerbee profited from uncertain defending to put their team 2-0 up.

The game's key moment came a minute before the break, when Rodney Fern's angled shot gave Leicester renewed hope and prompted a second-half barrage. Frank Large, a journeyman striker whose career thus far had been played out in the third and fourth divisions, was employed to great effect, with Leicester repeatedly powering long balls in his direction as he barged and bullied the City defenders. Large's snapshot put Leicester level and within ten minutes they were in the clear, as David Nish pounced on Large's flick-on to put them ahead before Large himself headed home from a corner.

A frenzied crowd helped their team see out the remaining time in the face of increasing pressure, with City's only reward coming from Bell's solo effort a couple of minutes from the end. The game's last action saw Shilton dive at the feet of Francis Lee to secure a famous victory in what, incredibly, was the seventh meeting between the two sides in cup competitions over the last three seasons – and Leicester's first win.

Leicester City: Shilton, Rodrigues, Bell, Roberts, Sjoberg, Nish, Gibson, Large, Stringfellow, Cross, Fern.

Manchester City: Mulhearn, Book, Pardoe, Doyle, Heslop, Oakes, Lee, Bell, Summerbee, Young, Coleman.

Player Of The Month
Trevor Brooking (West Ham United)

Having made his first-team debut in August 1967, Brooking hit his first West Ham goal in December and from an early stage marked himself down as a player of immense talent. In February, he gave further indications of what was to lie ahead with some typically skilful displays.

Fulham looked as though they could spring a surprise when they led at Upton Park after half an hour. However, prompted by Brooking, West Ham turned in an irrepressible display thereafter, with Brooking himself scoring twice in a minute in the 7-2 rout.

Brooking next put in an eye-catching performance in West Ham's unusually narrow defeat at Elland Road before excelling in their surprise 3-0 FA Cup win at Stoke City. Nominally a centre-forward but operating in a position slightly deeper than his shirt number indicated, Brooking helped set up two goals for John Sissons as West Ham recorded one of the results of the round.

Tall and elegant, Brooking gradually became the creative hub of the team, but retained the ability to score vital goals. His long West Ham career encompassed two FA Cup wins, the second of which, in 1980, saw him score the only goal in the final as the then second-division side saw off Arsenal.

Brooking made his England debut in 1974, beginning an international career which spanned eight years and brought him forty-seven caps. Despite England's lack of success during the period, he still produced some memorable moments, most notably his second goal in a World Cup qualifier in Budapest in 1981, a fierce left-footed drive which flew high past the keeper and wedged itself firmly against the stanchion. Brooking was more generally noted for his creativity than his finishing, and his graceful play was often the highlight of England's performances throughout this period.

A one-club man, Brooking amassed almost 650 appearances for West Ham. In an era of increasing emphasis on physicality, he is warmly remembered for his classy play and gentlemanly demeanour on the pitch, a throwback to earlier times.

MARCH 1968

Leeds' litany of near misses at last came to an end in the Football League Cup Final. Inevitably, in the eyes of their many detractors, the match was an ugly affair. A fraught, dour, physical contest was settled by Terry Cooper's first-half goal, which came about after a favourite Leeds tactic – Jack Charlton standing directly in front of the goalkeeper at a corner, preventing him from coming to claim the ball. It was a ploy which most critics and some but not all referees took a dim view of, but had brought Leeds some considerable success over the past couple of years.

While there was recognition that Leeds were due some success after so much heartbreak – and indeed had been the better of two uninspiring sides in the match itself – the nature of the contest and the still-to-be established stature of the competition meant that praise was hardly gushing. 'Wembley's wide-open spaces have seldom been more misused, as both sides reduced the size of the pitch to the size of a postage stamp, in a battle of brawn rather than brain…' Leeds, though, could hardly have cared less. They had broken their duck and few doubted that this would be the stepping stone for more prestigious honours to come.

After a solid 2-0 first-leg win against Gornik, Manchester United looked well set to reach another European Cup semi-final. Three days later, they welcomed Chelsea to Old Trafford, looking to extend their unbeaten league home record to thirty-eight games. Chelsea had recruited David Webb from Southampton, and the new centre-half made an impressive debut, defending superbly and instigating moves that led to Chelsea scoring twice, either side of Kidd's goal for United. The game's key moment then came when Best, well shackled by Harris throughout during one of the many Beauty and the Beast duels the two enjoyed during the era, blazed a penalty over the bar. Osgood soon hit Chelsea's third, condemning United to a defeat which looked even more costly when news of City's win at Burnley came through. It wasn't the first time that United had faltered immediately after a European Cup tie – would the search for their Holy Grail ultimately jeopardise their domestic chances?

Many United fans would have first heard of City's important win when they got back into Manchester to pick up their *Football Pink*. This particular issue told them everything they needed to know with one headline of glorious economy. *Lee Spot-on for 1-0 City*. Result, score, scorer and nature of goal all set out in just eighteen characters.

The Pink and its many regional counterparts were an institution and an essential part of the Saturday tea-time ritual, both for fans returning from games and for those who had spent their Saturday afternoons watching Mick McManus do battle with Jackie Pallo before nipping down to join the queue outside their local newsagents. Detailed move-by-move accounts of the first hour or so of the afternoon's big games would condense into ever more curt descriptions of the later action, and ultimately nothing at all from the last ten minutes unless a goal had been scored, in which case the marksman would be listed in the *Late Scorers* section. Often, scouring this list was the only way to determine the final outcome of games which had featured a few minutes of injury time, with the score in the classified results columns set out exasperatingly as Everton * Liverpool *.

At least United didn't have the FA Cup to distract them, and their conquerors, Spurs, took on Liverpool in the standout tie of the fifth round, surprisingly the first time the sides had ever met in the competition. A brilliant Greaves goal put Spurs on course to retain their trophy, but Hateley's header sentenced them to a daunting replay at Anfield where, as journalists never tired of reminding them, they hadn't won since the year the *Titanic* went down. And there would be more reminders to come in the future, as Spurs duly succumbed in a tightly contested game.

Still well placed in the league, Liverpool therefore remained in contention for the double, but this prospect paled almost into insignificance compared with Leeds' potential haul. With the League Cup already under their belt, they too had reached the FA Cup quarter-finals, were many critics' favourites for the league and had also advanced to the semi-finals of the Fairs Cup.

The performances of the round came from second-division Birmingham City. Having deservedly earned a draw at Highbury, they then finished the job in front of over 51,000 at St Andrew's, knocking Arsenal out for the second successive season. Barry Bridges, sold by Chelsea two years earlier, scored both Birmingham goals. Having won so impressively at Stoke in the previous round, West Ham disappointed their fans and no doubt many neutrals by losing at home to lowly Sheffield United. Pitch invasions had become all too commonplace and an unusual one occurred at Fratton Park, where a robust exchange between a West Brom player and some spectators caused a policeman to stride towards the player to issue some cautionary words. Referee Mr Dawes took immediate action, banishing the uniformed intruder back from whence he came. 'I told him

I wasn't having policemen coming on to my field and the matter was settled quite amicably.'

United had survived their trip to Poland, where a 1-0 defeat saw them through on aggregate, but they once again faltered on their return to league action three days later. Coventry's 2-0 win over the sluggish champions in front of a record 47,000 crowd at Highfield Road – many accommodated in a temporary stand after a fire had destroyed the original – enabled them to edge out of the relegation zone. Coventry's impressive gates throughout the season had allowed them to splash out in the transfer market, bringing in Ernie Hunt and Chris Cattlin at a combined cost of £140,000 immediately before the match.

Though now focusing fully on his new career in broadcasting, Jimmy Hill would no doubt have delighted in his old team's success, and would also have enjoyed the burgeoning sales figures of the weekly magazine to which he had lent his name. Circulation amongst younger readers had been increased by the recruitment of 'star writer' George Best, and their rivals at *Soccer Star* belatedly recognised that they needed to attract a similarly prestigious and charismatic recruit in order to remain competitive.

The household name they eventually went for was Arsenal's Ian Ure. With so many of the magazine's contributors wrapped up in their own intellectual superiority, perhaps it was Ure's outstanding performances in the first series of the BBC's *Quizball* which persuaded them of his credentials. Ure had been star man in the show's very first episode late in 1966, leading Arsenal – also represented by Bertie Mee, Terry Neill and celebrity supporter Ted Knott – to victory in a show in which the rules were so complicated that even quizmaster David Vine frequently seemed bewildered.

Arsenal went on to triumph in the final of the first series, battering Dunfermline 7-3, although Ure's personal highlight had been his four-goal semi-final salvo to sink gallant Leicester City and their celebrity acolyte and Filbert Street regular Lady Isobel Barnett.

Ure's first column saw him answering questions from the *Star*'s readers, most notably about his off-field relationship with Denis Law. Despite the fact that pretty much every Arsenal–United encounter saw them routinely kick lumps out of each other, often culminating in a full-blown fist fight, Ure insisted that the two of them were actually great friends. One could only wonder what sort of treatment the man dished out to his enemies.

With four teams locked within a two-point span, it promised to be the most exciting denouement to a title race since the war. Pivotal to the outcome would be the games the quartet still had to play against each other. At Elland Road, Manchester City started brightly but fell away after Leeds took the lead, and their 2-0 defeat meant that they travelled to Old Trafford four days later knowing that defeat in the derby would realistically end their title challenge. On their most memorable night for many years, they recovered from the shock of conceding a first-minute goal to secure a spectacular 3-1 victory. It was a win which not only put City squarely back into title contention, but also banished the inferiority complex which had been built up over the recent years of widely diverging fortunes for the two Manchester clubs. Malcolm Allison would later call it the greatest night of his life – and did he have some nights – marking it as the point where not just the critics but the players themselves recognised just how good they could be.

The cup quarter-finals saw Birmingham again produce the result of the round, as Fred Pickering's header was enough to beat a Chelsea side whose improved league form had raised hopes of reaching a second successive final. Another 51,000 sell-out St Andrew's crowd roared their side to victory and into their third semi-final in twelve years, all reached as a second-division club. For the fourth round running, Liverpool had been drawn away. For the fourth round running, they brought their opponents back to Anfield for a replay. Few expected West Brom to succeed where Bournemouth, Walsall and Spurs had all failed. Leeds and Everton were the day's other winners, Everton impressively disposing of Leicester whilst Leeds squeezed out a 1-0 win over Sheffield United as they ground remorselessly on.

Match Of The Month
27 March 1968, Division One: Manchester United 1 Manchester City 3

Postponed in February due to bad weather, this rearranged fixture had become much more than just another Manchester derby. City had remained strongly in title contention but, after defeat at Elland Road four days earlier, needed a good result here to restore belief that they really were good enough to stay the course. United were back on top of the table, strong favourites to retain their crown, and even stronger favourites to win tonight and put City back in their place.

The game started explosively, with Best pouncing on a mistake by Tony Book to put United ahead with less than a minute on the clock. It took a good ten minutes for the City defender to clear his head as United went for the throat, but they survived without further concession and started to play their way into the game. They were soon rewarded, as Bell's surging run saw him fasten on to Mike Doyle's through ball and lash the ball high past Stepney for a dramatic equaliser.

Confidence restored, City then took the game to United in a manner that the Stretford End can seldom have seen. United were pinned back by wave after wave of attacks, with Bell the inspiration in one of his finest ever performances. City's reward eventually came from an unlikely source, George Heslop's header from a Tony Coleman free kick being his only goal of the season.

United's efforts to fight back seldom troubled keeper Ken Mulhearn, apart from when a low cross driven across goal just eluded Law's full-length lunge, and City always carried the greater threat. Four minutes from time, they played Bell through to bear down on Stepney's goal, only to be scythed down by a desperate lunge from Francis Burns. Lee dispatched the penalty with aplomb, sealing City's emphatic win and announcing to the football world – and in particular to the United fans – that they had at last again become a force to be reckoned with.

Manchester United: Stepney, Brennan, Burns, Crerand, Sadler, Stiles, Fitzpatrick, Law, Charlton, Best, Herd (Aston).

Manchester City: Mulhearn, Book, Pardoe, Doyle, Heslop, Oakes, Lee, Bell, Summerbee, Young, Coleman.

Player Of The Month
Peter Osgood (Chelsea)

Osgood had burst on to the Chelsea scene in 1965 with dramatic impact, his elegant running and close control allied to composed and sometimes explosive finishing making him an instant crowd favourite. There were calls for him to be included in Ramsey's '66 World Cup squad, but his arrival in the spotlight had come slightly too late. When he continued his outstanding form in the early part of the following season, a call-up to the full squad looked imminent, but a broken leg sustained in a tackle with Blackpool's Emlyn Hughes put Osgood out for the rest of the campaign.

Osgood eased his way back into the Chelsea team after a lay-off of almost a year, and gradually his form and confidence came back. By March he was operating at full tilt, and his brilliant performance was the centrepiece of Chelsea's sensational 3-1 win at Old Trafford, United's first home defeat for thirty-eight league games. Osgood scored Chelsea's third and clinching goal with a low shot, setting himself up for a prolific month. His header put Chelsea on the way to a comfortable win over Sheffield Wednesday in the FA Cup replay and after a penalty contributed to a comfortable win against Leicester, he left the best till last with a superb winner at West Ham. Surrounded by defenders, his back to goal, he created just enough space to pivot and sweep home the game's only goal with a sweet finish.

Osgood's tally of seventeen goals was a season's best, and highly satisfactory given that he was still feeling his way back after such a bad injury. His skill and vision were such that he was often deployed in midfield by Dave Sexton, but by 1969/70 he was operating purely as a striker and with devastating effect. As well as netting twenty-three league goals, he scored in every round of the FA Cup, a feat which has never been repeated since. His form eventually persuaded Ramsey to give him a full cap, and he made his England debut against Belgium in February 1970. He impressed enough to be selected as part of the Mexico twenty-two, twice being introduced as a substitute, but afterwards made just one more appearance for his country.

Osgood enjoyed further success at Chelsea, making important contributions to their 1971 European Cup Winners' Cup triumph, including goals in the final and replay against Real Madrid. He continued to score spectacular goals for his club before, not for the first time, falling out with Sexton over his hedonistic lifestyle. Osgood was transferred in 1974 to Southampton, with whom he won another FA Cup winner's medal in 1976. He will, however always be synonymous with Chelsea, his status as 'The King Of Stamford Bridge' being confirmed forever when a statue of him was unveiled outside the ground in 2010, four years after his death.

APRIL 1968

The first leg of England's European Cup quarter-final against Spain attracted a full house to Wembley, and gave Alf Ramsey some interesting selection problems. Banks hadn't been at his best for Stoke, and his performance at Hampden, albeit on a treacherous surface, had been shaky. Hunt's England goal drought had continued and Summerbee's debut had been unconvincing. However, Geoff Hurst's injury made things a bit more straightforward, and both Hunt and Summerbee took their places in the forward line. Banks predictably retained Ramsey's loyalty, with Cyril Knowles getting the nod over Keith Newton to fill the still-injured George Cohen's shoes.

England dominated possession but were yet again dogged by poor finishing and, as the game progressed, Spain's counter-attacks became more threatening against a visibly tiring English side. Most fatigued of all had been Bobby Charlton, subjected over the last month to a demanding schedule of crucial games, but he somehow found the strength to fire England ahead with a goal five minutes from time. Banks justified Ramsey's faith with two superb saves, the second of which acrobatically denied Spain a last-gasp equaliser, but many critics doubted whether one goal would be enough for survival in Madrid.

Charlton returned to Manchester in time for his side's vital encounter at home to title rivals Liverpool. Best's early goal was the prelude to further United pressure, yet within fifteen minutes goals from Yeats and Hunt had overturned the deficit. The game remained end to end but as time wore on Liverpool's counter-attacks carried the greater menace and, but for some great saves by Stepney, their margin of victory would have been greater. After a thirty-seven-game unbeaten run in league matches at Old Trafford, United had now lost three in four.

A buoyant Liverpool returned to Anfield for their replay with West Brom and when Hateley put them ahead early on, their surge towards a double seemed to be gathering momentum. But Albion grew into the game impressively and Astle's header midway through the second half deservedly brought them level. Their composed football saw them create the better chances in extra time, but ultimately neither side could make the crucial breakthrough. A third match, scheduled for Maine Road, would now be necessary.

Concerned by Hugh McIlvanney's mental state after so many trials by tedium at Highbury, *The Observer* tried to lighten his mood by allowing him to take a little jaunt along the Thames to Craven Cottage. It didn't work. 'The only hope for spectators was that the clouds of dust which rose from the hard dry pitch might obscure a little of the welter of ineptitude.' The match between almost-doomed Fulham and Coventry ended all-square, with suggestions that Fulham's late equaliser had come about due to the low sun being in the defenders' eyes. 'Many of us in the stands would have welcomed a little temporary blindness

– about an hour and a half of it.' It was a shame they hadn't sent Hugh to Upton Park, where he would have seen West Ham destroy Newcastle 5-0, the centrepiece being a hat-trick by the increasingly influential Trevor Brooking.

The league's top two now turned back to European action. Real Madrid made their first visit to Old Trafford since their iconic team of the late 1950s twice put United out of the competition. This particular vintage wasn't quite of the same calibre, but still presented a formidable obstacle. Best's goal secured a narrow lead in a tense match, leaving United, like England in the Nations Cup, with a precarious lead to take to Madrid. Meanwhile, Leeds faced Rangers in the quarter-final of the Fairs Cup. After a goalless draw at Ibrox, the second leg brought fears of unrest. A record number of police were deployed, with Scottish fans without tickets urged to watch the closed-circuit broadcast set up at Ibrox. It was, however, the fans *with* tickets who caused the problems, bombarding David Harvey with missiles despite appeals for calm by their own captain, John Greig. Leeds came through the tie with relative ease, setting up a semi-final against Dundee, their third Scottish opponents in succession.

With four contenders still almost neck and neck at the top of the table, the three-match Easter programme carried even more weight than usual. With two of their games against the hapless Fulham, United looked to have the easiest schedule and duly took four comfortable points. Their other fixture, at Southampton, saw them recover from two down at half-time to earn a draw. Neighbours City took four points from their two home games, but their return fixture at Stamford Bridge saw Alan Birchenall score the only goal. Ironically, it was City's best performance of the three but the absence of Bell and some unusually wayward finishing proved costly.

Leeds' twenty-six-game unbeaten run was ended by Tottenham, but the real losers over Easter were Liverpool, who suffered a shock home reverse to Sheffield United and could only take a point from the return fixture. Things got even worse for them when they were narrowly ousted by West Brom in the second replay of their cup quarter-final. Criticised for too often playing the long ball to Tony Hateley – a tactic which all of his many employers struggled to resist – Liverpool were finally undone by Albion's more composed football. Bobby Hope was particularly influential, setting in train a fine move which saw Clive Clark score the winner after Astle and Hateley had shared first-half goals.

To complete a miserable week for Shankly's men, Martin Peters' goal then sentenced them to defeat at Upton Park and the title now looked like a shoot-out between the Uniteds of Leeds and Manchester. Manchester led by a point with just three left to play, but Leeds had a game in hand. City and Liverpool now needed slip-ups from the leaders – two of them in Leeds' case – if they were to have any chance, and time was fast running out.

Leeds' game in hand was at Stoke City, and classy strikes from Peter Dobing put the home side two up at the interval. Leeds launched a ferocious fightback after the break and within fifteen minutes Greenhoff and Charlton had pulled them back level. Dobing swept in from close range to restore Stoke's lead, only to prompt an even more furious assault on Banks' goal. England's number one was in inspired form, leaving his line time and again to catch or punch balls aimed at the Leeds strikers, augmented for the last twenty minutes by Big Jack Charlton. During an agonising seven minutes of injury time, Banks produced two fabulous saves and watched as Hunter's last-gasp header came back off the post. Somehow, Stoke had survived and boosted their prospects of beating the drop. Meanwhile, Leeds were left to reflect on a missed opportunity – even a point would have kept their destiny in their own hands.

They had just four days to reset their focus on the FA Cup semi-final against an Everton side deprived of Alan Ball due to suspension. It was a typically tense, cautious and physical encounter, ultimately settled by another of Gary Sprake's aberrations. His terrible clearance gave Husband the chance to chip the ball directly home. Jack Charlton back-pedalled to punch the ball over the bar but Johnny Morrissey scored the ensuing penalty, in those days punishment enough for such unsportsmanlike behaviour. The other semi-final was a strictly local affair, with West Brom taking on Birmingham City at Villa Park. Ultimately West Brom's greater class made the difference, goals from Brown and Astle easing them through to the final.

Neither Everton nor West Brom had too much time to celebrate their achievement in reaching Wembley. Just two days later, they were back in action in games which would give the title race yet another twist. Their opponents would be the two Manchester clubs. United's trip to the Hawthorns was their final away game, and with two straightforward-looking home matches to finish their season, a win over West Brom would surely see them retain their title. Having had the weekend off while their opponents were locked in semi-final battle, few expected them to falter. Instead, with just over an hour gone, they were 6-1 down as a shambolic defensive display was ruthlessly punished by an inspired Albion side. When the incredible news was transmitted over the tannoys at Anfield and Maine Road, both Liverpool and City redoubled their efforts.

Tottenham proved uncommonly durable at Anfield, holding out for a 1-1 draw which left Liverpool's hopes slender at best. City, though, secured a 2-0 win over Everton, which sent them to the top of the table. No one at Maine Road was getting too carried away: Leeds could still overtake them if they won their game in hand, and City's final two fixtures were tough assignments at Tottenham and Newcastle. It would, as Joe Mercer put it, 'be like climbing Everest and Mont Blanc in one week'.

Match Of The Month
29 April 1968, Division One: West Bromwich Albion 6 Manchester United 3

United arrived at the Hawthorns knowing that three wins in their final three games of the season would see them retain their title. They faced a West Brom side still on a high after reaching the FA Cup Final some forty-eight hours earlier, but surely bound to have suffered some reaction to their exertions. United, having had a rare weekend off, seemed almost too relaxed in the first half, and their performance was littered with defensive mistakes. Dunne's poor backpass allowed Astle to nip in and put Albion ahead after ten minutes, and a terrible mistake by Francis Burns set Ronnie Rees free to tuck away a second. Half-time came with a packed-to-the-rafters Hawthorns wondering whether Albion could keep it up. Most would have thought that a trademark United comeback was inevitable. Few, if any, could have foreseen what was actually about to unfold.

Counter-attacking with flair and pace as United fought to get back in the game, Albion played Rees through only to see Stiles cynically hack him down as he prepared to shoot. Brown scored from the twice-taken penalty and the floodgates opened. Astle headed a fourth and, after Law scored a penalty for United, seventeen-year-old Asa Hartford stroked in Albion's fifth before Astle powered home another header to complete his hat-trick. In the meantime, United had squandered a number of chances, and one of the night's enduring images was the sight of Denis Law walking fully twenty yards, head in hands, after a scarcely believable miss in front of an open goal. Kidd grabbed a couple of late consolations for United but the game was long since up as West Brom fans, already giddy after reaching Wembley, could scarcely believe their eyes. Yet even these reactions paled into insignificance compared with those at Maine Road and Anfield, as news of United's humiliation came through.

West Brom: Osborne, Clarke, Williams, Brown, Talbut, Fraser, Rees, Collard, Astle, Hope, Hartford.

Manchester United: Stepney, Dunne, Burns, Crerand, Sadler, Stiles, Best, Law, Charlton, Kidd, Aston.

Player Of The Month
Jeff Astle (West Bromwich Albion)

Jeff Astle was a 'typical' English centre-forward; tall, brave and strong in the air. He signed for West Brom from Notts County

– where he had been managed by Tommy Lawton and was often referred to as the great man's protege – and quickly became a crowd favourite at the Hawthorns. His exploits in April 1968 nudged him firmly towards the legendary status he would ultimately acquire.

In the FA Cup, Albion were faced with a daunting replay at Anfield, but Astle produced a superb performance, scoring their equaliser with a magnificent header in a game Albion ultimately deserved to win. In the third game, at Maine Road, Astle netted a crucial early goal, racing on to a through ball to fire low past Tommy Lawrence and then, late in the game, was pivotal in the slick passing move which set Clive Clark free to score the winner. The semi-final against Birmingham saw their second-division neighbours cause Albion plenty of problems, but again it was Astle who struck first, pouncing as Herriot could only parry Tony Brown's shot to put the Baggies on the road to Wembley. It maintained his record of scoring in every round, an achievement he would extend to its conclusion with the winning goal in the final.

Yet for all his heroic exploits in the cup, it was the league where Astle produced his most eye-catching display of the month. At home to champions Manchester United, Astle scored a fabulous hat-trick, including two thumping headers, as Albion shocked United and the football world with a 6-3 win on one of the Hawthorns' most famous nights. Incredibly, when Albion hosted West Ham just two nights later, he netted another three times on his way to an overall tally of twenty-six league goals for the season.

Astle continued to score prolifically for Albion over the next two seasons, and his achievement in becoming the first division's leading scorer in 1969/70 earned him a place in the final Mexico squad. He made his England debut, coming on as a substitute against Brazil, and quickly had a chance to become an instant national hero but instead fired wide of a gaping net. He won four further England caps but failed to get on the scoresheet, leading Ramsey to conclude that he wasn't quite of international class.

Not that this mattered to West Brom fans. Astle continued to lead their attack until 1974, scoring a total of 174 goals for the club, and is acknowledged as one of their all-time greats. His premature death in 2002 was ultimately attributed to industrial injury, specifically the traumas caused by repeatedly heading a football, something he did as well and as often as anyone of the era. The Hawthorns now has an entrance known as the Astle Gates, due recognition of one of their finest players.

MAY 1968

The title race entered its final two weekends with Leeds back in pole position, knowing that three wins would leave them uncatchable. However, their next game was at home to Liverpool, themselves still in with a shout, although they would need to win at Elland Road and hope for good news from elsewhere if they were to get their name back on the trophy.

Manchester United, stung by their extraordinary collapse at the Hawthorns a few days earlier, tore into Newcastle to register their biggest win of the season, with Best marking his election as Footballer Of The Year – at just twenty-one – by hitting a hat-trick in a 6-0 victory. Long before the end of the rout, their fans had been more concerned with the news from White Hart Lane and Elland Road, emanating from the plethora of transistor radios brought into the ground. There was a dramatic late twist at Leeds; with Revie's men 1-0 up and controlling the game, the familiar nerves and fear set in and they sat back in a bid to see out time. In the space of sixty seconds, Liverpool bundled home two of the scruffiest goals imaginable, both from goalmouth scrambles following corners, to inflict a terminal and cruelly unlucky defeat.

But for the last few minutes, it had been one of Leeds' best and most enterprising performances of the season. Don Revie was in self-pitying mood afterwards, stating that 'most people feel that a defeat for Leeds is a victory for attractive and attacking football'. It would take far more than an unlucky reverse in which they had attacked almost relentlessly for most journalists and indeed fans of other clubs to forgive Revie and his team for the systematic brutality, cynicism and disregard for the paying customer which had characterised their approach since they came into the top flight. There are many who still haven't forgiven them almost fifty years on.

The roars from Old Trafford on hearing of Leeds' demise were soon tempered when the final score from White Hart Lane came in. In the day's finest performance, City had produced a magnificent display to dismantle Tottenham. After absorbing early pressure, they increasingly dominated the game, taking the lead when Bell finished off a slick counter-attack. Bell struck again early in the second half and then turned provider for Summerbee's third. George Heslop's inexplicable handball allowed Greaves to net a late consolation penalty, with his dressing-room explanation 'their guy hit me on the funny bone and my arm just shot out' provoking first silence, then expletives and finally laughter from Joe Mercer. The upshot of the day's drama was that, for the first time, the title was City's to lose.

Leeds' already slim hopes were completely extinguished at Highbury three days later, where they equalised three times against Arsenal only to lose to a last-minute goal. In what was a meaningless match for the home side, it was noted in *The Guardian* that 'from the roar one would have thought Arsenal had won the championship, though it is one of the perverse British pleasures remaining to deny others success'.

Leeds had been forced to play the match despite the fact that Charlton, Cooper and Hunter were all absent with England in Madrid, in preparation for England's attempt to defend their 1-0 first-leg lead against Spain. Alf Ramsey had spent the previous Saturday afternoon at White Hart Lane, and there was speculation that Colin Bell's match-winning display would put him in line for a full England debut. However, a slight injury suffered late in the game ruled him out of contention and, with Banks out with flu and Hurst suffering from a septic toe, it was a chance for others to step up to the plate.

Bonetti was an obvious choice to replace Banks, but Ramsey surprised many with his inclusion of Norman Hunter in place of the stricken Hurst. It suggested that a policy of containment was on Sir Alf's agenda, but against high-quality opposition and with a crowd of 125,000 to contend with, it wouldn't be easy. Marshalled by a superb Bobby Moore, England's defence withstood Spain's expected early barrage, with Amancio, Pirri and the ageless Gento posing an incessant threat. By half-time, things were more even in a match of great skill and far less physical conflict than most had anticipated.

Early in the second half, Amancio lit the blue touchpaper with a gorgeous curling finish. As the stadium erupted with the feverish anticipation of seeing their team take out the world champions, it was time for England to show their mettle, and they did so superbly. Now taking the game to their hosts, Hunt forced a great save but from the resulting corner Peters, ghosting in in what was well on the way to becoming trademark fashion, flashed home a near-post header. The game then became end to end, with both sides living dangerously, but seven minutes from time England's hero emerged. To Ramsey's enormous credit, it was the unlikely figure of Norman Hunter who buried a fierce shot from Roger Hunt's cutback to confirm England's passage to the last four.

It was undoubtedly England's best performance and result since the World Cup Final, tellingly delivered when the chips were really down. The Spanish coach acknowledged that England had been 'so very, very good' and the result brought out a torrent of tabloid jingoism of the type last seen during the World Cup. *The Daily Express*'s headline 'Take that, Spain!' was followed by a eulogy to England's show of 'moving courage and wondrous football in the face of a screaming violent crowd and a referee who chastised every honest tackle and treated the Spaniards as though they were his favourite nephews.' No wonder some foreigners didn't seem to like us very much.

In a terrific team effort, Bobby Moore's display had stood out even above the general excellence on show. 'This was a magnificent performance by Bobby Moore,' stated Football League chairman Len Shipman. It was remarkable that England's performance had been delivered just four days after the majority of the team had taken part in crucial, full-blooded league fixtures, whilst the Spanish players had enjoyed a restful weekend.

For many of Ramsey's squad, there was an even more important round of fixtures to come on the season's final Saturday. Whilst most of the focus was on the thrilling battle for the title, there was similar intrigue at the bottom, with three teams in the frame to take the second relegation place and join Fulham in the second division. Stoke and Coventry both ground out goalless draws away from home and ultimately it was Sheffield United – strongly favoured to survive given that their fixture was at home against a team with nothing to play for – who failed to escape the trapdoor, Chelsea's 2-1 win having fatal consequences for the Blades.

So, who would take the title? City led United on goal average, with Liverpool a point further back. All three were in with a chance of winning the big prize, but most eyes were focused firmly on St James' Park. This is more than could be said for the *Match Of The D*ay cameras, which had been dispatched to Old Trafford. The decision was entirely defensible, having been made a few weeks earlier, when the table suggested that this day would almost certainly mark United's coronation, but it deprived viewers of witnessing the season's most dramatic game.

Seven spectacular goals illuminated a grey Tyneside afternoon, the upshot being that City squeezed home 4-3 to take the title. The game epitomised the way in which they had played all season, always on the offensive, and their refreshing style of play, contrasting markedly with the more cautious, functional approaches adopted by Leeds and Liverpool, made them popular champions. Few were more fulsome in their praise than Geoffrey Green. 'It was worth every yard for a southerner to make this long haul to the north-east on Saturday. In the event, it would have been worth it even on a bicycle, facing rain and a headwind, to see a title won in this style and in the grand manner.'

There was widespread delight for manager Joe Mercer, one of the game's most loved figures, and an appreciation for the part that coach Malcolm Allison had played. Almost exploding with ideas, Allison had got more out of his players individually and collectively than anyone could have imagined, and wasn't slow to let everyone know that this was just the start. 'We'll terrify the cowards of Europe' was the quote draped across the tabloids' back pages on Monday morning after a still-intoxicated Allison had regaled the press with boasts of his young team's potential.

For City, European adventures were something to look forward to, but their neighbours had more immediate priorities. The one consolation from their shock home defeat to Sunderland was that it wouldn't have mattered even if they had won, and they quickly turned their attention to their next engagement, the return match against Real Madrid.

To a man, critics feared that the 1-0 first-leg lead wouldn't be enough – a contrast with the modern mentality, where a win without conceding an away goal is all that home sides crave – and by half-time it seemed they would be proved right. Fluid attacking play saw Madrid take a 3-1 advantage and most in the ground expected the second half to be a formality. Geoffrey Green described the half-time scene. 'The vast crowd was in a symphony of sound. They resembled a man who has two bottles of wine inside him, pleasantly intoxicated and feeling that there is nothing wrong with life.' Although perhaps an unwitting reflection on the alcohol tolerance of sports journalists as much as the state of the spectators, the words convey beautifully a sense of complacency, of a job already done.

When they returned for the second half, Real Madrid's own players were no exception to the self-satisfied mood, visibly easing off even though United needed just one goal to be back in command of the tie. For good measure they scored two, one of them coming from Munich survivor Bill Foulkes, a man for whom winning the European Cup would have extra meaning. While the stunned crowd struggled to absorb the shock of what they had witnessed, United, after three previous semi-final failures, had at last reached the final.

United's date with Benfica meant that, uniquely, the FA Cup Final wouldn't be Wembley's most prestigious May date. The domestic occasion duly played down to its diminished billing, with Everton and West Brom, two teams capable of the most attractive football, both paralysed by fear of failure, as a dour spectacle numbed all but the most committed supporters. Things only got lively when fatigue allowed space to become more freely available, and Everton's Jimmy Husband missed a simple headed chance close to the end of normal time.

Everton had finished the stronger, but extra time saw Albion start with renewed energy. Astle had a shooting chance from just outside the box, but miscued his effort horribly. The ball rebounded back off an Everton defender straight into Astle's path, and without breaking stride he connected perfectly with a left-footer which flew high past Gordon West's left hand into the top corner of the net. Despite the prodigious efforts of the tireless Ball, Everton seldom looked like recovering, and West Brom's composure in possession saw them reap tangible and well-deserved reward for a season in which they had produced some memorable performances in both league and cup.

But now Wembley braced itself for a night of nights. It could only ever be an emotional highly-charged occasion, and at its epicentre were Bobby Charlton and Matt Busby, the Munich tragedy's two highest profile and most revered survivors. Charlton duly headed United into the lead, only for Graca to equalise for Benfica.

The game's pivotal moment came as full time approached, with Eusebio clean through on Stepney. As the nation held its collective breath, the normally deadly striker fired straight at the keeper and United were reprieved. In extra time, they ran away with it, Best flamboyantly rounding Henrique to put them ahead, before nineteen-year-old Brian Kidd put the outcome beyond doubt. Charlton put further gloss on the scoreline by clipping in a fourth and at the final whistle fell into the arms of his manager in a scene which would have melted the hardest of hearts.

It was also a scene witnessed by a few who wouldn't have expected to be there: rumours about there being scores of forged tickets in circulation meant that touts outside the ground struggled to offload their wares. In the end, with the game having kicked off, they ended up giving dozens away. A mounted policeman received about thirty, which he passed on to young children, who were thereby able to witness English club football's greatest triumph to date. The story of United's victory dominated the front pages of the following morning's papers, with so many of the words conveying a sense of emotion not commonly found in football reports. Many journalists hadn't just lived through the Munich tragedy, they had also lost colleagues and friends in it.

But Wembley's season wasn't quite over yet. To warm up for their forthcoming Nations Cup commitments in Italy, the FA had arranged a friendly against Sweden. England performed impressively, with Colin Bell making a highly promising debut, but the game's highlight was a superb goal from Bobby Charlton. Not only did it seal England's 3-1 win, it also saw him pass Jimmy Greaves to become England's all-time leading goalscorer, albeit having played some twenty-eight games more than his erstwhile team-mate.

There was much praise for England's performance, it being noted that the new players had slotted easily into the 'system' so condemned just two years earlier. Now, having a well-defined pattern of play was starting to be seen as a strength, at least by some. *The Guardian* referred to 'the now high standard of methodical play which has brought admiration and envy from so many foreign observers and officials', it also being noted that similar continental envy would be directed at 'the depth of England's talent, which in no way impairs by the introduction of fresh blood the overall impressive performance of the side as a whole'. The concept of a system of play into which different personnel could slot seamlessly was starting to be understood.

Match Of The Month
11 May, 1968, Division One: Newcastle 3 Manchester City 4

The thrilling season reached a climax on its final day, as Manchester City travelled to Newcastle knowing that a win would give them the title irrespective of how their neighbours fared at home to Sunderland. Newcastle were still in the hunt for a Fairs Cup place, admittedly a somewhat smaller prize, but with their impressive home record City could be under no illusion that they faced a severe test.

City approached the game as they had done most of their fixtures this season, opting for all-out attack. Summerbee's slick finish gave them the lead after a flowing move, but a stunning drive from Bryan Robson saw them quickly pegged back. A magnificent strike from leading scorer Neil Young restored the lead, but more uncertain defending allowed Jackie Sinclair to finish superbly with a dipping drive past a helpless Mulhearn.

A furious Allison wanted to lay into his players as he approached the dressing room at half-time, but thought better of it when he realised how fraught and nervous they were. Instead, he and Joe Mercer tried to calm them down and get them to do what they had been doing all season.

It worked. Young's second great strike of the afternoon restored City's lead, and they increased their advantage when Bell, instrumental in all four goals on this most crucial of afternoons, cleverly released Lee to clip the ball over McFaul before celebrating with the City fans behind the goal. A late McNamee header gave rise to a nervy last few minutes but City held on to take the title amid scenes of wild exuberance, as thousands of travelling fans surged on to the pitch to congratulate their heroes.

This final-day victory epitomised the way in which City – who exactly doubled their goal tally of the previous season – had gone about their business throughout the campaign and was just reward for the transformation in playing style which Mercer and Allison had brought about.

After the game, Mercer and Matt Busby were brought together by TV link-up on *Grandstand* and Busby warmly congratulated his rival and friend. These really were different times.

Newcastle: McFaul, Craig, Clark, Moncur, McNamee, Iley, Sinclair, Scott, Davies, Robson B, Robson T.

Manchester City: Mulhearn, Book, Pardoe, Doyle, Heslop, Oakes, Lee, Bell, Summerbee, Young, Coleman.

Player Of The Month
Bobby Charlton (Manchester United)

One of the most famous English footballers of all time, Charlton's career at United began in 1953. He made his debut in 1956, immediately becoming a regular in the side and a frequent goalscorer. After surviving the Munich air disaster, Charlton began playing again just three weeks later, helping his team reach the FA Cup Final. He was a member of England's World Cup squads of 1958 and 1962 and, by 1966, was a household name both at home and abroad. His reputation was enhanced further when a searing thirty-yarder broke the deadlock against Mexico, and his two goals against Portugal were enough to see England through to the final. Charlton's exploits were duly rewarded when he was named European Footballer of the Year.

Charlton continued as a central figure in the England side, and this month saw him help England through to the Nations Cup semi-finals with a memorable win in Madrid, before returning to Wembley for the friendly against Sweden, where his superb goal saw him overtake Jimmy Greaves as England's all-time leading scorer. But it was his exploits for his club which would make the month particularly memorable.

Charlton had won three league titles with United but, ever since the Munich disaster, his and the club's prime target had been to win the European Cup. May 1968 saw them reach their fourth semi-final and this time, on an emotional night in Madrid, they at last progressed to the final. This, though, was as nothing compared with the emotion surrounding the final, where three of the Munich survivors – Charlton, Busby and Bill Foulkes – would be involved.

Foulkes had already made his mark with a vital goal in Madrid to help his side recover from their half-time deficit, but the final belonged to Busby and Charlton. Charlton had always been renowned for his powerful long-range shooting, but his two goals on the evening showed different aspects of his armoury. The first was a precise glancing header, one of very few goals scored by Charlton with his head throughout his career, and the second a delicate near-post clip across the keeper. The embrace between Charlton and Busby at the end of the game is one of the night's – and indeed the competition's – enduring memories.

Although England were unable to prevail in the European Nations Cup the following month, hopes were high that Charlton could inspire England to retain their trophy in Mexico. However, the thirty-two-year-old consistently struggled in the draining conditions and his impact on the tournament was negligible. Perhaps mindful of his stellar reputation internationally, and his psychological effect on the opposition, Ramsey had started him in all four of England's games and received criticism for substituting him during the fateful match against West Germany. In retrospect, he might have been better served leaving Charlton out altogether.

Charlton's forty-nine England goals remained a record until 2015, and he also briefly held the country's appearance record before being overtaken by Bobby Moore. He played on with United until 1973, finishing with 199 goals in just over 600 games. His short managerial career was unsuccessful but he has remained in football as a Manchester United director, often picked out by TV cameras at their matches as well as at FA Cup finals with his friends. His iconic status is assured forever.

Summer 1968

Was this English football's high-water mark? The national team were world champions, and we could now boast the European club champions as well. The competition at league level was ferocious, with four teams in strong title contention even on the season's penultimate Saturday, and the crown ultimately going to a side whose style of football had been a breath of fresh air. Domestic crowds had risen again, with aggregate league attendances topping the 30 million mark for the first time in the decade. All that was needed now was for England to go to Italy and bring back the European Nations Cup, and England would have a full house. For all the carping about negative, defensive football, these were heady days indeed.

Having successfully and encouragingly come through the warm-up game with Sweden, the authorities had decided that the best preparation for England's European Nations Cup semi-final would be a match four days beforehand away from home against a side hell-bent on revenge for the perceived injustice they suffered in the World Cup Final. So it was that England took the field in Hanover against a German side who would have little regard for the forthcoming commitments of their opponents. As it turned out, it could have been worse – at least there were no serious injuries. Beckenbauer's late goal signalled West Germany's first win over England, as well as Ramsey's first away defeat in seventeen games as England manager.

England's defeat had been witnessed by Scotland manager Bobby Brown, whose team would themselves face the Germans in their bid to qualify for the Mexico World Cup. He was described as being 'cock-a-hoop' after the game, with the Germans' lacklustre performance even in victory convincing him that the Scots would qualify with ease. He obviously wound up Geoffrey Green, who unusually allowed his irritation to filter through to his words: 'But the Scots know it all. Having first revealed their inherent artistry to the world, they have always refused to look beyond that, hence their failures when it matters in the world game today.'

By the time England's game against Yugoslavia came round, the world seemed a much darker place. The day's radio and TV programmes had been interrupted at regular intervals to bring updates on the condition of Senator Robert Kennedy, shot in the early hours of the morning in Los Angeles. America may have been a long way away, but there was something about the Kennedys that resonated vibrantly in Britain, and the desperate sense of tragedy and loss transmitted itself vividly across the Atlantic. No amount of assurances that doctors were doing everything possible could mask the unspoken inevitability of the ultimate outcome, duly confirmed the following morning.

The game against Yugoslavia, hardly to be underestimated given that they had qualified from their group at the expense of the West Germans, took place in Florence, where just 25,000 could be bothered to attend. They witnessed an ugly, brutal clash, with the Slavs starting the fight but England more than prepared to respond in kind. One of the most depressing matches in English football history was settled five minutes from time, when Dragan Dzajic flashed a drive into the roof of Banks' net. Tempers became even more frayed after the goal, and when Alan Mullery retaliated after yet another cynical foul, he earned the dubious honour of becoming the first Englishman to be sent off in a full international. Nobby Stiles, whose many and varied misdemeanours over the years pushed many referees close to but not quite beyond the limit, would surely have felt the tiniest pang of jealousy at being denied that particular distinction.

Subsequent interviews with England players suggested that they had never before been subjected to such a level of physical intimidation, but the press considered things to have been more even-handed. It all came down to a matter of interpretation as to what was acceptable. 'But now the unfriendly critics who always pointed to Wembley as the reason for England's global victory in 1966 are hugging themselves. When it was all over, all that remained in the mind was a desert of frustration and ruthless tackling. But we at least were more honest in our misdemeanours,' said one. 'The only difference between the warring parties was that the English tackling was more open in view; the Slavs applied force with a subtle concealment which was just as damaging,' opined another.

Alf Ramsey said: 'When it comes to rough play, we have a great deal to learn. But I don't think we wish to learn to play that way.' Bobby Moore added: 'They say we're hard, and we are at times, but at least it's a fairly open sort of hardness, man to man. We don't set out to cripple people with every tackle. And we don't writhe about on the ground as if we've been shot if we catch one.'

The other semi-final was also a dismal, cynical affair, with 60,000 witnessing a goalless draw between Italy and Russia. To the delight of the crowd and the tournament organisers, desperate for home representation to maintain local interest, Italy won through to the final via the toss of a coin. Seldom can international football have produced two such barren matches in the final stages of a major competition. They were followed by another two, barely more appealing, Italy ultimately prevailing with a 2-0 replay win after the first game ended in a 1-1 stalemate.

The 1966 World Cup spectacle had had plenty of critics, in many ways marking the end of the age of footballing innocence, but there was also plenty to admire, enjoy, and get excited about. This mercifully brief tournament exemplified what many feared would be the game's natural progression, as professionalism and winning at all costs had become the *modus operandi* of all four participants – and of many of those who hadn't even made it this far.

Disappointment at the national team's failure to land the prize was tempered by the acknowledgement that the demands on key players had been abnormal, with so many vitally important club matches taking place throughout the month of May. Indeed, rather than criticising the team, some more reasoned voices thought they had done well to get so far, 'questioning what other national team manager would have to accept a situation in which national interest is often subservient to a league programme.' The contrast was particularly marked before the game in Spain, with most English players having played three hard games in eight days whilst those of their opponents had been adjusted to allow more preparation time. 'That's what happens in countries who value national prestige more than Britain does these days,' observed *The Times*.

So, the international summer may have left a sour taste in the mouth, but at club level things had seldom seemed so vibrant. We could boast the European champions, with Leeds also through to the Fairs Cup Final. The league championship had been thrilling and compelling, with attendances having increased significantly. And there was a range of managers who already were – or would certainly become – club legends, all in competition at the same time. Busby, Revie, Shankly, Mercer, Nicholson, Catterick… and with a young Brian Clough girding his loins to join them.

And for all the terrace violence, there was still a sense of fair play amongst the majority of supporters, unimaginable in the modern *schadenfreude*-laden game, where opposition teams are mocked and reviled as a matter of course, and the level of contempt is just a question of degree. Newspaper reports described loud applause at Old Trafford when news of City's decisive victory at Newcastle came through, which today seems hardly credible. United's defeat had ruled them out anyway, so perhaps their fans preferred the title to stay in Manchester? But to *cheer*? When City and Liverpool were neck and neck to take United's crown in 2014, Gary Neville was asked which of them he would prefer to prevail. 'It's like asking which of two blokes you would want to run off with your wife…'

1968/69:

Triumph of the Dark Side

AUGUST 1968

Maine Road had the honour of hosting the Charity Shield, and most of the attendees went home well satisfied as Manchester City thrashed West Brom 6-1. Debutant Bobby Owen, signed by City after impressing for Bury in a hastily arranged friendly to enable the championship trophy to be presented, scored in the first minute as fans and critics went away convinced that both he and his team were destined for great things once the season began in earnest.

City's title defence began at Anfield where, after taking the lead and hitting the bar, they were eventually overhauled by a robust Liverpool side who looked increasingly strong as the match wore on. Liverpool seemed none the worse for the absence of the dropped Tony Hateley, whose replacement Bobby Graham took his chance in every sense by netting their equaliser before Peter Thompson decided the match. The other Manchester–Merseyside encounter saw Everton unlucky to go down at Old

Trafford, due largely to an outstanding performance by Alex Stepney and the brilliance of Best, who interrupted a twenty-minute period of Everton dominance by firing home a superb goal. Ball's equaliser simply prompted more inspiration from the Irishman, as he cleverly set up Charlton to drive home what proved to be the winner.

The opening-day schedule didn't exactly scrimp on eye-catching fixtures, as the computer also brought together Spurs and Arsenal. Spurs frequently deployed Mike England up front but to little effect, and the consequent weakening of the back line allowed Arsenal to take a two-goal lead. Greaves touched home his customary goal, but Arsenal held on comfortably for a notable triumph.

Of the other likely contenders, Leeds made a strong start with an impressive performance at Southampton, having warmed up by earning a 1-0 first-leg lead in their Fairs Cup Final against Ferencvaros. Their performance at the Dell surprised observers not so much by the fact that they won but rather by the more enterprising style of their football. Don Revie had promised a more positive approach from his side this season, although it would take much more than one match to convince Leeds' denigrators that the dark arts were now to be consigned to history. An opening-day stroll on the south coast was one thing, a crucial late-season match against a title rival would be quite another.

Promoted QPR, shorn through injury of the talismanic Rodney Marsh, began their first ever top-flight campaign at home to Leicester City. Leicester's ranks had been bolstered by the expensive acquisition of Allan Clarke from relegated Fulham, and the striker spoiled the newcomers' party by scoring a smart equaliser. Still, the general consensus was that Rangers had acquitted themselves well, and would have enough about them – especially when their many casualties returned to action – to make a decent fist of life at the top table.

The success of *Jimmy Hill's Football Weekly* hadn't gone unnoticed, and the new season gave youngsters a new title to help satisfy their football cravings. From the same stable as the turgid *Charles Buchan's Football Monthly* – which, like *Soccer Star*, increasingly looked as though it belonged to another era – came the colourful and vibrant *Goal*. Full of varied articles, player interviews, opinion pieces, transfer gossip titbits together with posed and action photos, it also featured from the outset the major selling point of *Bobby Charlton's Diary*, straight in on page two, allowing Bob to treat his readers to ghost-written opinions on all aspects of the wide world of football.

A more innovative feature in *Goal* was 'Girl Behind The Man' in which players' wives would take a quick break from their domestic chores to pose in front of the kitchen sink or whilst leaning on the vacuum cleaner. Some of them even had jobs of their own. As the weeks went by, the ordinariness of even top players' home lives became charmingly apparent. The houses were far from palatial, the wives were typically girl-next-door teenage sweethearts. Like their counterparts of the modern era, many of them spent an inordinate amount of time in hairdressing salons – the difference was that the 1960s Wags actually worked there. The removal of the minimum wage had certainly improved the players' lot but, unless you were George Best, had only elevated them financially to the status of the average middle manager, if that.

The ever-increasing focus on footballers brought an unforeseen burden, with fanmail estimated at some 100,000 letters a week finding its way to the players. An England international said: 'I get nearly a thousand letters a week, most without stamped addressed envelopes. It costs me a lot of money to reply. If I were a film star earning thousands of pounds a performance, I could take on a secretary or two…as it is, I just couldn't afford it.' This was a genuine problem, as PFA chairman Cliff Lloyd acknowledged. 'Players are trained athletes, yet they are spending long hours attending to their fans,' he said. For the likes of Bobby Thomson, this had evidently been very much the case…

Back on the pitch, Manchester United got the chance to avenge last season's hammering at the Hawthorns – the night, in effect, when their title had been lost – in their first midweek game. They conspicuously failed to take it. After just eighteen minutes, they were 3-0 down and feeling glad they didn't play West Brom every week. Astle scored twice as he again terrorised a fragile defence and although United pulled a goal back, the result was never in doubt.

It wasn't the ideal preparation for the Manchester derby, although with City trying their best to throw away a 3-0 lead against Wolves – conceding two late goals and then having their woodwork struck – it looked as though their neighbours weren't in the best of health, either. Perhaps inevitably, the clash between the English and European champions proved to be a disappointing stalemate. City had the better of the play, United the closest of the misses, and both sides were ultimately happy enough not to lose.

West Ham had made a promising start with five points out of six, but were put in their place when Everton came to visit. Not for the first time, the expensive Bobby Ferguson failed to live up to his price tag, but Everton's composure in midfield, the energy of Ball and the increasingly formidable presence of young Joe Royle up front made them worthy winners, even if the 4-1 scoreline was slightly hard on the Hammers.

There was little consistency of performance to be found in the opening weeks, with the notable exception of Leeds United, who built on their impressive victory at Southampton to register a further three straight wins. Their next attempt to extend their 100 per cent record came to an abrupt halt at the City Ground, but it could have been so much worse. A half-time fire gutted Forest's main stand, also destroying the club offices and dressing rooms, but there were no casualties amongst the crowd. The Leeds team bus was trapped behind a phalanx of fire engines, and the players, many of whom had lost their clothing and valuables, were forced to travel home in a fleet of taxis, still in their kits. The damage at the City Ground was such that Forest would be forced to play out their next few home matches across the Trent at Meadow Lane.

West Ham's golden trio: a gleaming trophy with smiles to match

Heroes at the Cottage: Ball, Cohen and Wilson on the season's opening day

Nothing, but nothing, gets past the world's greatest goalkeeper

Another near-post run, as Geoff gets ahead of the Chelsea defence

Manchester Monopoly: United celebrate after clinching the title at West Ham…

…and City follow suit twelve months later

Nobby's bulldog spirit thwarts England's finest striker…for now…

Stepney beaten again as Jeff Astle sticks another one past his favourite opposition

Derby chairman Sam Longson introduces his new bright young thing to the media...

...while Don Revie poses outside Elland Road with his team's admirers from the press

Jack Charlton's first commandment: Thou shalt not pass...especially if thy name be Osgood

Denis Law in full flight; even Bobby Moore is forced into desperate measures

They used to play on grass: the 1970 League Cup finalists step onto Wembley's hallowed turf…

…and, five weeks later, Revie gees up his exhausted players for one last push

They think it's all over…it is now: England's dejected captain contemplates the end of an era

Manchester City were finding the mantle of champions to be an onerous burden, suffering heavy beatings at Leicester – for whom Clarke struck a fine hat-trick – and Arsenal, where Radford excelled as his team romped to a 4-1 victory. City ended the month with an uninspiring draw at QPR and while it was no great surprise to see Rangers at the foot of the table, few would have expected City to be their partners in the drop zone. Gallows humour was never far away from Maine Road, and there were plenty who recalled what happened the last time City had been champions in 1937 – they were relegated the very next season.

Things were little better across at Old Trafford, with United winless since the opening day. Inspired by Peter Houseman, visitors Chelsea were ahead within a minute and from then on picked off United at will. Chelsea's 4-0 win caused many to observe that some of the United team seemed to have aged overnight, as if at last taking the European Cup had left them with nothing to drive for. Fortunately, their next opponents were their old friends from Tottenham, who so often seemed to inspire United to hit the heights. With the returning Law in supreme form, United recorded a thrilling 3-1 victory, allowing their fans to wallow briefly in the illusion that business as usual had been restored.

That certainly appeared to be the case when they stormed into a 4-2 lead in their next game, at Hillsborough, but Wednesday came back to record an extraordinary 5-4 victory in one of the most famous games ever staged at the stadium. But when it came to the following morning's headlines, even Wednesday's five couldn't compete with another man's six. In Swansea, Gary Sobers made history when he hit six sixes in an over playing for Nottinghamshire against Glamorgan. Bowler Malcolm Nash at least had the dubious consolation of knowing that his name would forever be a part of sporting history.

West Ham's World Cup trio had already achieved that distinction, and now they were striving to elevate the rest of their team-mates to a similar status. Undeterred by the heavy defeat by Everton, they had dropped back into their merry cavalier ways and when they hammered Burnley 5-0, Hurst and Peters were joined in the goalscoring fun by the blossoming Trevor Brooking. Four days later, West Brom arrived in the East End and received similar treatment, Martin Peters netting a hat-trick in a 4-0 rout. The league table showed West Ham tucked just behind Arsenal at the summit, and after the years of northern domination – and the inevitable challenge to come from the usual suspects as the season unfolded – *The Observer* suggested that the league table be buried in a time capsule and preserved for posterity. And for all the excitement that the unpredictable start to the season had brought, there remained one constant. Lurking ominously, with a fire-ravaged game in hand, were unbeaten Leeds United.

Match Of The Month
31 August, 1968, Division One: Sheffield Wednesday 5 Manchester United 4

Almost 52,000 spectators crammed into Hillsborough, wondering which Manchester United would turn up. The one which had succumbed so pitifully to Chelsea a week earlier, or the one which thrillingly beat Tottenham four days later? In the end, the fans were spoilt rotten, ending up with two Uniteds for the price of one.

The game began at a frenzied pace, fired by an early goal by Jack Whitham for Wednesday. Ten minutes later, United were in front with strikes from Best and Law, only for John Ritchie to glance home a header to put Wednesday back on terms. Fifteen minutes gone, two apiece, and a crowd barely able to catch its breath.

The game then settled into a pattern, with United attacking with all their old flair and deservedly regaining the ascendancy with tremendous goals from Law and Charlton. After months plagued with niggling injuries, Law looked as sharp and mercurial as ever, in this era of thrilling players without doubt the most thrilling of them all.

Showing great resilience, Wednesday fought back towards half-time and after Stepney had been forced into two great saves, Whitham pounced on a defensive mix-up to put Wednesday back in the game seconds before the interval. Seconds after it, they were back on level terms, as Nobby Stiles headed into his own goal from a testing free kick.

Roared on by a raucous crowd, Wednesday now attacked relentlessly, and after Megson's goal was disallowed, Whitham tapped them ahead after a fumble from Stepney. Rather than sitting back, Wednesday went for the kill but couldn't find the goal to give them breathing space, and towards the end United put the home goal under siege. Somehow, Wednesday came through the last few minutes unbreached, and the final whistle was greeted firstly with relief and then with fulsome appreciation for the magnificent spectacle the twenty-two players had served up.

Sheffield Wednesday: Springett, Young, Megson, Ellis, Mobley, Eustace, Whitham, McCalliog, Ritchie, Ford, Fantham.

Manchester United: Stepney, Brennan, Dunne (Burns), Fitzpatrick, Sadler, Stiles, Morgan, Kidd, Charlton, Law, Best.

Player Of The Month
Martin Peters (West Ham)

But for thirty seconds and a dubiously awarded free kick, Martin Peters would have become a national icon, at the same time diminishing his team-mate Geoff Hurst's place in football history. Nevertheless, he will always be remembered as one of England's World Cup heroes, as well as one of West Ham's glorious triumvirate.

Peters made his West Ham debut in 1962 at the age of eighteen, and had been a regular in the side ever since. For the first time in several years, 1968 saw West Ham make a strong start to the season, and it was Hurst and Peters – whose on-field relationship bordered on the telepathic – who were the driving force. Unusually, it was Peters who outscored his team-mate throughout this dizzying spell, beginning with the opening goal in the Hammers' impressive 2-0 win at Stoke City. He also scored West Ham's consolation goal in their one reverse of the month, at home to Everton, before really coming into his own.

Another away win, this time at Coventry, was put in train by Peters' early goal before Burnley and West Brom were both put to the sword at Upton Park. Peters smashed home a thirty-yarder to put West Ham on the way against Burnley, coming close on several further occasions as his team coasted to a 5-0 win. Then, against West Brom, a magnificent team performance was capped by three assured strikes from the England man. A calm one-on-one finish after being put through by Redknapp, a header from a Hurst cross, and a close-range shot set up by Hurst saw West Ham to a comprehensive 4-0 victory.

Peters would go on to score a personal best nineteen league goals over the course of the season, and his career would be characterised by an abnormally high scoring rate for a midfield player. He reached double figures for the season no fewer than eight times over his long career. In March 1970, he moved to Tottenham Hotspur, with whom he won two League Cups and a UEFA Cup, before being transferred to Norwich City. He stayed at Carrow Road for another five years and, by now well into his thirties, was twice voted the club's player of the year. A brief stay at Sheffield United brought his magnificent twenty-year club career to a close, his longevity enhanced by his clever and economical style of play.

Seldom has a player slotted into the national team as seamlessly as Peters. His appearance in the 1966 quarter-final was just his fourth cap, but he immediately became one of Ramsey's indispensables. He and Alan Ball were the two youngsters of the World Cup-winning side and, whilst both had an enormous impact, they could hardly have been more different in their on-field demeanour. Ball, with his shock of red hair and relentless energy, was always a centre of attention whereas Peters' craft and clever movement meant that he could sometimes pass through a game almost unnoticed and yet still exert a vital influence.

Nicknamed 'The Ghost' for his ability to glide undetected into scoring positions, defences at both club and international level so often recognised the danger only when it was too late. He won sixty-seven caps for England, scoring twenty goals, many of them crucial, and none more so than the one that so nearly proved to be the World Cup winner.

SEPTEMBER 1968

Buoyed by their excellent start to the domestic season, Leeds travelled to Budapest to defend their 1-0 Fairs Cup first-leg lead against Ferencvaros. Revie's men produced a typically resolute performance to claim the trophy with a goalless draw, secured largely by a superb performance from Gary Sprake. Now with two prizes under their belt after so many near misses, Leeds looked set fair for plenty more. But could they, as Revie had promised they would, succeed in a way which spectators and critics might find a little more palatable?

If Leeds were aspiring to become more enterprising, West Ham appeared to have taken on just a smidgen of Leeds' resilience. Their bid to show that they had acquired a hitherto elusive consistency took them next to Old Trafford, and an impressive performance saw them come away with a thoroughly deserved draw. Unusually, West Ham's defensive display took most of the plaudits, although young winger Harry Redknapp also caught the eye, setting up Hurst for the Hammers' equaliser and providing a constant threat.

They then entertained Spurs at Upton Park, and another superb match also ended all square. It must have been good, as even Hugh McIlvanney enjoyed it, describing the game as one of 'exhausting pace and vibrant excitement'. And this with scarcely a Scotsman in sight…

So, what had changed at Upton Park? After Nat Lofthouse's Bolton had been ripped apart in the League Cup, he was moved to comment that 'that team would have beaten England!' West Ham had always been capable of hitting heights that few others could aspire to, but to do it so consistently over even ten games had previously been beyond them. Geoff Hurst attributed the improvement to harder work, citing the fact that the wingers were now tracking back and harassing the opposition rather than making token gestures at defending. The penny seemed to be dropping even with the Hammers that skill and flair on their own weren't enough.

For all West Ham's impressive form, there was still a sense that if London was to make a concerted challenge for the title then Arsenal would be the likeliest contenders. They weren't pretty – apart, perhaps, from Jon Sammels, perpetual winner in the *Football League Review*'s pin-up poll amongst its female readers – and their methodical, primarily defensive approach still saw them tagged repeatedly as the southern Leeds. Their chance to test themselves against the real thing came with a fixture at Elland Road, and although they acquitted themselves well, they ended up well beaten. Jack Charlton once again excelled at both ends of the pitch, taming Bobby Gould whilst finding time to nod home a trademark goal from a corner.

The win saw Leeds installed as favourites to become champions, and they next travelled to Maine Road to meet the current incumbents. City had at last awoken from their slumbers with a resounding 4-0 win at Sunderland, although significant damage had been done throughout their period of hibernation. Already way off the pace in the league, their hopes of progressing through even one round of the European Cup were hanging by a thread after a frustrating goalless draw at home to Fenerbahce. Malcolm Allison's 'terrify Europe' quote was coming back to haunt him, with more than one critic observing that the only people they had been terrifying so far this season were their own supporters.

Today, though, City were at their most irresistible, ripping into Leeds from the outset and reminding everyone how and why they had won the title last season. Two smart close-range finishes from Bell and a twenty-five-yard screamer from Neil Young saw them through to a comfortable victory, condemning Leeds to their first defeat of the season.

Liverpool had so far been imperious at Anfield, but travelled to newly promoted Ipswich looking for a first away win in five attempts. Goals from Graham and St John saw them get off the mark, and on their next journey they announced quite emphatically that their travel sickness had been cured. The game against Wolves marked eighteen-year-old Alun Evans' first return to Molineux since his £100,000 transfer to Liverpool and he was given the traditional traitor's reception as the teams took the field.

At the end of the game, the jeers were replaced by warm applause both for Evans and his team-mates, after Liverpool powered to a 6-0 victory, with the newcomer scoring twice. Evans had brought greater fluidity and variety to Liverpool's attack, allowing Shankly to send the one-dimensional Hateley on to the next stage of his UK tour at Coventry City. Roger Hunt and Peter Thompson also each scored twice as Liverpool inflicted Wolves' heaviest home defeat since the war.

Everton were also moving into top gear, crushing Sheffield Wednesday before taking a measure of revenge for their cup final defeat by thrashing West Brom 4-0. Their midfield trio of Ball, Kendall, and Harvey gave the team a beautiful balance, combining flair, pace and poise with energy and commitment, and the contrasting qualities of the muscular Joe Royle and the pacy Jimmy Husband offered genuine goal threat. Ball had proved to be a prolific scorer from midfield ever since his arrival on Merseyside, and it was he who did most to put West Brom to the sword with a classy hat-trick.

Manchester United had continued to struggle, and there were some suggestions that they were being distracted by their impending date in Argentina to take part in the World Club Championship. The previous year's edition, Celtic against River Plate, had produced more of a war than a football match, five players being sent off amid scenes of almost perpetual intimidation, retaliation and all-round violence. With the Argentines' display against England in the World Cup also still fresh in the public's memory, there were many who wondered whether United's pursuit of this unofficial world title would prove to be more trouble than it was worth.

The first leg of their tie against Estudiantes was in Buenos Aires, and United's route there from Manchester – via London, Paris, Madrid and Rio de Janeiro – was an ordeal in itself. But nothing compared with the experience awaiting them on the appalling pitch at the intimidatingly named Stadio Bombonera. 'If we're kicked or punched, we've just got to take it,' said Pat Crerand before the game. 'The boss has made this quite clear.'

Kicked and punched they certainly were, as well as receiving the occasional headbutt, being spat at, having their hair pulled and having to dodge missiles thrown from the crowd. Whilst hooliganism amongst fans was hardly confined to South America – indeed United fans themselves were amongst the worst offenders domestically as the authorities still struggled to find ways to suppress terrace violence – the brutality meted out on the pitch made Leeds look like blissfully stoned hippie pacifists.

United players were routinely subjected to off-the-ball assaults, the vast majority of which went unpunished, and were still in a state of shock a day later. They lost by the only goal, also seeing Stiles sent off for retaliation as, at last, he snapped under the most intense provocation. Some took the view that he had merely received a taste of his own medicine, others that he had been a marked man from the minute he had walked off the plane. It was clear, though, that definitions of acceptable on-field behaviour differed so widely between the two continents that civilised competition between their teams was unlikely to be achieved, and that for the world game to prosper something needed to be done to bring the two codes of conduct closer together.

British viewers had been able to watch the atrocities on a special edition of *Sportsnight with Coleman*, whose eponymous presenter was establishing himself as the nation's most familiar sporting voice. He, from time to time, took on commentary duties on *Match Of The Day* and by the next season would also become its studio presenter, but it wasn't just his expanding array of gaffes which drew public comment.

The League's new agreement with the BBC for *Match Of The Day* stipulated that seven matches per season must be from outside the first division, so as to advertise the quality of football available throughout the levels. After a shocker of a lower-league game had been screened on a Saturday night a few weeks earlier, Coleman made a gentle joke on the following midweek's *Sportsnight* show to the effect that 'at least we've got some decent football tonight', mentioning that the requirement to dip beneath the top division had been imposed by the Football League.

This slight on the quality of football produced by two of its clubs – and the suggestion that the Football League rather than the BBC had been responsible for inflicting it on the viewers – predictably incurred the wrath of the hyper-sensitive *Football League Review*. The magazine had a dig at the BBC for labelling its show *Match Of The Day* when, on many occasions, it would inevitably be anything but. But couldn't they see that calling the show 'Boring Football From Rotherham' would hardly help to pull in the viewers?

ITV's football offerings had continued to take the form of a range of regional games shown on Sunday afternoons, but with Jimmy Hill now fully on board the time had come for them to offer something a bit more showbiz. *The Big Match* was duly launched on London Weekend Television, hosted by Brian Moore, who also provided commentary on the main feature game, with brief highlights of a couple of games from the other regions also being shown.

Moore's commentary style couldn't have been further removed from that of the calm and unflappable Kenneth Wolstenholme: the merest sniff of penalty-area action would elevate his volume and pitch, and goals, near misses and half-decent saves would produce a reaction bordering on the hysterical. Moore's style had the effect of making games seem far more exciting than they actually were, and with Jimmy Hill in the studio providing expert analysis – in particular using slow-motion replays and freeze-frames to assess controversial refereeing decisions – the overall package was highly appealing to an audience used to receiving little embellishment of the pictures they saw on the screen.

For better or worse, *The Big Match* gave birth to the TV pundit. Hill would repeatedly receive criticism that he was undermining referees by showing them to have got decisions wrong, but this was just what viewers – especially fans of the wronged team, who could then have their 'we wuz robbed' claims officially validated – wanted to see. Televised football would never be the same again.

Match Of The Month
21 September 1968, Division One: Leeds United 2 Arsenal 0

The division's two unbeaten sides took the field at Elland Road on a blustery Yorkshire day, with Leeds taking the opportunity before kick-off to show their fans the recently acquired Fairs Cup, as well as the League Cup won against the very same Arsenal earlier in the year. Whether this display was also something intended to wind their opponents up is something only Revie would know. That League Cup Final had been widely vilified, one critic going so far as to describe it as a gruesome spectacle, and others rather illogically using the poverty of the football served up to condemn the League Cup competition as a whole. Throw the two most unappealing sides in the league together on an occasion filled with tension, one without a trophy for fifteen years and the other without a trophy full stop, and what else could you reasonably expect?

But now, the climate was slightly different. Revie's vow that Leeds were ready to play a more expansive game had been borne out to an extent by their early-season performances, even though the team's foundations were still built on robust defending. Arsenal had also produced some encouraging displays, even if the team remained noticeably short on flair.

In the end, the match was largely one-sided. Leeds showed enterprise and imagination and used the flanks to great effect, with Mike O'Grady and Terry Hibbitt a constant menace. Arsenal threatened early on, but were slowly pressed back as the hosts, driven forward by the relentless Bremner, took a grip on the game. Mike O'Grady, likened to a 'human torpedo', opened the scoring with a magnificent diving header before Jack Charlton brought out his party piece once more, trampling on Bob Wilson's toes before nodding home from a corner.

Even Leeds' sternest critics were forced to admit that the spectacle had been rather more palatable than most of the two teams' recent encounters, and Revie's men were now being widely tipped as prospective league champions.

Leeds: Sprake, Reaney, Cooper, Bremner, Charlton, Hunter, O'Grady, Lorimer, Jones, Madeley, Hibbitt.

Arsenal: Wilson, Storey, McNab, McLintock, Neill, Simpson, Armstrong, Sammels, Gould, Court, Jenkins (Johnson).

Player Of The Month
Terry Paine (Southampton)

Terry Paine joined Southampton in 1956, made his first team debut in 1957 and went on to become the record appearance holder for the club. As captain and their major on-field influence, Paine steered Southampton into their first ever division one campaign in 1966 and had the honour of scoring their first ever top-flight goal in a 1-1 opening-day draw against Manchester City. Paine excelled in what was a highly satisfactory debut season for the Saints, providing a regular supply of crosses for Ron Davies and Martin Chivers to attack to great effect. In addition, Paine scored eleven goals himself, the eighth time he had reached double figures as a winger.

The following year saw Southampton consolidate their position in the league and they began the 1968/69 season hoping to progress further still. September saw them suffer a narrow home defeat to leaders Arsenal, although Paine scored the best goal of the game, putting Southampton ahead with a classy finish after a penetrating run. The following week, Paine's precise cross set up Davies to earn Southampton a point at Manchester City, before he produced an outstanding wing display to help his team crush Newcastle in the League Cup. Paine then struck a late equaliser at Loftus Road, denying QPR a first win of the season, as a trademark run to the far post went undetected by the Rangers defence.

Despite then being a second division player, Paine had first been called up for England in 1963 and went on to play nineteen times for his country. His ability to score goals from wide positions was a major factor in him earning the call-up, and he showed that he could transfer this knack to a higher level, scoring seven times for England, including a hat-trick against Northern Ireland. His final cap came in England's first 1966 group game against Uruguay, after which he became a victim of Ramsey's wingerless strategy.

Southampton's style of play was already starting to change as they sought to maintain their first division status and Paine's role within the team evolved with it, as he increasingly assumed a 'hard-man' persona in a more central position. The team achieved notoriety as an uncompromising physical outfit, quite at odds with their style when they first won promotion, and it was a pity for Paine to be tarred with this brush after having provided such stellar service. It seems safe to assume that his record of 716 appearances for the club will never be beaten.

OCTOBER 1968

Manchester City's return to domestic form fuelled hopes that their European Cup trip to Istanbul would be profitable, but a daunting test lay ahead. The Fenerbahce ground was packed with hours to go to the kick-off, with rabid Turkish fans thirsting to acclaim what would be the greatest night in their country's football history. City were braced for the occasion and, having weathered an early storm, took the lead through Tony Coleman. The away goal meant that Fenerbahce needed two to win, and

City went into the interval well satisfied both with their own performance and the muted atmosphere in the stadium.

The game turned immediately after half-time, when Fenerbahce equalised to spark a frenzied reaction from the crowd, some of whom invaded the pitch and, after congratulating the players, remained on the pitch perimeter for the rest of the game. In an increasingly intimidatory atmosphere, City fought hard to retain their slender away goal advantage but after numerous close shaves, disallowed goals and further pitch invasions, finally conceded again to make an inglorious exit from their first ever European campaign.

There were no such problems for United in disposing of feeble Waterford, but their eyes – and those of the press – were already turned to the imminent return leg against Estudiantes. The build-up to this unofficial world title match exceeded even that of their European Cup Final, as the match-up between continents and footballing cultures captured the imagination of football fans everywhere. Matt Busby was concerned primarily with the need for controlling the emotions of the crowd, writing to sports editors asking them to help create a calm atmosphere and impressing on United supporters that 'our visitors' style of play is quite the normal thing in South America'.

The programme for the preceding match, against Arsenal, emphasised that serious misconduct by fans could result in the game being abandoned and awarded to the opposition. The fans' response on the day wasn't the most encouraging, as they showered the Arsenal goalmouth with coins and debris, forcing the referee to threaten to abandon the match. The game itself had brought back echoes of the previous year's encounter, when Law and Ure were dismissed; now, the United forwards reacted tetchily to Arsenal's robust tackling, hardly inspiring confidence in their ability to withstand the far more severe provocation heading their way.

United's last game before the Estudiantes showdown was at Anfield and six of the players who would play against the Argentines, including Best and Law, were rested. Busby insisted that medical certificates could be provided if necessary, but for all six to be suffering injuries which would keep them out for just a single game seemed an almost preposterous scenario. It was a strange display of priorities from United, apparently attaching more importance to the prestige of winning a glorified friendly than to a vital league game against their fiercest rivals. Liverpool duly secured a routine victory in a match bereft of the normal competitive edge, and now all eyes turned to Old Trafford.

The capacity crowd was fully installed well before kick-off, its patriotic fervour raised further still by the overnight 400m hurdles triumph of David Hemery in the Mexico Olympics, seen by millions on *Good Morning Mexico* before they went off to work and school. The race had also delivered a bronze for John Sherwood, not that commentator David Coleman seemed to care too much. But almost as soon as the action in Manchester started to unfold, the misgivings about the match and the competition itself proved well founded.

The best that can be said is that at least the crowd behaved themselves. United tackled hard, Estudiantes hacked harder. Law was forced off with a badly gashed shin and, at one stage, after being crunched knee-high with the ball two yards away, Best handed the ball to his assailant as if to say 'this is what you're meant to play with'. The Irishman's patience expired midway through the second half as he lashed out in retaliation, an outcome the Argentines had so obviously been seeking from the outset. Both he and Medina were dismissed, with the Argentine – maintaining the South American trait seen so distastefully in the World Cup – seeking to continue the fight as he was escorted reluctantly from the field. The goals – one each, giving the title to Estudiantes – seemed almost incidental, as journalists debated the wider repercussions of a second successive outbreak of intercontinental warfare.

There were inevitable calls for the competition to be discontinued. And yet, the fixture at Old Trafford had captured the public imagination in a way that even their great European nights couldn't match. Fired up by tabloid bloodlust, there was a real curiosity as to how methods of play could differ so much. Were these guys really the assassins they were made out to be? And for United, this tournament *really* mattered. Would it have meant the same to any other English club? The thirst for international prestige was in United's DNA. In the 1950s, they had entered the European Cup against the League's wishes; now they sacrificed two vital league points in pursuit of the cachet of becoming 'world champions', and in 2000 they would elect to withdraw from the FA Cup in order to compete in the inaugural and evidently worthless Club World Championship. Trailblazing on behalf of English football or unadulterated self-obsession?

Back on the domestic front, Everton's sparkling form continued. They had the better of the drawn Merseyside derby at Anfield, before producing a magnificent display to come away from the Dell with a 5-2 victory. An excellent month ended with another away win at Wolves, leaving them well in touch with Leeds at the top. Their only setback occurred in the League Cup, in which they followed in Chelsea's footsteps by losing to Derby County at the Baseball Ground. Brian Clough's young team were going well in the second division and a number of their players – in particular centre-half Roy McFarland – were attracting the interest of top-flight clubs.

Leeds had generally continued on their relentless way, although the fallibility they had shown at Maine Road resurfaced when they faced Burnley at Turf Moor. Totally out of sorts, they suffered a 5-1 thrashing from a vibrant young side and, at the same time, gave hope to their rivals that the title race might not be the procession many were predicting.

At the other end of the table, QPR's fortunes had at last started to turn. Though still missing Marsh, they had gained their first ever top-flight win at the thirteenth attempt with a 2-1 victory over Ipswich, and now followed it up by beating Sheffield Wednesday. Despite the result, which took Rangers off the bottom of the table, it was a performance fraught with nervous fallibility. Rangers were 3-0 up with two minutes left, yet still contrived to concede two goals and were indebted to a goal-line clearance to hold on to the points.

To no one's great surprise, West Ham's form had started to drop off, but their goalscoring prowess remained undiminished. When Sunderland came to Upton Park, they were on the receiving end of a fearsome battering, with Geoff Hurst scoring a hat-trick in each half as the Hammers racked up an 8-0 victory. Hurst later confessed to having punched one of his goals in, but with the others featuring a header, a long-range shot and clean finishes to a couple of great team moves, he also showcased the full range of his striking abilities. Hurst might not have been as eye-catching as some of his peers, but as an all-round striker he was without a weakness.

On a good day for London forwards, Tommy Baldwin scored a hat-trick for Chelsea against Leicester and in the game of the day, Jimmy Greaves' two crafty efforts saw Spurs edge past Liverpool at White Hart Lane. The second, decisive, goal came from a quickly taken free kick as the Liverpool wall was retreating, prompting comparisons with Leeds' disallowed goal in the cup semi-final eighteen months earlier. With so few matches being televised, it was difficult for anyone – including referees themselves – to assess whether the laws of the game were being interpreted consistently, but the Spurs game featured on *Match Of The Day* and no doubt prompted a few expletives from embittered Yorkshire folk.

Greaves' brace took his league tally to eighteen, prompting further calls for his reinstatement to the England squad for their first game of the season. But Ramsey's mind had long been made up, and Greaves remained firmly on the sidelines. Nobby Stiles and Jack Charlton were also omitted from the squad to face Romania in Bucharest, which meant that only Bobby Moore of England's World Cup outfield defensive unit remained in situ. Knee problems had brought George Cohen's career to a premature close and Ray Wilson had also been plagued by injury over recent months. Charlton's replacement would be the experienced Brian Labone, who had already indicated his intention to retire before the 1970 World Cup but was thought to be open to persuasion. With Mullery seemingly firmly established in Stiles' place and Blackburn's Keith Newton settled at right-back, the first-choice Mexico team was starting to take shape. But gaps and doubts still remained: in particular, Roger Hunt's continued lack of international goals was a major concern and, having turned thirty with a game based on hard running, could he really be a potent force in the Mexican heat?

Match Of The Month
19 October 1968, Division One: Burnley 5 Leeds United 1

Burnley were having a moderate season but when a series of injuries forced them to introduce a string of youngsters into the side, things suddenly took a turn for the better. They promptly put together three straight wins leading up to the arrival of league leaders Leeds, a side with whom they had had a number of testy encounters in recent years. With some of the casualties now recovered, it was expected that Harry Potts would turn back to experience for this toughest of tests, but he stuck with the youngsters and was rewarded with an astonishing display of fluid attacking football.

With Ralph Coates, relocated inside from the wing, pulling the strings in a virtuoso display, Burnley's pace, energy and ingenuity were all too much for Leeds. On the flanks, eighteen-year-old Dave Thomas and nineteen-year-old Steve 'Kangaroo' Kindon gave Reaney and Cooper a rare chasing as Burnley created chances at will. Coates opened the scoring with a twenty-five-yard screamer before crossing for Frank Casper to head a second just three minutes later. Leeds were stung into a fierce rally, and when Bremner fired home from close range the game was briefly back in the balance. Early in the second half another teenager, John Murray, pounced on a loose ball to restore Burnley's two-goal lead and this time there was no let-up. Murray played a crafty ball for Kindon to power through what remained of the Leeds defence and smash the ball past Sprake, and the final indignity came when Casper cut inside from the right to float a delicate chip over the flat-footed keeper.

Leeds' day was made worse by an injury to Terry Cooper, thought to have been in line for an England call-up, but it was far too late to influence the result. A full-strength Leeds side had been ripped apart by an outfit with an average age of just twenty-two. Don Revie took the defeat with good grace, admitting that 'Burnley were a revelation', and his side were also well behaved on the pitch, never resorting to the brutality so often seen when things weren't going their way. But would this result tempt Revie to go back to his tried and tested methods?

Burnley: Thomson, Smith, Latcham, Dobson, Waldron, Blant, Thomas, Murray, Casper, Coates, Kindon.

Leeds: Sprake, Reaney, Cooper (Lorimer), Bremner, Charlton, Hunter, O'Grady, Giles, Jones, Madeley, Gray.

Player Of The Month
Ralph Coates (Burnley)

Coates made his Burnley debut in 1964 and quickly established himself as a first-team regular. As Burnley's championship side of 1960 faded away, the club embarked on a policy of bringing players through from the youth team, but were still able to compete effectively enough to achieve four more top-four finishes.

However, by autumn 1968, the team was struggling and a combination of injuries and loss of form meant that the side frequently featured as many as six youth products. Players such as Steve Kindon, Dave Thomas, John Murray and Martin Dobson, together with the now-established twenty-two-year-old Coates, gave the side an immediate lift and they promptly won eight games in succession, attracting a lot of positive sentiment. Coates scored Burnley's clinching goal in their 3-1 win at Stoke and then put in a superb performance as Leicester were brushed aside in the League Cup. *The Guardian* correspondent claimed not to have seen a more impressive midfield player all season as Coates inspired his side to a 4-0 win. The energy and enthusiasm of the young side was taking teams by surprise and next to suffer were the mighty Leeds United, who took a 5-1 hammering on one of Turf Moor's most famous afternoons. Central to Burnley's stellar performance was Coates, again playing in a more central position to accommodate the inclusion of Kindon and Thomas on the flanks. Coates opened the scoring, crossed for Casper to head the second and generally dictated play against Burnley's much-vaunted opponents.

Coates had established himself as one of Burnley's key players, and continued to impress in wins against Leicester and, in the League Cup, Crystal Palace. However, once the sequence of victories ended, results for the rest of the season became inconsistent, hardly surprising for such a young side. There would be further memorable performances: equally, there were some shockers, and the season saw Burnley lose 7-0 at both Spurs and Manchester City, as well as suffering a 6-1 reverse at Elland Road as Leeds exacted full revenge for their humbling experience at Turf Moor.

Coates had already won several under-23 caps and was eventually called into the full squad, making his debut against Northern Ireland in April 1970. He was included in England's squad of twenty-eight which travelled to Mexico, only to become one of the unlucky six discarded before the tournament began. He won three further caps after the World Cup, but the fierce competition for midfield places saw him gradually fade from the England reckoning.

The promise of the exciting young side had led Burnley to be dubbed 'the team of the 70s', but when the decade duly arrived the team struggled, and they were relegated in 1971. Coates was then transferred to Spurs for £190,000, where he stayed for seven years, being part of the team which won the UEFA Cup in 1972 before scoring the winner in the 1973 League Cup Final.

NOVEMBER 1968
News came through from the USA that the fledgling Soccer League had foundered after less than two years. Apathy amongst

the public had soon equated to multi-million pound losses and the rapid withdrawal of sponsors, and the Americans were criticised for trying to sell 'instant football' as if it was some household commodity, rather than systematically building up interest from grassroots level. Once the foreign stars had taken their leave, the American public showed little appetite for a game with little local tradition, played by players they had never heard of. The British press reported the news with a thinly disguised 'told you so' smugness. But, certainly according to its administrators, the English game had plenty of problems of its own.

The grey old men of the Football League had never been happy about the removal of the maximum wage. They consistently used their mouthpiece, the *Football League Review*, to bemoan the ills which had befallen the beautiful game as a result of Jimmy Hill's victory for the common footballer. Clubs were in debt because of spiralling wage bills; players with more money than sense were being tempted into dubious lifestyle choices; the increase in petulance and violence on the field was simply because the stakes were now so high. What was needed was a return to the good old days of serfdom, a restoration of the natural order. The League duly put forward a proposal to the clubs for the reintroduction of a maximum wage, with a ceiling set at £50 per week compared with the £20 which applied until its abolition seven years previously.

It wasn't difficult for even slightly insightful commentators to discern the true driver for the League's proposal. Year by year, the degree of control which these excruciatingly self-important pensioners exercised over the game and its players was diminishing. As players at last forged decent livings of their own, some going beyond that with their flash cars, their growing fame and adulation, bitterness and jealousy built up amongst these would-be autocrats. The League's proposals never stood a chance. The maximum wage horse had long since bolted, and the clubs overwhelmingly voted to retain the existing set-up.

It did, however, mean that many of them would need to find further new ways of generating income if directors' bank accounts weren't to be bled dry. One possibility manifested itself with the news that, in Austria, the first examples of shirt sponsorship had emerged, with players in a number of club sides wearing company names on the front of their shirts. But to the Football League, few things could have seemed more vulgar than the desecration of the club shirt. Alan Hardaker, Football League secretary, said: 'If one of our clubs requested permission to adopt a similar advertising method, it would be considered extremely bad taste.' For now, at least…

Results of recent games between Manchester United and Leeds resembled a binary sequence – five 1-0s, two 1-1s and two 0-0s interrupted only by a 3-1 win for Leeds in 1966. It therefore came as little surprise to anyone that the latest encounter, at Old Trafford, ended up goalless. There were moments of excitement, with Sprake making two great saves and Madeley and Lorimer coming close for Leeds. Both sides were evidently satisfied with their point, although goalless draws were starting to become a habit for Leeds, this being the second of three in succession.

Goals were also in short supply at international level, as England's game in Bucharest produced a 0-0 draw. And it was a classic, drab 0-0 draw at that. England's struggles to score in recent matches had been put down to poor finishing rather than an inability to create chances. This time, however, opportunities for Hurst and Hunt were virtually nil as England were dominated by an average Romanian side. On the positive side, England's defence excelled, with Labone and Keith Newton outstanding, but their reluctance to press forward left enormous gaps in midfield and contributed to a disjointed, underwhelming performance. Romanian manager Nicolescu was 'sad to see a World Championship side so timid', whilst Sir Alf declared himself 'most disappointed'.

QPR's continuing struggles persuaded chairman Jim Gregory to dispense with the services of Alec Stock – two promotions and a glorious League Cup triumph in the previous two seasons evidently counting for little – and he somehow persuaded Tommy Docherty to relocate from Rotherham to

West London to fill the vacancy. The Doc's influence wasn't immediately apparent, as Rangers' first two games under his leadership failed to produce a goal, but they got off the mark with a 2-1 win at home to Nottingham Forest. With plenty of discontent around following the recent Autumn Budget, *The Observer* just couldn't help itself. 'With everything else going up, there was a certain fascination in watching two teams that looked so likely to go down.' In a horribly scrappy game, Rangers were indebted to two blunders from Forest keeper Peter Grummitt for their first goals and points under the new boss.

Liverpool, Everton and Leeds remained locked together at the top of the table, although Liverpool were lucky to scrape through a bizarre game at Sheffield Wednesday. With Liverpool leading 2-1 late on, Wednesday's Gerry Young got the ball in the net. Surrounded by protesting Liverpool players, referee Homewood disallowed the goal, only to then find himself besieged by even more vehemently protesting Wednesday players. Unable to placate them, he eventually gave up the ghost and made his way down the players' tunnel, bombarded by missiles and cushions at every stride.

With crowd and players uncertain as to exactly what was going on, the debris was cleared from the pitch and Mr Homewood eventually returned to a torrent of catcalls, followed by the players. Four minutes later, he blew the final whistle to provoke yet more crowd abuse, since virtually no time had been added for the various periods of treatment in what had been a very physical game. Any Argentinians who had accidentally strayed into Hillsborough would have permitted themselves a wry smile. 'This lot are worse than we are...'

Everton remained in imperious form, seeing off Sunderland with ease before heading to Elland Road to take the ultimate test. They deserved to extend their unbeaten run of sixteen games, and when Joe Royle's delightful header equalised Giles' soft penalty, it looked as though they would do so, but Eddie Gray's fine finish sealed Leeds' 2-1 win. Eric Todd, amongst others, wasn't terribly impressed with Leeds' cautious approach and unimaginative passing. 'If the goals had been on the touchline, Leeds would have done nearly all the attacking,' he commented. It appeared as though the chastening defeat at Burnley had prompted Revie to get his team to revert to their old ways; the New Improved Attractive Leeds had proved to be a predictably short-lived experiment.

Chelsea continued on their erratic path. Despite being down to ten men for almost an hour, they still comfortably saw off Manchester City at Stamford Bridge. Their next home game saw them face a Southampton side which year by year since promotion had become progressively less attractive and more physical – 'usually as destructive and boring as a Peace rally' according to the ever-topical *Observer* – and Chelsea were short-odds favourites to extend their unbeaten twenty-match home run. However, inspired by Mick Channon, a home-grown player who had replaced Martin Chivers with sufficient success to prevent the Saints seeking an expensive external replacement, Southampton again took the spoils at Stamford Bridge, hanging on for a 3-2 victory.

It hadn't been Peter Bonetti's finest afternoon, but he made up for it the following week with an heroic display against Arsenal. Hugh McIlvanney was deemed to have recovered sufficiently from previous ordeals to be allowed into Highbury once again, but after a first half of 'paralysing sterility' there must have been fears that a further period of convalescence would be required.

Fortunately, the second half produced a dramatic improvement, with Bonetti the standout performer on 'one of those marvellously adhesive afternoons when it seems he could catch a pound of wet cod if it were fired from a cannon....' If Bonetti missed out on the World Cup squad, at least he would be a shoo-in for GB's *Jeux Sans Frontieres* team. For now, though, he was more concerned with earning his team the points and restoring a reputation somewhat damaged by a number of indifferent recent displays. After Houseman had scrambled Chelsea ahead, Bonetti made terrific saves from Armstrong,

Sammels and Radford to preserve the lead and keep Chelsea, just, on the fringes of the title race.

Match Of The Month
2 November 1968, Division One: West Ham 4 QPR 3

Although West Ham's blistering start to the season had not been maintained, they were still handily placed in the table and well in contention with Arsenal, Chelsea and Spurs for the annual consolation prize of London's highest finisher. QPR's ambitions were simple and straightforward – to stay up.

On a mudbath of a pitch, the tempo of the game never let up, fired by an early goal by Barry Bridges for the visitors. Bobby Moore then took matters into his own hands, carrying the ball forward before surprising the Rangers defender by unleashing a 30-yarder that flew past Peter Springett. Not to be outdone, Hurst and Peters both had their names on the scoresheet by half-time, each heading home to put West Ham in what appeared to be the comfort zone.

Rangers' fans were in a familiar state of dismay but their star striker, the almost-recovered Rodney Marsh, had rather more faith, insisting to the press box hacks alongside him that Rangers would get back into the game. And get back into it they did, two headers from Mick Leach drawing them level with twenty minutes to go. The Rangers revival had been inspired by Les Allen, with an energetic, driving performance.

Sadly for Rangers, parity would be restored for little more than a minute. Hurst turned provider this time, crossing for Harry Redknapp to power home a searing volley which, for all Rangers' desperate late assaults, proved to be the winner. It also proved to be the last goal witnessed by Alec Stock as Rangers manager. Three days later, he was sacked by Jim Gregory, a move which was greeted by shock and consternation after the incredible success achieved by the team over the previous two years. At least his final match had been a memorable one, moving *The Observer* to state that a spectacle so captivating was 'the reason why grown men become as children in the pursuit of a mere game...' Not that this would have been much consolation to Alec Stock.

West Ham: Ferguson, Bonds, Charles, Peters, Stephenson, Moore, Redknapp, Boyce, Brooking, Hurst, Hartley.

QPR: Springett, Watson, Harris, Keen, Hunt, Hazell, Bridges, Leach, Allen, Wilks, R Morgan.

Player Of The Month
Joe Royle (Everton)

Royle had first broken into the Everton side as early as 1966 as a sixteen-year-old, and scored three goals in four games to illustrate his potential as an 'old-school' centre-forward. He became a regular during the 1967/68 season, the first of five in succession in which he would finish as the club's top scorer.

By 1968, he had already been called up for the England under-23 squad and was one of the most prolific strikers in the league. November saw him hit the best form of his career so far. Two thumping headers at Ipswich earned a point for his team, and a penalty against QPR put the seal on a 4-0 win. A fine diving header at Elland Road couldn't prevent Everton's narrow defeat – their first league reverse since August – but the following week saw him score a hat-trick in the 7-1 drubbing of Leicester City. Once again, much of the damage was done with his head, as crosses from both left and right were powerfully dispatched, but his game on the ground was also developing, as illustrated by the explosive drive which delivered Everton's first goal.

Royle's aerial power provided a focal point for an Everton side capable of attacking on all fronts, but the interplay and craft of Ball, Harvey and Kendall enabled them to resist the temptation to overdo the long ball up to the striker. Instead, he benefitted from the team's ability to get the ball wide to Johnny Morrissey in particular, providing a fruitful supply of crosses for Royle to attack. Despite continuing his outstanding form throughout the following season, a vital component of

Everton's championship-winning side, Royle was unable to force himself into the Mexico squad, with a place in the final forty being as far as he got. The more experienced Allan Clarke and Jeff Astle had forced themselves slightly higher up the pecking order. Eventually, though, Ramsey could no longer resist Royle's claims, and he won his first full cap against Malta in 1971. He went on to make just six appearances for his country, like several of his ilk generally considered to be a highly effective club player but not quite of true international class.

Royle was transferred to Manchester City in 1974, and enjoyed a highly successful three years with the club, including a League Cup win in 1976. He also went on to have an impressive managerial career, notably at Oldham Athletic, whom he brought into the first division for the first time since 1923, as well as enjoying great success in cup competitions. He eventually returned to Manchester City, leading them to successive promotions after their demotion to the third tier of English football, before taking on further managerial roles with Ipswich and Oldham, as well as indulging in a spell of TV punditry.

DECEMBER 1968

The rate of manager turnover had reached an unprecedentedly high level. Within the space of a month, Matt Gillies at Leicester, Ronnie Allen at Wolves, Bobby Robson at Fulham and Tommy Cummings at Villa had joined Alec Stock in the ranks of the unemployed. The final straw for Gillies was Leicester's 7-1 humiliation at Goodison, after which he fell on his sword after ten years at the helm. Gillies was a former Justice of the Peace, and spoke openly. 'A lot of what goes on in soccer makes me cringe. I feel sorry for the way the game is going and I want no part of the thuggery and gamesmanship which, to my mind, goes to the point of cheating.'

Perhaps Gillies' moral outrage had been provoked by feeling forced to jump before he was pushed, but a couple of days later there was a tone of disgust both in broadsheets and tabloids as they reacted to the news of Johnny Carey's dismissal from

Nottingham Forest. Carey, who had led Forest to the cusp of a double just eighteen months earlier, hadn't seen it coming, professing himself shocked and bewildered. Forest's form had certainly been poor, but a raft of injuries and the fire which forced them to play their home games away from the City Ground were surely mitigating factors. The dismissal sparked plenty of 'what is the game coming to?' articles, with Hugh McIlvanney describing the wave of sackings as 'a mindless process of repetition from which nothing whatsoever has been learned'.

Incredibly, the next day brought another managerial change as Tommy Docherty quit QPR after just a month at the helm. Docherty had reportedly given chairman Jim Gregory an ultimatum – give me the money to buy Brian Tiler from Rotherham or I'll accept the offer to go and manage Athletic Bilbao. So it was that The Doc said goodbye to West London and booked himself in for a crash course of Spanish lessons.

With resounding home victories over Spurs and West Brom, Manchester City had rediscovered the home form which had taken them to the title. When Burnley, a side always vulnerable to a collective off-day, arrived at Maine Road, they were swept aside in as ferocious an attacking display as City had ever produced under the Mercer/Allison regime. With Alf Ramsey watching proceedings intently, alongside Ted Heath – a man whose hopes of garnering electoral support in the Moss Side area were surely misguided – City's forwards had the chance to stake their claim for a place in the England side to face Bulgaria in four days' time. And how they took it. Although Summerbee was forced off injured, the victim of progressively more desperate Burnley tackling, Bell, Lee and Young were all in superb form. The elegant yet ferociously powerful Young may have been rather too languid and inconsistent to fit in with Ramsey's work ethic, but was an essential part of the City side. The goals were spread around, and a double-figure tally would have been brought up but for Harry Thomson's brilliance and an extraordinary penalty miss by Lee, whose effort skewed comically towards the corner flag.

Ramsey, though, wasn't too concerned about penalty takers – he had Hurst at his disposal and, in any event, England had only been awarded one penalty in the last six years. Lee was duly selected to make his debut in the Bulgaria game, with Bell alongside him. Ramsey's only other change was to give Everton's Gordon West a chance in goal, suggesting that Bonetti's erratic form had seen him supplanted as Banks' understudy.

The game produced another disappointing result, this time 1-1, although England's performance was much improved and they were unfortunate not to win, with Bobby Charlton having one of his finest games. England attacked relentlessly, twice struck the woodwork and were thwarted by numerous last-ditch deflections and interceptions. Bulgaria seldom escaped from their own half, but did so on one occasion to great effect, a brilliant breakaway goal from Georgi Asparoukhov putting them ahead and drawing waves of applause from a generous Wembley crowd. Within two minutes, Hurst forced home an equaliser but for all England's excellent approach work and Charlton's powerful shooting, the winner just wouldn't come.

Manchester United were suffering a post-Estudiantes reaction – or was it something more permanent? A narrow but deserved win over Liverpool on a frostbound Old Trafford pitch raised hope of a revival, but their next game, at Southampton, brought a limp failure. John Arlott – a man who, like so many sports journalists and commentators of the era, valued doing things the right way far more than the outcome achieved – was depressed by what he had witnessed. 'Some of them behaved petulantly and at times viciously, like men tired of football, galled by failure to achieve their accustomed success and indifferent to their club's high and carefully nurtured reputation.'

Having fallen behind to early goals from Davies and Channon, United initially fought by legitimate means to get back into the game. When the breakthrough remained elusive, they dismayed Arlott with their behaviour, three times deliberately kicking opponents after the ball had gone. 'There were at least a couple of punches and half a dozen squalid arguments...' Arlott's conclusion was that this was much more than a loss in form. 'This time the trouble is more serious: it is in the mind.'

The League Cup delivered more spectacular giant-killing feats, this time from third-division Swindon Town. Having already dismissed Coventry City and Derby County, they went to Burnley to face a side in prime form, having won eight and drawn one of its previous nine games, and pulled off a shock 2-1 victory. Burnley redressed the balance in the second leg, but the play-off saw Swindon produce a tremendous display to win 3-2 and earn a place at Wembley.

The other semi-final brought together Spurs and Arsenal. John Radford's late goal had given Arsenal a narrow first-leg lead and he repeated the trick at White Hart Lane, equalising on the night to put Arsenal through to Wembley. A competitive game had naturally been expected, but both sides overstepped the mark by a distance, with a vicious clash attracting headlines such as 'The Shame Of London'. The trouble eventually spread to the terraces, with scores of children being hauled to safety amongst scenes of increasing unrest. More than one journalist commented that the spectacle was just as bad as the sort of thing we so denounce from foreign teams, and that English football needed to put its own house in order before it started flinging mud at others.

Whatever the means adopted – and Spurs had been equally guilty – the result emphasised the progress being made at Highbury. And although most had expected Arsenal's challenge in the league to fade away, they remained in contention as the turn of the year approached. A superb performance – cited as their best and most entertaining for many years, though this is not necessarily the most fulsome praise – saw them beat Everton 3-1, and against Manchester United on Boxing Day they were almost as good again. Over 62,000 saw them dominate the second half, and their three goals were fair reward for an impressive display. When George Armstrong scores with a header, you know you're having a good day. Arsenal had conceded just thirteen goals in twenty-four games – a record even more miserly than that of

Leeds and Liverpool – and on the rare days when they delivered a little more adventure at the other end of the pitch, they were almost guaranteed a victory.

Bertie Mee, like Revie and Shankly before him, had built his team from the back, having recognised from the outset that this was the most important factor in achieving consistent performance. In contrast, the two Manchester clubs' philosophies were far more enterprising, frequently delivering dizzying highs, but both teams were also far more vulnerable to losses of form by key individuals. With half the season gone, they were both languishing in the bottom third of the table, a fate which it was impossible to envisage befalling either Leeds or Liverpool. But then how often had those two clubs' supporters witnessed scintillating football that would live in their memories forever?

Don Revie's dossier-based approach ensured that his team were always well prepared for every game, but his players wouldn't have needed much reminding of the qualities of their next opponents. Burnley came to Elland Road to face the backlash for their 5-1 win at Turf Moor a couple of months earlier, and backlash is what they got. Showing an unusual thirst for goals rather than sitting back on what they had got, Leeds subjected Burnley to a fearsome battering, and their 6-1 win put their visitors firmly in their place.

Tommy Docherty's absence from football after his ill-fated flirtation with QPR and his second thoughts about moving to Spain was curtailed by an offer from Aston Villa's new chairman, local businessman Douglas Ellis. Docherty was evidently the go-to man for teams stuck at the bottom of division two – two years previously, he had been appointed at similarly-placed Rotherham, now plying their trade in the third division as The Doc's prescription became progressively less potent – and Mr Ellis promised that the new manager would have 100 per cent control in his bid to keep Villa out of the third division. Three wins in succession, the second achieved in front of over 41,000 at Villa Park, was a pretty good start.

Another outspoken individual who had inherited a side in danger of falling into the third tier was Brian Clough. Although his first year hadn't produced the transformation he and the directors desired, this season was looking ever more likely to end in celebration. Clough, still just thirty-three years of age, had signed an assortment of highly promising young players – Roy McFarland, Kevin Hector, Alan Durban, John O'Hare – and the recruitment of Dave Mackay from Spurs had brought crucial on-field experience, leadership and drive. Boxing Day saw his team face Middlesbrough in a clash of the top two, and on a difficult pitch the sides produced a superb match, with Derby edging it by the odd goal in five.

Match Of The Month
7 December 1968, Division One: Arsenal 3 Everton 1

Arsenal had made significant progress in Bertie Mee's time at the helm, but their relative success so far this season had been greeted with grudging admiration, if any at all. Based on the league's meanest defence – quite a feat given the increasing emphasis placed by teams on being hard to beat – they were a team of little flair but ever-increasing efficiency. Meanwhile, Everton were the league's leading scorers and their stylish, fluent football had won them many admirers.

As if to make a point, Arsenal chose the occasion to put on their best display of the season, focusing from the outset on attack rather than containment. John Robertson, recently signed from Spurs, provided a new threat on the wing, and in Gould and Radford had willing, if not necessarily aesthetically pleasing, targets to hit. Gould set up Radford to put Arsenal ahead, and after Bob Wilson had been severely tested, David Court gave them breathing space. Jon Sammels had prompted Arsenal's attacks with guile and subtlety, but when he departed with injury the shape of the game changed.

The golden trio of Ball, Kendall and Harvey started to control proceedings, and concerted Everton pressure culminated in Ball forcing home from close range, after a series of ricochets involving both woodwork and defenders. The goal marked the cue for Arsenal to revert to type and seek to close out the game. For all Everton's class and ingenuity, they foundered repeatedly on the rocks of McLintock and Ure, and close to the whistle George Graham calmly made the points safe after a defensive slip.

It was a heartening win for Arsenal – and for London football in general, as the northern powers were yet again threatening to make the title race a private battle – and emphasised how far they had come since Mee's appointment. It would take a while yet for them to reach their peak, but when they did they would certainly make it count. Despite the day's disappointment, Everton's zenith would arrive slightly earlier.

Arsenal: Wilson, Storey, McNab, McLintock, Ure, Simpson, Radford, Court, Sammels (Graham), Gould, Robertson.

Everton: West, Wright, Brown, Kendall, Labone, Harvey, Husband, Ball, Royle, Hunt, Morrissey.

Player Of The Month
Emlyn Hughes (Liverpool)

Hughes' career began as a half-back for Blackpool, where he made an impact sufficient for Bill Shankly to publicly covet the player before signing him for Liverpool in 1967. Settling quickly into the Anfield side, Hughes added a vibrant energy and commitment to the Liverpool midfield and helped them to challenge for the league title year after year. One of his trademarks was his capacity to make surging runs from his own half of the field, on occasion culminating in spectacular individual goals.

Liverpool came into December in a particularly strong run of form, with Hughes by now a central part of the team. His twenty-yard drive opened the scoring against West Ham, enabling Liverpool to extend their run of consecutive wins to six and putting them four points clear at the top. After suffering a narrow defeat at Old Trafford, Liverpool returned to Anfield to face Spurs, a game in which Hughes made two decisive contributions. Firstly, he cleared Mike England's header off the line and then, a few minutes later, carried the ball at full pace from the centre circle to the edge of the area before crashing a drive past Jennings for a breathtaking winner.

Hughes won his first full England cap against Holland in December 1969 and did enough to win a place in Ramsey's final twenty-two for Mexico. He didn't feature in the tournament, but became a regular in the England side immediately afterwards, going on to win sixty-two caps as well as fulfilling Shankly's 1966 prophecy by captaining his country. His career spanned an unfortunate time for the national side, which failed to qualify for three tournaments in succession.

Hughes, however, enjoyed prodigious success during his Liverpool career. He captained the side to four league championships, an FA Cup and two UEFA Cups, as well as the European Cup in 1977. He was also named Football Writers' Player Of The Year in 1977, when Liverpool so nearly completed the treble. Despite his success and popularity with the fans for his exuberant playing style and enthusiasm, there were frequent suggestions that he was rather less popular in the Liverpool dressing room.

Hughes joined Wolves in 1979, and a year later captained them to the one trophy he failed to win during his Liverpool career – the League Cup. After retiring, he went on to acquire broader fame in his long-standing role as a *Question Of Sport* captain, where his exaggerated high-pitched laughter and 'infectious' personality delighted some and infuriated others.

JANUARY 1969

The unfailing ability of the balls in the velvet bag to deliver FA Cup ties laced with intrigue was demonstrated yet again when Tommy Docherty's Aston Villa were drawn away at QPR, the club he had walked out on in a huff just a few weeks earlier. A bad-tempered match at Villa Park saw Villa continue their new manager bounce with a 2-1 win. With Rangers still at the foot of division one, this was hardly a shock of seismic proportions but the Docherty angle saw the match garner plenty of column inches. Rather more startling was the outcome at Roker Park, where Fulham, bottom of division two and without an away win all season, crushed Sunderland 4-1. However, the result of the greatest consequence would come in the midweek replays, where favourites Leeds were beaten at home for the first time all season, losing 3-1 to a superb Sheffield Wednesday.

Three days later, Manchester United came to Elland Road and the bitter rivalry between the two sides was reflected in a first half of all-too-familiar violence and petulance. Stepney's blunder allowed Jones to head Leeds in front but Bobby Charlton drilled home an equaliser before the game's real flashpoint emerged. After a foul on Charlton gave United a free kick on the edge of the Leeds box, Best curled it gloriously into the top corner only for the referee to award a goal kick, stating that the free kick had been indirect. This was certainly news to the United players, as no signal had been given, and prompted the rare sight of football's modern-day gentleman, Bobby Charlton, protesting vehemently to the referee.

United fans in the ground were incensed, edging menacingly towards the touchline and creating fears for the referee's safety, but order was just about maintained, with Leeds rubbing salt into the wound when O'Grady's fierce shot gave them the winner. The free-kick incident would be debated fiercely after the game and in the press over the following days, with opinion pretty much unanimous that United had been hard done by. Leeds, though, would doubtless have felt that the perceived injustices they had suffered over recent seasons merited a change of fortune. Perhaps this really would be their season.

For United, however, there were other things to think about. Though still involved in the FA and European cups, there had been a marked decline in their performances this season. Speculation about Matt Busby's future had been rife for some time, and intensified when a press conference was called at Old

Trafford for later in the week. The event attracted even more cameramen and journalists than were seen at a typical home game, and confirmed what most had suspected – Busby had decided to retire at the end of the season. Aged 59, and after 23 years at the helm, what more was there for him to achieve? He would 'move upstairs' to ensure continuity, but the day-to-day running of team affairs would pass to a younger man.

But which younger man? United had taken the unusual step of advertising the position externally, with the club stating that they were looking for an experienced candidate between the ages of 30 and 45 for a job attracting a salary in the region of £10,000 a year. Would it be an insider or an outsider? The heads of both shortlists were quickly removed from contention, with Jimmy Murphy and Don Revie both ruling themselves out of the running. Touted external candidates included Noel Cantwell, Alan Ashman, Dave Sexton, Malcolm Allison, Brian Clough and Ken Furphy.

One man who certainly wouldn't be applying was Sir Alf Ramsey, whose search for the perfect Mexican blend went on. The performance against Bulgaria had been encouraging even if the result disappointed, but for Romania's visit to Wembley he decided to restore some of his World Cup stalwarts – Stiles, Hunt and Jack Charlton. Arsenal's John Radford was brought into the squad; a hardworking player with a decent but hardly sensational goalscoring record, he was certainly in the Ramsey mould, but did he have the class to succeed at this level? A penny for Jimmy Greaves' thoughts.

England's performance was a bitter disappointment. Hunt's England goal famine – which by now had extended to his club, where he had failed to score for six games – continued, Radford was quiet, Hurst well shackled, and England's only goal came from the Jack Charlton corner kick routine. A late penalty allowed Romania to equalise and left Ramsey with much to ponder. Just four goals in the last six games left little doubt as to where the major concern lay. According to *The Express*, the purveyors of wondrous football just seven months earlier had now descended into a dispirited rabble, and subjected the 80,000 present to an evening of 'Soccer shame'.

But within the predictable tabloid over-reaction could be found a grain of truth. There was recognition that some of the players might have had at least one eye on important forthcoming club matches and this, after all, had only been a friendly. But where was the pride in pulling on the shirt? Shouldn't England matches, even friendlies, always be the pinnacle of a player's season? Evidently not. With certain managers beginning to earn notoriety for pulling players out of England squads, only for them to play for their clubs three days later, the status of England caps awarded for friendly matches was starting to diminish.

Roger Hunt, as usual, bore much of the critical brunt for England's attacking failings, but three days later at last had something to cheer about when his goal helped Liverpool to a vital win at Chelsea and saw him break the club goalscoring record. It was also a significant day for young Alun Evans, who had struggled to maintain the promise suggested by his spectacular start at Anfield, but here capped a fine performance with a beautiful finish, curled around Bonetti with the outside of his foot, to seal Liverpool's 2-1 win. When news of the other leaders' results came, through, none of them managing a win, Bill Shankly was in bullish mood. 'What's going to stop us now?' he asked of the assembled hacks, all too reverent to mention the name of Don Revie's men.

The fourth round of the cup again saved its big stories for replay night. Having earned a draw against Sheffield Wednesday at Hillsborough, Birmingham once more claimed a top-flight scalp with a win in front of a customary St Andrew's full house. Yet again, Fred Pickering was on the scoresheet in a game that Birmingham thoroughly deserved to win. After seeing off Leeds in the previous round, the defeat was a desperate disappointment for Wednesday, a mid-table side whose season was now effectively over before the end of January.

Keeping Tommy Docherty out of the news remained almost impossible, as his Villa side continued their spectacular renaissance. They went to the Dell and stormed into a two-goal lead, only to be pulled back and forced into a replay. Over 59,000 crammed into Villa Park – the sort of attendance usually reserved only for cup semi-finals rather than their own matches – to see goals from Martin and Broadbent power Villa through to another famous victory. The feisty, outspoken Docherty wasn't to everybody's taste, but he had an undeniable ability to shake things up for the better – at least temporarily.

Other replays saw both Manchester clubs come through, United having initially been held at Old Trafford by an impressive Watford side whose manager, Ken Furphy, was said to be heading the list of external candidates to succeed Matt Busby. City, meanwhile, came through a tough tie at Newcastle before putting on a sparkling display at Maine Road. Other than Leeds, all the fancied teams had made it through to the last sixteen.

Match Of The Month
8 January 1969, FA Cup Third Round Replay:
Leeds United 1 Sheffield Wednesday 3

Leeds had held Sheffield Wednesday to a 1-1 draw at Hillsborough, taking an early lead through Peter Lorimer's penalty but being pegged back by John Ritchie's equaliser in a frantic tie played out in front of more than 52,000 spectators. Elland Road was similarly sold out for the replay, with most expecting Leeds to finish the job in their customarily efficient fashion.

Ahead after just five minutes through Albert Johanneson, making a rare appearance in place of the injured Mike O'Grady, Leeds again made a perfect start, but any thoughts of a comfortable evening were soon disabused as a confident Wednesday, inspired by Peter Eustace, took the game to them. Eustace endured several heavy tackles as Leeds employed their traditional techniques in an attempt to diminish his impact, but Wednesday were undeterred and eventually Brian Woodall chipped over Sprake to level things up.

A few minutes after the resumption, Woodall struck again to give Wednesday a shock lead. With Giles absent and Bremner forced off with injury, Leeds struggled to impose themselves as Wednesday's experienced side kept possession well. The tie was put to bed when John Ritchie strode through a dishevelled defence late on to roll home a third goal, sealing a famous victory and much the most famous moment of Brian Woodall's brief professional career, which would see him score just twice more for Wednesday before drifting back into the lower leagues.

Whilst a result of great significance in that it removed the cup favourites from the competition, for Leeds it would prove to be a blessing in disguise. So often victims of the most unmanageable fixture congestion as they fought on several fronts towards the end of the season, this early exit – following a similarly premature demise in the League Cup – gave them the breathing space to focus on the prize they craved above all others.

Leeds: Sprake, Reaney, Madeley, Bremner (Belfitt), Charlton, Hunter, Gray, Lorimer, Jones, Bates, Johanneson.

Sheffield Wednesday: Springett, Smith, Megson, Ellis, Mobley, Young, Irvine, McCalliog, Ritchie, Eustace, Woodall.

Player Of The Month
Peter Thompson (Liverpool)

Thompson signed for Liverpool from Preston in 1963, and played a crucial role in the side that won two league titles and an FA Cup in the mid-1960s. He was first capped for England in 1964, and was part of the initial twenty-eight selected for the 1966 World Cup, only to become one of the discarded six.

Thompson remained a fixture in the Liverpool side, performing with remarkable consistency for a winger, and with his team putting together a good run of form as they came into 1969, his influence remained as great as ever. The FA Cup saw Liverpool face a Doncaster side that tried to bridge the class divide by applying overly physical tactics, and it took two moments of class from Thompson to break their resistance, setting up goals for Hunt and Callaghan. Back in the league the following week, an impressive West Brom threatened to take at least a point away from Anfield until Thompson pounced to fire home the only goal a few minutes from time.

Liverpool next faced a visit to Stamford Bridge, where Eddie McCreadie generally managed to keep Thompson quiet, but the winger made the most of the few occasions on which he escaped the Scotsman's clutches. His fierce shot was parried by Tommy Hughes for Hunt to put Liverpool ahead, before he set up Alun Evans to clinch the points for the visitors. Back in the cup, Thompson then starred against Burnley, forcing two great saves from his near-namesake in the Burnley goal as Liverpool moved into the fifth round.

Having established new momentum, Liverpool lost only once more as they made Leeds fight all the way for the title, and Thompson remained an ever-present throughout the run. Indeed, given the rough treatment he routinely received, his appearance record was remarkable, missing just ten league games over the seven seasons where he was a first-team regular. He ultimately made over 400 appearances for Liverpool, also featuring as a substitute in the 1971 FA Cup Final, before moving on to Bolton in 1973.

Thompson had continued to feature in Ramsey's squads in between the World Cups, although his appearances on the pitch were sporadic. He achieved a unique and unwanted double when he was included in the twenty-eight initially selected for Mexico, only once again to find himself one of the unfortunate six. His England career came to an end against Holland in 1970, his sixteenth cap.

Genuinely two-footed, he was one of the most dangerous and effective wingers of his generation but, as with all his counterparts, found his England chances restricted by Ramsey's tactical preferences.

Frequently referred to as 'too nice' to make the absolute maximum out of his talents, he nevertheless had an outstanding career and is regarded as a true Liverpool legend.

FEBRUARY 1969

The FA Cup fourth round had one more dramatic tale to deliver. After being spared by floodlight failure when 2-0 down, Preston returned to Stamford Bridge a week later determined to make the most of their lucky escape. They took a first-half lead, hit the woodwork, and with the match approaching injury time hundreds of Chelsea fans were streaming out of the ground, muttering about their team's poor performance and the terrible injustice of it all. Those who remained inside then witnessed two Chelsea goals within sixty seconds, causing almost the whole Preston team to slump to their knees. Cruel on the night, but in the overall scheme of things justice had been served.

The following weekend saw a nationwide freeze, allowing just four matches to be completed in England. None of the fifth-round cup ties were played, resulting in a quarter-final draw featuring a full complement of eight either/ors. The *Match Of The Day* team reacted with commendable alacrity to ensure that their devoted audience had something to watch, managing to get their cameras to Ninian Park to record division two promotion challengers Cardiff crushing bottom-of-the-table Oxford 5-0.

The poor weather returned the following weekend, and saw the pools panel, formed and previously only utilised during the big freeze of 1963, power back into action. Including such luminaries as Tommy Lawton, Tom Finney and referee-turned-dipstick-wielding *It's A Knockout* adjudicator Arthur Ellis, the panel was faced with the task of deliberating on twenty-three postponed matches. Of their five first division forecasts, their most surprising verdict was for Leicester to hold Everton; when the games were actually played, it proved to be the only one they had got right.

Liverpool must have sorely regretted the efforts made by staff and volunteers to get the Anfield pitch playable for the visit of Nottingham Forest. Forest, in real danger of relegation just two years after their valiant bid for the double, came to face a Liverpool side unbeaten at Anfield for over a year. Even though Forest had a new manager, with Matt Gillies having been appointed to replace Johnny Carey, home bankers hardly came more solid. When Roger Hunt hit a post within ninety seconds, few could have imagined what was about to unfold. Forest struck just three minutes later and displayed a confidence and composure totally at odds with their performances throughout the previous six months. Barry Lyons' goal sealed a victory vital for Forest, but even more damaging for Liverpool's title hopes. Whilst Liverpool were suffering, Leeds ground their way to a narrow win over Chelsea on a pitch described as resembling a well-groomed coalyard.

The next round of league fixtures was also destroyed by the weather, although Liverpool's game again survived, and they fought back to earn a point at West Ham. On a day when the only three division one matches were all played in London, Bobby Tambling's four goals against Sunderland at least gave the Sundays something to write about.

The FA Cup ties were fitted in when weather permitted, and first port of call for a prospective upset was White Hart Lane, where Tommy Docherty's Villa were fired up to continue their spectacular recent form. An impressive first-half display failed to deliver the lead they deserved, and they eventually succumbed only by the odd goal in five. Instead, the shock came elsewhere. Those early-season suggestions that West Ham had acquired a new resilience and consistency were put into proper perspective as the soft-touch Hammers came back with a vengeance at a rocking Field Mill.

Mansfield hardly got a kick in the early stages, but once the visitors had declined several opportunities to dampen the home crowd's fervour, the match became more even. Two superb finishes saw Mansfield into a healthy half-time lead, but with an almost disbelieving crowd expecting their team to face a second-half onslaught. Instead, Mansfield struck again within four minutes and West Ham's play descended into what *The Guardian* referred to as 'shambling mediocrity'. It was the most famous night in Mansfield's history, the first time they had ever made the cup quarter-finals, but a shocker for West Ham. So much talent, so much early-season promise, but another season of woeful underachievement.

Strongly fancied to create another upset were Birmingham City, drawn at home to Manchester United. In a thrilling match, they were forced to settle for a 2-2 draw before being ruthlessly dismissed at Old Trafford, where Denis Law continued his majestic recent form with a hat-trick in United's 6-2 win. Joining them in the quarter-finals were neighbours City, whose game at Blackburn finally took place at the fifth time of asking. Lee and left-winger Tony Coleman both scored twice as City marched convincingly into the quarter-finals.

Lee was by now assuming a more central role, with Summerbee restored to his more natural wing position, and he and Coleman had created havoc down the flanks. And City were hardly alone in eschewing the 'wingless' approach of the England manager. Indeed, those fearing that the winger would become an extinct species had been pleasantly surprised, as most top club sides continued to utilise them to great effect. Leeds and Arsenal, two of the era's most well-organised and defensively-orientated sides, still employed Albert Johanneson then Eddie Gray and George Armstrong respectively; Liverpool Peter Thompson and Ian Callaghan, Everton Johnny Morrissey, Manchester United John Aston and George Best. Not all of them played on the wing all of the time, but certainly did so often enough to show that there had been no slavish following of the world champions' template.

Equally, there were many teams which *had* gone down the more compact 4-3-3 route and Bill Nicholson, one of the game's most astute tacticians, gave a newspaper interview which distilled the essence of the approach. '4-3-3 creates space on wings, taking players away so that others can fill that space. But this tends to mean putting square pegs into round holes.' This was often an inevitable consequence of this so-called 'method football', where players were subjugated to the tactical needs and shape of the team. The days when managers finished their team talks with 'just go out there and enjoy yourselves' were coming to an end, and several of the great stars of yesteryear, notably the great Tom Finney, were happy to earn a few bob by telling the newspapers how they wouldn't have enjoyed playing in modern-day football, notwithstanding the relative riches available.

Despite their indifferent league form, United remained football's big draw and their game at Portman Road attracted Ipswich's all-time record attendance, with several hundred more taking a vantage point on the roof of a nearby multi-storey car park. United again disappointed John Arlott, who despaired of Nobby Stiles' 'compulsive need to build up a hate relationship with his audience', but the bulk of the crowd were well satisfied with the game's outcome, determined when Tony Dunne sliced a clearance into his own net. Their league placing might have been moderate, but United were still European champions and this was a famous victory for Ipswich, which also took them above United in the table.

Chelsea gave a debut to seventeen-year-old Alan Hudson in their game at Southampton, but it proved to be a painful experience for him and his side. David Webb's return to the Dell saw him get on the scoresheet just before half-time, but it only served to put his own side 3-0 down as the ball flashed past a helpless Bonetti. Two second-half goals from Ron Davies completed a 5-0 rout which saw the Saints overtake Chelsea to move to fifth in the table. They had no realistic prospect of moving any higher, but it was still an impressive achievement for a side which epitomised the way that the 'smaller clubs' were moving: difficult to beat at home, at a tightly packed stadium, and physical, defensive and uncompromising away from the Dell.

Footballers continued to be slated for their on-field misdemeanours, and all too often the implied criticism took the form of a comparison with the behaviour of the so much more civilised and respectful rugby union players. But when a Five Nations match saw a player openly punch an opponent yet receive no disciplinary action, Brian Glanville was quick to pounce on the hypocrisy. 'Where soccer's villainies tend to be performed in the light, rugby's usually go on in the dark recesses of the scrum, where all things seem to be permitted. I have nothing basically against rugby, providing it keeps in its place; which is that of a rugged and somewhat primitive minor sport, whose artificially low level allows ex-public schoolboys to become national figures, where in soccer they would remain nonentities.' Ouch.

An ex-public schoolboy himself, Glanville closed with his view that soccer was becoming fashionable – chic, even. 'Working-class boys who had made their mark in theatre, films, journalism and literature have stayed loyal to the game they loved as children.' There would be peaks and troughs throughout the following decades, but even Glanville could never have foreseen just how fashionable the game would ultimately become.

Match Of The Month
11 February 1969, FA Cup Fifth Round: Birmingham City 2 Manchester United 2

Second-division Birmingham's FA Cup exploits over the previous two years had seen them dispose of Chelsea and twice see off Arsenal, all in front of full houses at St Andrew's. The fifth-round draw now gave them another chance to see off a top-flight side, and their prospective victims were the most charismatic of them all – Manchester United. With United not the force they were, Birmingham were favourites in the eyes of many. And how close they came to living up to their billing.

On a treacherous pitch and in driving sleet, the two sides produced football of a quality beyond the reasonable aspirations of any of the 52,000 attendees. United looked far superior in the early stages, forcing several great saves from Herriot before eventually going ahead through Law's trademark hanging-in-the-air header. Beard, on as a substitute, scored with his first touch to leave things all square at the interval, with most of the crowd now expecting United to become just another first division victim.

United, however, were determined to prove that they weren't yet just another first division team. Kidd, a handful throughout, struck a post before Charlton's through ball was killed by Best, who crashed home a ferocious drive to put United back in front with just ten minutes remaining. But the confidence instilled by their recent cup exploits ensured that Birmingham weren't about to fold. They got their reward when Best, disorientated by finding himself in his own penalty area, handled to give them the chance to secure a ticket to a lucrative Old Trafford replay. Twenty-year-old Dave Robinson calmly converted the spot kick and, as United set themselves up for the restart, Nobby Stiles could be seen putting a consoling arm round a distraught Best.

Birmingham's share of the proceeds from the usual 63,500 FA Cup crowd at Old Trafford no doubt provided a degree of compensation for the 6-2 drubbing they went on to endure in the replay.

Birmingham: Herriot, Martin, Green, Page, Robinson, Wylie, Vincent, Greenhoff, Pickering, Hockey, Thwaites.

Manchester United: Stepney, Fitzpatrick, Dunne, Crerand, James, Stiles, Morgan, Kidd, Charlton, Law, Best.

Player Of The Month
Terry Cooper (Leeds United)

Initially a left-winger, Cooper made his Leeds debut in 1962 but it wasn't until the 1966/67 season that he began to feature regularly in the first team. He played a major role in Leeds' relentless search for honours, and scored the goal which gave them the first trophy in their history when his volley beat Arsenal to win the League Cup in 1968.

A classy full-back, Cooper was one of the more popular Leeds players with the public, forming a productive left-sided partnership with Eddie Gray and seldom being cited in the litany of accusations of dirty play and sharp practices associated with Revie's team. With Ray Wilson's international days clearly numbered, Cooper increasingly became the critics' favourite to replace him with a series of consistently impressive club displays.

February saw Cooper and Leeds in peak form, as they gathered momentum in their bid to take the league title. Their four league games delivered maximum points without a goal being conceded, with Cooper making important contributions at both ends of the field. Against Ipswich, he crashed a drive against a post and helped Leeds survive several dangerous attacks on a treacherous surface; at Forest, his energetic display helped subdue the in-form Barry Lyons as well as create several good chances for his own team. Leeds ended the month on top of the table and as warm favourites to take the title.

Cooper was duly called up for his first cap against France the following month, performing impressively in a 5-0 win and almost instantly being recognised as the ideal full-back to fit into Ramsey's preferred formation. As a former winger, he was more comfortable and competent than most of his peers when it came to making overlapping runs and putting in accurate crosses, providing the team with a natural attacking width.

Cooper was first-choice left-back in Mexico, although, like many, he suffered in the heat and altitude, particularly against West Germany, where the impact of a series of exhausting overlapping runs proved to be an important factor in allowing the German wingers freedom to create danger later on. Cooper went on to win twenty full caps, a total which would have been significantly higher but for a broken leg suffered in 1972, which kept him out for over eighteen months and effectively ended his international career. Cooper stayed with Leeds until 1975, but never seemed to regain the pace and fitness which had been such a part of his game before his injury. He went on to feature for Middlesbrough and both Bristol clubs – initially as player-manager – before becoming another of his era to embark on a largely unsuccessful managerial career.

MARCH 1969

West Ham's season may have petered out in familiar fashion, but at least they were leading the way in taking steps to deal with trouble amongst spectators. Protracted discussions with police now allowed them to segregate fans, with visiting supporters shepherded into a specific part of the ground. As a result, they reported 'far fewer incidents and far less tension' and signposted the way ahead for managing potential trouble between rival supporters inside stadia. The prospects of more sinister violence in the vicinity of the stadium also receded with the news that the Kray Twins had been sent down, no doubt allowing one or two of the bubble-blowing fraternity to breathe more easily from now on.

Cup quarter-final day saw Manchester take centre stage, with over 110,000 attending two games which promised to be classic encounters. In the end, both failed to deliver. At Maine Road, a Spurs side heavily beaten in their previous two visits underwent a one-game-only tactical transformation to the extent that spectators must have wondered whether they were watching Southampton in disguise. From the start, they sought to intimidate and injure, with England and Mullery the main transgressors. City could make little headway in a tense encounter with minimal goalmouth incident, until an opportunist strike by Lee squeezed past Jennings to enter the net via the inside of a post. Spurs managed not a single threat on Dowd's goal throughout the entire ninety minutes.

Across at Old Trafford, a similarly tight and lifeless match also produced just one goal, with an Everton side unusually reluctant to open out the game sneaking through when Joe Royle bundled home a horribly scrappy goal. The game spilled over into fisticuffs towards the end when Best and Morrissey threw punches at each other, but were both allowed to stay on the pitch.

Elsewhere, holders West Brom produced an impressive display to win at Stamford Bridge after falling behind early on, probably just as well after an extraordinary piece of refereeing from Jim Finney almost cost them the tie. Astle's header was handled on the line by Harris, but bounced back into the net off Peter Bonetti's body. In the split second between the handball and the ball entering the net, Finney had blown for a penalty and refused to overturn the decision even though it patently disadvantaged the recipients of the award. West Brom's fury was exacerbated when Brown's spot-kick was saved by Bonetti, but justice was ultimately done.

Meanwhile, cup favourites Liverpool, a round behind due to the weather, emerged safely from Filbert Street with an Anfield replay to look forward to, only then to squander a series of great chances, including a penalty, as Shilton produced a memorable display. Andy Lochhead's header from a rare breakaway gave Leicester a shock win, and the following week they squeezed past Mansfield to make their way into the semi-final. The draw dismayed most neutrals, with City and Everton paired together in a tie which most had hoped would have been saved for the final.

In the second division, Derby County were now striding away from the field, receiving stellar reviews for the quality of their football, which was consistently attracting broadsheet journalists to the Baseball Ground. Dave Mackay continued to be an inspiring leader to a group of high-energy young players who had gelled into what most agreed was the best footballing side seen in division two for many years. Blackburn were their latest victims, as four goals and a succession of near misses reaffirmed the attacking flair of Hector, O'Hare and Hinton et al.

England's next opportunity to regain some scoring form came with the visit of France to Wembley. The fixture congestion which followed the devastation of February's programme meant that Everton, Chelsea and Manchester United, amongst others, had rescheduled fixtures which now clashed with the international, and the clubs were given precedence to keep their international players in their sides.

The absentees gave Ramsey the chance to get to know a few fringe players a bit better – the likes of Peter Eustace, Alan Oakes, Jim Montgomery and Ralph Coates – but the name on most people's lips when the squad was announced was the one conspicuous by its absence. Jimmy Greaves, despite continuing to score regularly for Spurs and remaining the darling of the southern press, was again omitted in what appeared to be a definitive statement from Ramsey that the door to a return for the country's most instinctive, talented and prolific goalscorer had been bolted firmly shut.

The side ultimately selected saw a debut for Leeds' left-back Terry Cooper and a second cap, almost six years after his debut, for his Leeds team-mate Mike O'Grady. O'Grady was the closest thing to a conventional winger to be seen in an England shirt since England last met France almost three years earlier, and marked his return with a superb volley to put England ahead in the first half. A poor French side were then swept aside, with Hurst scoring a hat-trick, albeit with the help of two penalties, and Francis Lee opening his international account with a fine solo goal. Lee and Colin Bell were both highly impressive, suggesting that their Manchester City partnership might also bear fruit at international level.

The 5-0 win and fine performance were well received, even though it was acknowledged that the opposition was somewhat short of top class. There was also an appreciation for what Ramsey was doing tactically. Grady was regarded as a winger and Lee had often played there, but whilst they both often took up wide positions there was immense flexibility in their movement. They switched sides, they came inside, sometimes they were both on the same flank. They both gave the side plenty of width, but weren't touchline-hugging wingers as were seen in days gone by.

Another of the teams whose players were excused England duty was Arsenal, allowing John Radford and Bob McNab time to prepare for their forthcoming League Cup Final against Swindon Town. It evidently didn't help, as for the second time in three seasons the cup went to a third division side. Swindon's 3-1 extra-time win was widely feted, with Don Rogers in particular being tipped for bigger things, almost echoing the reaction to Rodney Marsh two years earlier. Swindon were also well placed to follow Rangers by winning promotion, giving Rogers a bigger platform on which to shine. It was a bitter disappointment for Arsenal, without a trophy since 1953, but a further illustration that they still lacked the attacking invention to move up to the next level.

Marsh himself was now fit and back in the Rangers side, but their fate had long been a foregone conclusion. They remained marooned at the foot of the table and their 8-1 drubbing at Manchester United was indicative of a side which had given up the ghost. They had had bad luck with injuries, but two promotions in two years had taken them a step too far, given the limited resources available to spend on bolstering their squad.

At the top of the table, Leeds were threatening to pull away, a comprehensive 5-1 win at Stoke the highlight of a strong, unbeaten month. Liverpool were by now their only realistic challengers, but would need to rely on favours from Leeds' future opponents. Although Everton's fine season had continued, they had fallen a little off the pace and their hopes of silverware now rested with the FA Cup. Their semi-final against Manchester City was one of the most eagerly anticipated of recent years, bringing together teams with as much attacking flair as any in the country.

Yet again, however, the weight of the occasion prevented either side from playing their natural game. Everton were particularly affected, not so much by players freezing on the day but more by a predetermined tactical approach focused more on containing their opponents than giving full expression to their own talents. Eventually, they succumbed to two pieces of brilliance. As full time approached, a rare flowing City attack saw Young hit a searing drive which cannoned to safety off Gordon West's shoulder. The resulting corner, however, proved decisive as some intricate play in the penalty area culminated in Tommy Booth firing home from close range.

For the second year running, an Everton side normally so full of flair and enterprise had failed to express itself on the big cup occasion. It was a team that appeared to have everything, perhaps the most well-balanced in the country, strong in all areas – you name it, they had it. But that elusive commodity – bottle – seemed to be the missing ingredient.

The other semi-final saw lowly Leicester City produce another surprise, squeezing past West Brom in a scrappy encounter. Again, the only goal came very late, with Allan Clarke's low shot squirming past John Osborne to give Leicester a Wembley date to look forward to – and hope it would enhance rather than detract from their attempts to avoid relegation.

Match Of The Month
15 March 1969, League Cup Final: Arsenal 1
Swindon Town 3 (after extra time)

Arsenal returned to Wembley as hot favourites to make amends for their turgid defeat by Leeds in last year's final. For Swindon, most assumed that they would have a good day out, enjoy the occasion and return to Wiltshire proud of their achievements but bereft of silverware. Once again, however, a Wembley full house witnessed a major shock.

Full of energy, Swindon not only held their own in the first half, but took the lead through a comedy goal when a series of deflections saw Roger Smart inadvertently wrong-foot Bob Wilson as the ball rolled into the corner of the net. Arsenal were well on top in the second half, attacking relentlessly but suffering increasing frustration as goalkeeper Peter Downsborough played the match of his life. Just as hope was beginning to run out, a defensive mix-up took the keeper out of the game and presented Bobby Gould with a simple equaliser.

Swindon had been chasing the ball for almost all of the second half, and the need for extra time seemed certain to play into the hands of their fitter top-flight rivals. Instead, showing extraordinary resilience on a heavy pitch, Swindon not only resisted Arsenal's pressure but created chances of their own. Wilson was now the busier keeper and was beaten again when Don Rogers joyously fired in from close range. The second half of extra time saw a deflated, fatigued Arsenal struggle to put together any concerted pressure, and their hopes were extinguished when Rogers broke away, contemptuously waltzed round Wilson and stroked the ball home to seal a fabulous, famous victory.

Some questioned whether two third division wins in three years was evidence that the top sides weren't taking the competition seriously: the desolation etched on the faces of the Arsenal players at the final whistle refuted these suggestions far more eloquently than any words could.

Arsenal: Wilson, Storey, McNab, McLintock, Ure, Simpson (Graham), Radford, Sammels, Court, Gould, Armstrong.

Swindon Town: Downsborough, Thomas, Trollope, Butler, Burrows, Harland, Heath, Smart, Smith (Penman), Noble, Rogers.

Player Of The Month
Peter Shilton (Leicester City)

Peter Shilton shot to national prominence as a seventeen-year-old at Leicester City, when his prodigious talent and promise persuaded the club that they could afford to dispense with the services of Gordon Banks. Despite Leicester's struggles, Shilton had continued to fulfil his promise and now, at the age of nineteen, he kept four FA Cup clean sheets in a month to do more than anyone to propel his team to Wembley.

At home to Liverpool, Shilton made three crucial saves to keep his team in the tie: at Anfield two days later, he surpassed even this display with a stunning performance which included a spectacular penalty save from Tommy Smith. Evans, Callaghan and Hughes were all denied by Shilton as Liverpool laid siege to Leicester's goal, and Andy Lochhead's header was enough to see Leicester through to the quarter-finals. Five days later at Mansfield, Shilton was less busy but still able to keep out an opposition which had blitzed West Ham in the previous round. In the semi-final against West Brom, Leicester were generally on the back foot, but their defence performed superbly with Shilton, other than for one fumble which he bravely rectified, once again unflappable. Leicester's relegation fight had been forced to take a back seat whilst they played through their FA

Cup backlog, but the three league games they fitted in saw just one goal conceded, with Shilton again in outstanding form as critics widely tipped him to follow Banks into the England team.

In the end, he became Banks' successor at Stoke as well as for England, as his career proved every bit as stellar as the early prognosis had suggested. Making his full international debut in October 1970 at just twenty-one, he would go on to win a record 125 caps during an England career that spanned twenty years. Shilton's longevity was in part attributed to his obsessive fitness regime, although his bulky frame was sometimes cited as a reason for an occasional lack of flexibility, most notably when he allowed a shot from Domarski to slither beneath his dive in the vital World Cup qualifier in 1973. Indeed, despite his record-breaking career, the two incidents for which Shilton is most vividly remembered are both goals he conceded, the other coming from the hand of Diego Maradona.

Shilton's club career took a major upturn in 1977, when Brian Clough identified him as the player he needed to enable newly promoted Nottingham Forest to become a real force. In his first season, they won the first division title and the next two both saw them lift the European Cup, extraordinary achievements in which Shilton played a crucial part. It was this signing more than any other which convinced clubs that goalkeepers were just as important as outfield players and should command transfer fees to match.

Shilton later went on to star for Southampton and Derby County, eventually racking up over 1,000 league appearances in his 30-year career.

APRIL 1969

Leeds continued to home in on their first title, but by now had reverted totally to the playing style which had made them so unpopular in their earlier first division days. Away fixtures saw them seek to grind out draws, and during the month of April they would achieve no fewer than five – four of them goalless. Spectators paying to witness the champions elect might reasonably have expected to see something more than a lesson in the art of defending but, with the big prize so close, this was no time for anything so frivolous as trying to entertain.

Not that title rivals Liverpool were much better. They too were a tough, uncompromising team founded on a solid defence, and this season more than any other had been referred to as 'a machine'. 'Looking at Liverpool on Saturday was about as inspiring as watching a concrete mixer at work' was a typical appraisal of the Anfield experience. Efficiency was the byword for both contenders in a title race which felt like the polar opposite of the thrilling climax witnessed only last season. Then, the two Manchester sides tilted for the title in a blaze of attacking football, both scoring and conceding freely; now, Leeds and Liverpool ground on relentlessly with little or no regard for the paying customer. Winning – or, away from home, drawing – was all that mattered.

The Easter programme saw Leeds maintain their advantage, beating Manchester City 1-0 at Elland Road, whilst Liverpool saw off Wolves by the same scoreline at Anfield. 'At the best of times, they are not the most artistic of sides. When their technical efficiency betrays then they can be unutterably boring.' This was one of those evenings. Alun Evans' brief early flurry of goals and charisma had given way to a series of uninspired performances as he struggled with the heightened burden of expectation.

The Easter period also saw a return of the violent seaside scenes previously seen some three years ago, as mods and rockers staged a nostalgic revival. Newspaper reports claimed that some of the brawls on south coast beaches involved youths who had travelled all the way from Liverpool, presumably desperate to escape the brain-numbing experiences to be found at Anfield. It was at least a reminder that gratuitous teenage violence wasn't confined to football grounds. The reporting of football hooliganism had been less prevalent this season, partly because it was by now less of a novelty, but also because the nature of the thuggery was evolving. Gangs were increasingly seeking trouble outside rather than inside the grounds, away from public view.

The link between behaviour on the pitch and trouble amongst spectators was now accepted as more tenuous, it being recognised that football matches merely delivered a convenient location and opportunity for those of like-mindedness to meet.

There were still occasional incidents of spectator violence inside grounds, and when Stoke City secured a goalless draw at Upton Park by not always legitimate means, one fan was sufficiently incensed to come on to the pitch and attack the referee at the end of the game. 'Mrs Sheila Wood, aged 30, who had been sitting in the stand with her two children and had forced her way down to the terraces, ran on to the pitch and went for him with both fists...' Mrs Wood was 'pounced on' by two policemen and escorted away, although she escaped charges, perhaps on the grounds that such a show of emotion on the back of an utterly meaningless game suggested that not all her chairs were under the table.

Although Liverpool were still well in the title race as they welcomed Ipswich Town to Anfield, an indication of the impact of the lack of entertainment provided by the team was that such an important game – and on a very pleasant April Saturday afternoon – attracted their lowest gate of the season. Those that stayed away missed one of Liverpool's better performances, albeit against feeble opposition, but with Leeds also winning against relegation strugglers Leicester, Liverpool remained five points adrift with a game in hand. They still had to face Leeds at Anfield, but firstly it would be their neighbours' turn to have a go at Revie's men. Bill Shankly said: 'We would be grateful if our dearest and closest friends at Everton would beat Leeds on Tuesday, giving us a good chance for the title we so richly deserve.'

Everton gave it their best shot, but foundered as had so many on the rock of the Leeds back four, as Revie's men ground out another goalless draw in a display of 'remorseless all-round efficiency'. With Liverpool unable to force a win at relegation-threatened Coventry – another goalless draw which saw Maurice Setters and Alun Evans sent off for fighting – Leeds were almost there, needing just a point from their last two games, the first of which would be at Anfield.

Before then, the FA Cup Final brought some welcome relief to Leicester City, still embroiled in a struggle for first division survival. While Manchester City's players had been going through the motions in a succession of irrelevant league games, their primary objective being to preserve their limbs for the once-in-a-lifetime big day, Leicester's had been forced to go at full throttle week after week. Joe Mercer's team were undoubtedly favourites, but would their players be able to turn on the style at will after weeks of taking it easy?

The answer, generally, was yes, although Leicester had several great chances to upset the odds, with Allan Clarke outstanding and Lochhead always a threat. In an entertaining final, the only goal came from a typically fierce drive from Neil Young in the first half. City made little attempt to sit on their lead, instead striving to make the game safe with a second goal, but their failure to get it meant that the match retained its intrigue right to the end.

As usual, both BBC and ITV televised the game live, both employing new gimmicks to attract viewers. And, as usual, the BBC won out resoundingly, still by far the more trusted source of football coverage, despite the high-profile presence of Jimmy Hill in the ITV ranks. One of the BBC's innovations was to have interviewers parked close to the touchline near the managers, intermittently interrupting them to ask for soundbites on how they thought the game was going. The output was less than illuminating, with both Mercer and O'Farrell rather more concerned with watching the game, and the experiment was dropped immediately.

City were deserved winners of a sporting contest, the spirit exemplified by Joe Mercer's first port of call after the game being to seek out and console Leicester captain David Nish before celebrating with his own men. After failing miserably to live up to the mantle of champions, and suffering bitter humiliation in Europe, City had cemented their status as one of the finest teams of the era. For Leicester, though, there was little time to mope – they still had five league games remaining to save themselves from relegation.

Two days later, attention turned to Anfield, where Leeds secured the point they needed to take the title. They were forced to defend for long periods, but as usual resisted manfully and were generously feted by the Kop at the end of the game. Eric Todd summed up public sentiment perfectly. 'Leeds United, whether you like it or not, whether you love them or hate them, are champions of the Football League.' Few could deny that, after so many near misses, they deserved their success, but grudging admiration was still the best that they could aspire to. They were the only league champions in history to have scored fewer goals than they accumulated points throughout a season, and would remain so until the introduction of three points for a win. Not that any of this bothered Don Revie, who immediately looked forward to next season's challenges. While falling short of Malcolm Allison's 'We will terrify Europe' prediction, he was nevertheless bullish about Leeds' European Cup prospects, not unreasonably given their consistent record of success in the Fairs Cup. However, his ultimate ambition went one step further than that – to win the World Club Championship. Somehow, this unofficial brawlfest had become the new Holy Grail.

Match Of The Month
28 April 1969, Division One: Liverpool 0 Leeds United 0

Leeds arrived at Anfield needing just a point to take their first league title; for Liverpool, victory would keep them in the race, but they would then need to win their two remaining away games as well as relying on Nottingham Forest earning at least a draw at Elland Road later in the week. Liverpool's hopes were faint, but with Leeds' history of last-gasp failures, Shankly knew that a win would get nerves jangling at Elland Road.

Liverpool's approach reflected the 'now-or-never' situation in which they found themselves, as they attacked relentlessly with a verve and commitment so often lacking in their recent displays. With Tommy Smith driving them on, they created several passable chances, the best of which were blazed over the bar by young Alun Evans. Leeds attacked only sporadically, but had the game's outstanding performer in Billy Bremner who, as in the recent away games at Arsenal, Everton and Wednesday in this most difficult of run-ins, epitomised the defiance which Revie had instilled into the club. The last twenty minutes saw Leeds man the barricades, almost counting down the minutes to the final whistle. When that whistle finally came, the Leeds players were warmly congratulated by their opponents, and then, as they walked towards the Kop, surprised and delighted to receive the most fulsome ovation from the Liverpool fans. Revie and his players, unused to any kind of affection from anyone other than their own supporters, were visibly moved by this display of sportsmanship, and warmly commended the Liverpool supporters in interviews after the game.

Leeds duly beat Forest in their final match, establishing a new record points total for a first division season. They may not have been the most popular champions, but no one could deny that they were thoroughly worthy ones.

Liverpool: Lawrence, Lawler, Strong, Smith, Yeats, Hughes, Callaghan, Graham, Evans, St John, Thompson.

Leeds United: Sprake, Reaney, Cooper, Bremner, Charlton, Hunter, O'Grady, Madeley, Jones, Giles, Gray.

Player Of The Month
Jack Charlton (Leeds United)

Charlton made his first-team debut for Leeds in 1953 at just seventeen years of age, but his career was almost immediately interrupted by a two-year stint of national service. On his return to Elland Road, he quickly became a regular starter, and was central to Leeds' emergence as a major force.

April was the key month for Leeds as they homed in on their first ever league title. Revie's early-season promise that Leeds would play a more attractive style of football had long since evaporated as the stakes became higher, and it was on their much vaunted defence that their hopes would now rest.

Although Leeds looked to have a decent margin over their challengers, their eight-match April schedule contained trips to Sheffield Wednesday, Arsenal, West Brom, Everton and their closest pursuers Liverpool. Their defence performed superbly throughout, conceding just two goals as the team remained unbeaten. Central to this in every way was Jack Charlton, who, faced with some of the division's most feted forwards – Ritchie, Radford, Astle, Royle and St John – repeatedly blotted them out of the game. His one mistake came at West Brom, where his backpass presented Krzywicki with the opening goal, but he remedied this in unconventional fashion, galloping down the wing to cross for Eddie Gray to equalise. Two exemplary defensive displays on Merseyside, both producing goalless draws, clinched the title, with Charlton marshalling the defence superbly at Anfield in particular as Liverpool threw everything at them in a bid to keep their own hopes alive.

Charlton was also an important goal threat at the other end of the field, scoring seventy goals over his Leeds career. He pioneered the controversial tactic of standing in front of the goalkeeper at corner kicks, preventing him from coming to claim the ball, and this ploy produced many goals for Leeds and, on occasion, for England. It was a tactic seen as unsportsmanlike by many observers and opposition teams, adding further to the enmity with which Leeds were regarded throughout the game.

Charlton's first England call-up came relatively late in his career. He was 29 when he won his first cap in 1965 but instantly became a regular – his no-frills defensive attributes seen by Ramsey as the ideal complement to the more cultured Bobby Moore – and played in all six games of the '66 campaign. He continued to figure in Ramsey's plans, but injuries and advancing years meant that his appearances became less frequent. He was named in the Mexico party, but played only once, with Brian Labone by now being Ramsey's first choice. His thirty-five-cap

England career ended on his return from Mexico, but he went on to play for Leeds until 1973, amassing 629 appearances.

Charlton turned to management once his playing career ended, and he was by far the most successful of his Leeds and England contemporaries, notably at Middlesbrough and then most famously with Ireland, where the team's World Cup exploits made Big Jack a national hero.

MAY 1969

The domestic schedule had been brought forward in order to accommodate a new experiment in which the home international championships would be played out over an eight-day period in early May. With England then undertaking a four-match tour of Central and South America, the month would allow Alf Ramsey the sort of time with his players only previously available for the World Cup itself. Furthermore, such a demanding schedule would simulate the demands of playing repeatedly over a short period, the closest the players would get to a tournament scenario.

The FA's best-laid plans weren't totally realised, as the winter weather disruptions had caused several key rearranged domestic fixtures to drift into May, with the second relegation place still to be settled. Leicester had left Wembley with the consolation of knowing exactly what was required of them in their remaining five fixtures, since the teams they were trying to catch had all finished their schedule. Seven points were needed to overtake Coventry, and two of them were secured with a win over Spurs at Filbert Street. A loss at Ipswich was a setback, but victory against Sunderland brought renewed hope, leaving them with three points to garner from games against Everton and Manchester United. Forbidding fixtures normally, but with neither opponent having anything to play for and their players eager to hit the beach, there were many who expected the great escape to be realised.

Almost 40,000 turned out at Filbert Street to see Leicester take on a full-strength Everton side, but things looked grim when the visitors took an early lead. A scrappy equaliser saw a throng of small boys invade the pitch in jubilation, and Leicester's desperate efforts to force a victory were boosted when Colin Harvey was dismissed with ten minutes remaining. The winner, however, wouldn't come, meaning that Leicester needed to win at Old Trafford to save their skins.

United had other things to think about before that, welcoming AC Milan to Old Trafford for the second leg of the European Cup semi-final, with the Italians 2-0 up from the first leg. On a night of almost unbearable tension, United pressed forward throughout, but the Italians' mastery of all aspects of the defensive arts – plenty of them on the dark side – brought increasing exasperation for players and fans alike.

Things got out of hand when Milan keeper Cudicini fell to the turf after being struck by a missile from the Stretford End, and the referee was forced to warn the crowd that a repetition would have severe repercussions. Just when belief was starting to fade, Charlton produced a blast from the past to leave United with twenty minutes to find an equaliser. Despite one or two close shaves, notably a goalmouth scramble in which many observers felt the ball had crossed the line before being smothered by Cudicini, Milan held on to end United's reign as European champions.

To their immense credit, United then took on Leicester less than 48 hours later and gave a performance of sufficient commitment to win 3-2, thereby relegating their opponents. The Matt Busby era thus ended with a victory, even if the occasion wasn't quite the momentous one that he and United's supporters would have wished for.

The home international experiment featured staggered kick-off times so that all six games could be televised live. It would be a real test of the nation's capacity for watching live football, but appetites were whetted by the Saturday afternoon game at Ninian Park, which saw Scotland register an exciting 5-3 victory over Wales. The Saturday-evening game in Belfast saw England eventually overcome a spirited Northern Ireland side, with the outstanding Lee scoring one, making one and winning the penalty from which Geoff Hurst sealed England's 3-1 win. There were more than a few problems at the back, with Brian Labone given a tough time by Derek Dougan and Best escaping Mullery, his supposed shadow, all too frequently in the first half. Bobby Moore, however, was his customary assured self, as was Gordon Banks, who made several important saves. 'We'll have to do a lot better than this,' said Ramsey afterwards, sentiments echoed by those who had witnessed the match.

Not that there had been too many of them in the flesh. The game attracted only 24,500 to Windsor Park compared with the usual 55,000 sell-out. The Irish FA would be well compensated for allowing the match to be shown live, but the poor attendance was grist to the mill for the TV naysayers, convinced that the option of watching a game from the comfort of the fireside would always be too great a temptation for too many.

For the midweek game against Wales, Ramsey took the opportunity to look at other players, awarding a first cap to Jeff Astle and recalling Terry Cooper at left-back. England again started slowly, falling behind to a Ron Davies header, but in the second half produced an inspired performance. Bobby Charlton had been going through such a poor spell that some were starting to question whether a permanent decline had set in but now, in tandem with the effervescent Lee, he turned the game around. Charlton's spectacular drive brought England level before Lee, who had earlier missed a penalty, smashed in a close-range winner.

For the visit of Scotland, it was back to Ramsey's 'A-team' and the most telling selection was Ramsey's retention of Terry Cooper at left-back instead of Bob McNab, a clear indication that the Leeds man had moved to the top of the pecking order. England produced a dynamic performance, with Peters scoring two beautiful goals. The first saw him glide past a defender before firing home from an angle; the second came from a clever one-two with Alan Ball, which set him up to stroke the ball precisely into the corner from twenty yards. Hurst also scored twice, the first coming after a superb move between Charlton and Lee. It was Ramsey's first success against Scotland, and could hardly have been more impressive. After months of sterility, England's attack looked vibrant and threatening. Lee had provided additional drive and energy, and seemed to have inked himself in as Roger Hunt's replacement. Hurst was at the peak of his scoring powers, Ball and Peters were improving year after year and Charlton evidently still had something left in the tank. Behind them, Moore had been imperious throughout the series, Banks was as commanding as he had ever been and Mullery's combative energy made him look like a more than adequate replacement for Stiles. The squad set off for the tour of Central and South America in a mood of real optimism.

Meanwhile, the authorities were left to reflect on whether the revamped home international tournament had been successful. The two games at Wembley produced healthy gates, although not full houses. In particular, the Scotland game could have accommodated a further 10,000. However, grouping the games together at the end of the season had produced a real 'tournament' feel rather than having matches played almost randomly throughout the season. It also allowed Ramsey to spend a worthwhile chunk of time with his players rather than just a couple of days. The format was deemed a great success and would be continued for several years. What was more contentious was the question of live television coverage and in the future, as in the past, only the England–Scotland game would be deemed worthy of such treatment.

There remained one outstanding club issue to be resolved. The Inter-Cities Fairs Cup's 'one club, one city' rule had denied entry to Everton, Tottenham and Arsenal and enabled Newcastle United to take their place, despite having finished only tenth in last season's table with just forty-one points from their forty-two games. Newcastle had made the most of their good fortune by progressing to the final against Ujpest Dozsa, where two goals from skipper Bobby Moncur helped his team to a commanding 3-0 advantage.

When Ujpest pulled two of them back before half-time in the return leg, it looked as though Newcastle's unlikely dream would be quashed, but Moncur came up with an away goal which totally demoralised the opposition. Newcastle powered on to a 3-2 win in Hungary to take the trophy on a 6-2 aggregate. Extraordinarily, Moncur's three goals in the final matched his total tally of league goals over almost 300 games. It would be another six years before the one club, one city rule was abolished, and Newcastle will remain forever its most grateful beneficiaries.

Match Of The Month
17 May 1969, Division One: Manchester United 3 Leicester City 2

Fixture congestion following February's big freeze and United's protracted involvement in the European Cup meant that a league season originally scheduled to finish in mid-April had dragged on for a further four weeks. But now, at last, the season's final match arrived and, for Leicester, it could hardly have been more crucial. A win would see them retain their top-flight status; any other result and they would be down.

United's agonising defeat in the European Cup semi-final two days earlier was the best possible outcome for Leicester, who arrived at Old Trafford hoping to capitalise on the inevitable mood of dejection and fatigue. United, however, would be playing their final game under Sir Matt Busby, and their incentive to get a result was enhanced by their friend and former colleague Noel Cantwell being in charge at Coventry City, whose hopes of survival now rested squarely on United's shoulders.

The game had an extraordinary start, with three goals in the first three minutes. Leicester's win-or-bust situation was reflected by the fact that their captain David Nish found himself in the United penalty area after just forty seconds. It proved to be a worthwhile venture, as he swept the ball home from Clarke's pass. But Leicester and their fans would inhabit dreamland for less than a minute. George Best produced a piece of brilliance to fire past Shilton from twenty yards, and United capitalised on their opponents' deflation as Kidd immediately forced home a second goal.

Leicester gradually overcame their shock and created a number of good chances in a very open match, but when Law increased United's lead early in the second half the game was up in every sense. Fern pulled a goal back with twenty minutes left, but Leicester's gallant fight was over. There was plenty of sympathy at seeing such a fine side relegated, but also an element of relief that the integrity of the league hadn't been compromised, with many – especially those residing in the Coventry area – fearing that United might fail to put in the requisite effort in what for them was a meaningless and no doubt rather irritating engagement.

Manchester United: Rimmer, Brennan, Burns, Crerand, Foulkes, Stiles, Morgan, Kidd, Charlton, Law, Best.

Leicester City: Shilton, Rodrigues, Woollett, Nish, Manley, Cross, Fern (Matthews), Gibson, Lochhead, Clarke, Glover.

Player Of The Month
Francis Lee (Manchester City)

Lee's move to City from Bolton Wanderers in October 1967 had delivered even more than even this super-confident character could have imagined. Within eighteen months of his arrival, he had helped his new club win both the Football League title and the FA Cup, as well as picking up a couple of England caps. After a fine display against France brought his first England goal, he now looked to consolidate his position in the national side in the home international programme.

Buoyant after City's FA Cup win, Lee got straight into the groove at Windsor Park a week later with a man-of-the-match display. His free kick found Peters to nod England ahead before he scored a tremendous individual goal to restore England's lead in the second half. His final significant contribution saw him win the penalty from which Geoff Hurst made the game safe.

The following Wednesday, some beautiful interplay saw Lee set up Bobby Charlton to fire home a spectacular equaliser, before Lee himself smashed home the winner. He then contented himself with setting up goals for Hurst and Peters in the 4-1 drubbing of Scotland, and his three excellent performances saw him cemented into Sir Alf's first choice XI ahead of the Central and South American tour. After returning briefly to Manchester to score a superb winning goal against Liverpool, he continued his inspired spell with England with another outstanding performance, including a goal, in the victory over Uruguay. By now, he was firmly established as Ramsey's first choice to partner Geoff Hurst in Mexico.

Lee duly started three of England's four games in the tournament, but despite some lively performances failed to get on the scoresheet. He continued as an England regular for another two seasons before finishing his England career with ten goals from his twenty-seven caps.

Back at Manchester City, Lee went on to be a key player in the team's double cup success of 1969/70, and his thirty-three league goals in 1971/72 were a post-war record for the club. His tally included thirteen penalties, an all-time record, and with two successful conversions in cup competitions he achieved a 100 per cent success rate for the season. He wasn't quite so reliable on England duty, failing to score on both occasions he was entrusted with the responsibility.

Lee signed for Dave Mackay's Derby in 1974, scoring freely as he helped his new team to win the league title in 1975, and taking particular pleasure from a stunning winner at Maine Road, a goal immortalised by Barry Davies' *Match Of The Day* commentary. Always more than capable of looking after himself, he produced another memorable TV moment when his spectacular altercation with Norman Hunter saw the two of them sent off, only to continue their argument with a flurry of punches as they made their way to the tunnel.

Lee came back to City as chairman in the 1990s, fuelled by the fortune built up in the waste-paper business he had set up as a player with Bolton. Rapturously received initially, his tenure failed to shake the club out of its malaise and the disastrous appointment of his old pal Alan Ball as manager saw many fans turn against him. He ultimately left the club with his stock diminished rather than enhanced, but is still remembered as one of City's all-time greats, as well as one of the finest and most charismatic players of his era.

Summer 1969

After the highly encouraging home international series, England set off for their exploratory tour of Central and South America. The objectives were to experience at first hand the conditions they would face in a year's time and also to test themselves against two strong South American sides who had qualified for the tournament. It was a tour with much more of a purpose than was usually seen at the end of a season.

After a week of acclimatisation, England took the field in the Mexico City midday sun against a home side roared on by over 100,000 fans. Apart from the absence of Banks, for whom Gordon West deputised, it was the same side which had trounced Scotland, confirming the impression that Ramsey now had a firm idea of his optimal eleven. The team acquitted itself well, although the heat and thin air meant that much of the game was played at walking pace. The 0-0 draw was a satisfactory outcome, but a composed performance and the knowledge that opponents brought up in the conditions also struggled to deal with them were more positive still. Each side was permitted two substitutions, as would be the case in the World Cup itself, but Ramsey was more interested in seeing whether his players could cope with the conditions for a full ninety minutes, and his only change came when Tommy Wright replaced the injured Keith Newton.

The party then moved on to Guadalajara, where an 'England XI' took on their Mexican counterparts in a game without full international status. Ramsey took the opportunity to rotate his squad, although Moore, Peters and Ball remained from the first game. In a hugely encouraging performance, England earned rave notices for their display, with Clarke and Astle both scoring twice in a comprehensive 4-0 win. The later kick-off time and lower altitude helped, although Ramsey conceded that his players had still been affected by the heat. Well, at least some of them. Alan Ball was disappointed at being substituted late on: 'I could have gone on for ever; you can breathe here at Guadalajara.' Alan Mullery also had cause to regret the decision to substitute Ball; it was he who replaced him and, three minutes from the end, he found himself being sent off.

The trip to Mexico had been largely a fact-finding and public relations exercise, but the second leg of the tour was intended to provide a better indication of England's ability to compete against top sides in hostile surroundings. Against Uruguay, an accomplished display was rewarded with a 2-1 win, which impressed friend and foe alike. Lee again excelled, setting up Hurst's winner after scoring the first himself, and England's performance was such that many of the 70,000 crowd applauded them off the field. After all the friction between British and South American clubs at both club and international level in recent years, it was a welcome relief and gave cause for optimism that England's reception in a year's time might be less hostile than many had feared.

Finally, England moved on to face Brazil in Rio. Having watched the Uruguay game, Brazil's new manager Joao Saldanha was moved to describe England as an almost perfect side, better than the one which won the World Cup. For sixty minutes, they gave every suggestion that he was right, their 1-0 lead through Bell's early goal scant reward for a highly impressive display in front of 125,000 at the Maracana. The game's turning point came when Charlton blasted a great second-half chance wide and, as England tired, Brazil for the first time started to dominate possession. Even they would have been surprised to score two goals in a minute, but Tostao and Jairzinho pounced to give Brazil a win which bore little reflection to the overall balance of play.

It was nevertheless a reminder that Brazil possessed sufficient individual talent to overcome even the most accomplished and organised of sides, although Saldanha continued his charm offensive by stating that luck had very much gone against England. Ramsey commented that 'no one disappointed me in the way they played…we will not mind playing Brazil anywhere if this is an indication of their strength.' But Brazil, too, had a year to improve under their new manager and a Pele whose appetite for international competition was slowly returning after the brutal kicking he had received in England. Not that Alan Mullery had been particularly impressed: 'He's a very clever player but he strolls about too much…'

1969/70:

Return of the School of Science

AUGUST 1969

The new season started with the public still entranced by the Apollo moon landing some three weeks previously but, amongst the footballing fraternity, fascination with Neil Armstrong's small step for man soon gave way to the anticipation of Wilf McGuinness's small step for Manchester United, as he moved up from reserve team manager to replace Matt Busby in charge of the first team.

McGuinness's introduction to the spotlight came at newly promoted Crystal Palace, who could hardly have picked more glamorous opposition for their first ever top-flight fixture. It enabled Selhurst Park to attract its highest ever attendance, with receipts to match, in what for the first and so far last time saw the ground attract English football's highest crowd of the day. Palace responded admirably, leading at half-time before being pegged back for an honourable draw. However, for United, things would deteriorate rapidly.

Their first midweek game saw them outplayed by Everton, although it seemed unlikely that they would be the only ones to suffer such a fate this season. Less palatable by far was the rout which followed three days later at the hands of Southampton and the head of Ron Davies. The Old Trafford crowd was stunned by the ineptitude of United's performance, as Davies helped himself to four goals against a defence unable to cope with his aerial power.

United weren't too much better up front and Denis Law, King of the Stretford End, suffered the indignity of being jeered by his subjects for his anaemic display. He wasn't alone, although by the time the fans had made their way home their anger may have given way to a stark realisation that their team was seriously over the hill and in need of major surgery.

It wasn't quite the inheritance that Wilf McGuinness would have dreamt of, but his team selection for the next game, at Goodison Park, at least demonstrated that he wasn't scared to make big decisions: six players were dropped after the Southampton debacle, including the hitherto untouchable Charlton and Law. It may have got a message across but it hardly improved things on the pitch as Everton coasted to a comfortable 3-0 victory, maintaining their 100 per cent record whilst leaving their victims with just one point from their opening four games. United acted quickly to bring in defensive reinforcements, signing Ian Ure from Arsenal for £80,000. If nothing else, it would at least have the benefit of reducing the likelihood of Denis Law being sent off in future, although the King's immediate concern was just to get back into the side.

Consolation, however meagre, for United fans came from the fact that their neighbours were in almost as bad a position, their opening-day win over Sheffield Wednesday having been followed by three straight defeats. Two of the reverses had come against Liverpool, who thereby joined Everton in completing a double over Mancunian rivals. Even as early as the second week of the season, it seemed inevitable that the North West's main challenge for the title would come from Merseyside.

The following weekend brought the season's fifth East Lancs Road derby, and Everton looked well set to extend Merseyside's winning sequence when Johnny Morrissey put them ahead after just three minutes at Maine Road. City, though, hadn't been playing quite as badly as their results suggested, and they came back strongly to earn a point with a towering header from young Ian Bowyer. The game at Maine Road also featured a one-man pitch invasion, as a lone City fan reacted to the referee's failure to award his team what looked an obvious penalty by storming on to the field, grabbing the official's shirt and, according to *The Guardian*, 'making a sign clearly indicating that he thought the referee should be in a mental home'.

Defending champions Leeds had started the season slowly, with four draws in their first six games. They remained undefeated, however, and in doing so passed Burnley's run of thirty unbeaten first division matches, a record which had stood for forty-five years. They had strengthened their ranks with the acquisition of Allan Clarke, who for the second season running had responded to relegation by putting in a transfer request. And, for the second season running, he commanded a fee which broke the British transfer record, with Leeds shelling out £165,000 for his services. Clarke had always been a prolific scorer even for struggling sides and surprised no one by getting off the mark straight away. He scored to help Leeds beat Manchester City in the Charity Shield, and found the target again on his league debut in a comfortable win over Tottenham.

Leeds' unbeaten sequence came to an end at Goodison Park; indeed, when Everton went 3-0 up just after the interval, the champions looked set for humiliation rather than mere defeat. But, in an emphatic demonstration that they never gave up without a fight, they pulled two goals back in the second half and came within inches of saving themselves. Everton's flying start had continued, but even in defeat Leeds had given everyone a reminder that they remained the team to beat.

Brian Clough's Derby, aided admittedly by a favourable set of early-season fixtures, had made a great start to first division life, cementing the impression that they were capable of far more than mere survival. Dave Mackay's inspirational leadership on the pitch was very much in evidence and with plenty of eager young legs to do the running for him, his relative lack of mobility seemed less of a handicap than it had been in his later days at Tottenham.

Also starting well were Wolves, whose three straight wins to begin the season were inspired by Peter Knowles, a scorer in all of them. Flashy at times but immensely skilful, his partnership with the equally flamboyant Dougan looked like the real thing. With under-23 caps already under his belt and in the form of his life, Knowles was being tipped by some to make a late bid for Ramsey's World Cup squad.

Arsenal looked like delivering yet another season low on excitement, as it took three games until their fans had a goal to cheer. It was, however, well worth the wait, as it came from the feet of eighteen-year-old Charlie George, who had immediately become a terrace favourite after spending many of his formative years alongside those who now cheered him on. Along with Jimmy Robertson, signed from Tottenham, he promised to bring an element of flair to this hitherto most colourless of teams.

The new season also saw the launch of yet another weekly football magazine, as the perceived appetite for football information, particularly amongst youngsters, still hadn't reached saturation point. The newcomer, *Shoot!*, cost just one shilling – sixpence less than its competitors – and was more obviously aimed at younger consumers than the other three weeklies already on the market. 'Terrific new football paper for boys' blared the front page of the first issue, with its implicit suggestion that girls had no place taking an interest in the rough, tough world of soccer and really ought to stick to *Bunty* and *Jackie*. The paper went straight to the top with its proud boast that 'Bobby Moore writes for you' and the England captain's first column mentioned that he was looking forward to running into his old pal Jimmy Greaves again. Whether this was on the pitch or in a nearby hostelry was not made clear.

Features which would become legendary included Paul Trevillion's *You Are The Ref* and the *Focus on...* section, which asked star players about their lives away from football. First to fill in the *Focus* questionnaire was Forest's Terry Hennessey, revealing himself as the proud owner of a Triumph Spitfire to go with his Vauxhall Viva. A big fan of *Till Death Us Do Part*, Terry loved to spend his spare time decorating and gardening. Whilst the favourite meal amongst footballers of the era would go on to reveal itself overwhelmingly as steak and chips, Terry's more sophisticated preferences to accompany his fillet were creamed potatoes, mushrooms and braised celery. Fans accustomed to seeing Big Tel ruthlessly scythe down anything within swinging distance would never have guessed that such a gourmet lurked beneath that rugged exterior.

Manchester City's Tommy Booth had shot to prominence after his cup semi-final winner, but his moment in the *Focus on...* spotlight possibly came a little too soon for him to have fully grasped the concept of the feature. Tommy played his cards very close to his chest. *Favourite player?* 'Haven't got one.' *Favourite other team?* 'None'. *Car?* 'Trying to pass test!' *Best friend?* 'Quite a few.' *Biggest disappointment?* 'None yet.' Tommy's invitation to appear on *Parkinson* must have got lost in the post.

Match Of The Month
30 August 1969, Division One: Everton 3 Leeds United 2

Fixtures in the first month of the season seldom came as eagerly anticipated as this one. Everton, league leaders with five wins and a draw from their first six games, against Leeds, league champions and on a thirty-five-match unbeaten streak. And the spectacle didn't disappoint.

Everton, with a performance described as 'incessantly thrilling', spent the first hour of the match relentlessly attacking the visitors, prompted as ever by the inspirational Alan Ball. Their rewards matched the quality of their play, as they built up a commanding three-goal advantage. A scruffy first goal after just five minutes led to recriminations between Giles and Hunter, and it wouldn't be the first time that Leeds players would argue amongst themselves during the afternoon. The week-by-week pressure of trying to maintain a long unbeaten run was clearly taking its toll.

The likelihood of Leeds extending their sequence receded sharply twenty minutes later, when Joe Royle headed home after his first effort came back off the crossbar, and Everton came close several times to increasing the lead before half-time. When Royle got a second with a delicate finish early in the second half, a thrashing looked on the cards, but Bremner's soft goal from a seemingly innocuous corner totally changed the mood of the game.

Everton's self-belief visibly wilted as Leeds sensed the chance of an unlikely escape, and when Clarke fired home with fifteen minutes still remaining, the celebratory air around Goodison gave way to a fraught tension. The final whistle arrived to cheers as much of relief as ecstasy, but the nervous finale couldn't mask the superiority which Everton had demonstrated for much of the game. And their five-point lead over the reigning champions was a handy cushion for the long slog that lay ahead.

Everton: West, Wright, Brown, Jackson, Labone, Harvey, Husband, Ball, Royle, Hurst, Morrissey.

Leeds United: Sprake, Reaney, Cooper, Bremner, Charlton, Hunter, Madeley, Clarke, Jones, Giles, Gray (Lorimer).

Player Of The Month
Roy McFarland (Derby County)

Having started his career at Tranmere, McFarland was one of Brian Clough's first signings after he took the Derby job in 1967. A strong but classy centre-half, capable of standing up to rough treatment without lapsing into unnecessary foul play, McFarland made an immediate impact and was a key figure in Derby's promotion in 1969. Derby made a superb start to their first season back in division one, August seeing them go seven games unbeaten with just three goals conceded. McFarland starred at both ends of the pitch, being singled out for praise after the goalless opening-day draw against Burnley before netting his team's first goal of the season with a header from Alan Hinton's corner to clinch a 1-0 win at Ipswich Town. Four days later, he followed it up with a goal at Highfield Road as Coventry were held to a draw. McFarland again earned press plaudits for his performance in helping Derby achieve the most impressive result of the sequence, a 2-0 win at West Brom in which the free-scoring Albion attack were held at bay with few scares.

It was clear that Derby's defensive organisation under Clough was at a level beyond that normally seen from newly promoted sides, and much of the credit for this naturally went to the leadership qualities of Dave Mackay. However, there was also plenty of praise for McFarland's performances, it being recognised by all who watched him that he was a certainty to win full England caps.

McFarland was always a threat from set pieces, also having the knack of scoring important goals in tight games, and the season saw him go on to net further winners against Newcastle and Manchester City as Derby finished the season in a highly impressive fourth position.

He was too young to make the squad for Mexico but after five appearances for the under-23s he won his first full cap in 1971 against Malta. He went on to appear twenty-eight times for his country, including all four games in the ultimately ill-fated qualifying campaign for the 1974 World Cup. Injury took him out of the game for a year, but for which his tally of caps would have more accurately reflected the qualities of a man described by Brian Clough as 'a Rolls-Royce of a defender'.

When Colin Todd signed for Derby in 1971, he and McFarland immediately formed an impressive partnership which helped Derby to their surprise title win in 1972, and they remained together when the team repeated the feat under Dave Mackay's management in 1975. McFarland went on to have a long but relatively undistinguished managerial career, a couple of lower league promotions the only additions to the more prestigious titles he won as a player.

SEPTEMBER 1969

Derby's great start to the season had earned plaudits galore, but there were plenty who wanted to see them face top opposition before taking a firm view on their qualities. Manager Brian Clough was prominent amongst them and welcomed the visit of leaders Everton to the Baseball Ground as a proper gauge of where his team was at.

A thrilling match saw Derby demonstrate that they were much the best side to emerge from the second division since Revie's Leeds came so close to winning the title at their first attempt in 1965. Against a full-strength, confident and competent Everton, Derby's high-energy play and outstanding teamwork saw them take a grip over the Merseysiders' much-vaunted midfield, and frequently bring the devastating flat-with-pace crossing of Alan Hinton into play.

Hinton's set-piece deliveries were also as good as any in the division, and it was from his corners that headers from O'Hare and Hector put Derby two ahead. A superb strike from Howard Kendall brought Everton back into the game, but Derby, inspired as ever by Dave Mackay, held on for a famous win which knocked Everton off the top and, not for the last time, put Clough and his men into the headlines.

Derby next went to Newcastle and came back with the points through Roy McFarland's header, again from a set piece, but it was the following week that saw them make their most eloquent statement so far. On an emotional day for Dave Mackay, his old team Tottenham came to the Baseball Ground and were put to the sword like seldom before, as Derby's precise and inventive football saw them surge to a 5-0 win. Admittedly, Spurs weren't in the greatest form, but this humiliation reverberated around the country. Spurs fans certainly didn't take too kindly to it, some 250 of them being thrown off their train back home following yet another exhibition of mindless violence.

Wolves and Forest produced a thrilling 3-3 draw at Molineux, but the following day's headlines made little reference to events on the pitch. After the game, Peter Knowles announced firstly to his team-mates and then to the press that he was quitting football to become a Jehovah's Witness. Few believed it was little more than a whim, with Bill McGarry insisting that Knowles' playing kit be left out for the following Monday, and none of his team-mates wishing him farewell. But he never returned. Beneath the exterior of a player who appeared to thrive on the adulation he received lurked a man ill at ease with big-time football and the behaviours it encouraged. 'When I look at some of the things I did, it makes me ashamed of myself,' Knowles said.

There were signs of life at Old Trafford, and when United's old foes Liverpool came to town defending a proud unbeaten record, it was a throwback to happier days. After striking the woodwork three times, United finally forged ahead through Willie Morgan, although it was Best who stood out with a fabulous display. But the man receiving most of the credit for United's revived fortunes was Ian Ure – since he came into the side, they had gone six unbeaten on the back of a new defensive solidity.

The next week saw a big day for Ure – his first return to Highbury in United colours. It looked set to be a grim one when a training-ground routine – a corner played in low, a step-over and a drilled shot from George Graham, a move which would be reprised by Teddy Sheringham on numerous occasions decades later – put Arsenal ahead, and they doubled their lead through Sammels before half-time. Best, though, was having one of those spells where he was playing teams on his own; he scored one, set up another, and United came away with a point.

Even though the papers had been spoilt for choice for lead stories throughout this most eventful start to the season, there was one recurring theme – the defensive nature of away teams, time and time again setting up with nine behind the ball and using overly physical play and timewasting tactics. Goals per game in the first division season just gone had reached a post-war low, and the decline had been rapid and marked – just seven years previously, the average had been a full goal per match higher. Broadsheets, tabloids, magazines, TV – concern was being expressed everywhere that the negative tactics routinely and increasingly adopted would drive spectators away. But what could be done? Hardly a day seemed to pass without some suggestion for brightening the game, for making it more entertaining. Changes to the offside law, points for goals, additional points for an away win…these and many more outlandish suggestions were dissected and debated.

The game was hardly short on star names and attacking talent, but so much more of the focus was now on suppressing it by whatever means teams could get away with. Life was becoming increasingly difficult for flair players. Not only would they be systematically kicked, bullied and intimidated on the pitch as never before, but if they succumbed to the often intense provocation and retaliated it would be they, not the initial offenders, who would incur the referee's wrath. And then that of the FA disciplinary committee, still itching to teach these *nouveaux riches* upstarts a lesson. If the hatchet men didn't put the ball players out of commission, the FA would, and the game's biggest crowd-pullers often spent significant spells on the sidelines for one reason or another.

Matt Busby, now able to take a marginally more detached view, acknowledged that there had always been 'hard men' but the difference now was that there were far more of them. 'You wouldn't expect one team to have more than one or two,' Busby said. 'Nowadays you have entire sides that base physical hardness as their prime asset. They use strength and fitness to neutralise skill and the unfortunate truth is that all too often it can be done. And it's true that there are a few teams who believe the game is still about talent, technique and imagination but for every one of those you'll find ten who rely on the runners and the hard men.'

Busby's comments illustrated the thinking of so many through this era. Previously, it was almost as if skill and effort were mutually exclusive attributes in a footballer. Nowadays, it wasn't that there was no place for skill in the modern game, but rather that skill on its own was no longer enough. However gifted you were, you now had to work hard for the team or else you wouldn't get into it.

It was inevitable that the link with Ramsey's approach would be made, and Hugh McIlvanney paid him a back-handed compliment. 'No national team had ever been brought to such a point of commando-like fitness and selfless commitment. The irony is that Ramsey long ago started building something much finer on his foundation of functionalism, leaving his hordes of imitators with an oily, ugly chassis while his England goes forward like a Rolls-Royce.' Even England and Ramsey's biggest detractors couldn't deny that the likes of Bobby Charlton, Ball, Peters and Moore were players of immense individual talent, but they still wouldn't be selected if they failed to comply with Ramsey's work ethic.

The evolution of several first division sides supported both Busby and McIlvanney's views. On their promotion in 1966, Southampton played an attractive brand of football, pulled off some spectacular results and were always welcome visitors where fans were looking for a decent afternoon's football. Their approach saw them survive though not truly prosper, but they had noticeably changed their style of play to the extent that they were now seen as the league's most cynical and uncompromising side, at least away from home. An occasional burst of brilliance from Ron Davies would alleviate the tedium of watching them, but the likes of Hollywood, Fisher, McGrath and even the redeployed Terry Paine were all renowned for excessive physicality.

Burnley had undergone a similar transformation. So recently the breeding ground for attractive bright young things, they had reacted to receiving several severe beatings the previous season by adopting a more pragmatic style of play. Their reputation had now descended to such an extent that the Kop bellowed 'We want football!' even before their match at Anfield had kicked off. As it turned out, Burnley delivered rather more football than the locals would have liked, scoring three times to overturn Liverpool's 2-0 lead, before a late equaliser saw the spoils shared. An irate Shankly scolded his team for their 'arrogance'.

The month's final Saturday saw a series of results which again illustrated the competitiveness of the league, as all three of the bottom sides achieved eye-catching victories. To Sheffield Wednesday fell the honour of being the first club to lower Derby County's colours, as Alan Warboys' shot was enough to earn the points at Hillsborough. Sunderland capitalised on Tottenham's recent disastrous form by sneaking a 1-0 win at White Hart Lane, secured by an own goal from Mike England. And Ipswich won away at Burnley, whose descent into a side that few wanted to watch was reflected by the dismal crowd of 12,000 at Turf Moor.

Stoke's signing of Jimmy Greenhoff had added a touch of class to what, Gordon Banks aside, was a workmanlike side short on glamour. However, patrons of the Victoria Ground were compensated for the ordinary fare usually on offer by the visit of the most glamorous name of all. Santos had for many years been undertaking European tours as a means of raising funds, although they hadn't been seen in England since 1962. Now, though, Stoke had been prepared to stump up the £12,000 appearance money – conditional on the inclusion of Pele in the starting line-up – and 23,000 were persuaded to pass up the attractions of Monday night's *Decidedly Dusty* in order to witness the world's greatest player in the flesh.

They weren't disappointed. Pele scored two breathtaking goals as Santos edged a 3-2 win in an entertaining game which was almost a throwback to more innocent and happier footballing times. Denis Smith would later claim he had been told not to dish out his customary treatment to Pele – 'the crowd have come to watch him, not you' – and the spectacle certainly appealed to the watching Geoffrey Green. 'A pity we cannot see more like this, with the thrills and all the artistry crowned with an absence of all that is crude.' For Stoke, Eastham excelled and Greenhoff impressed Pele to such an extent that the great man queried why he hadn't yet been picked for England. He wouldn't be the last to ponder this anomaly.

Match Of The Month
20 September 1969, Division One: Derby County 5 Tottenham 0

Dave Mackay's impact at Derby had been phenomenal. His inspirational leadership had seen them power their way to the second division championship, as well as being rewarded with a share of the Footballer of the Year award. Now, with Derby riding high after ten games unbeaten, he was demonstrating the same qualities back in the first division, causing many to question whether Spurs had been premature in allowing him to leave. His old club's visit to the Baseball Ground gave Bill Nicholson the chance to assess the situation for himself.

Urged on by a record crowd of over 41,000 – a figure which would never be surpassed at the Baseball Ground – Derby produced their finest display of an already highly impressive season. Within twenty-five minutes, they were three up, admittedly aided by some catastrophic defending from a Spurs side punching below its weight so far this season. Mike England's misplaced pass was seized on by Alan Durban, whose angled shot ripped into the far corner of Jennings' net, and a few minutes later Kevin Hector displayed skill, pace and composure to slide home a second.

Spurs' only serious riposte came from a moment of brilliance from Greaves, juggling the ball on the edge of the area before striking a fierce volley, only to see it not just saved but caught almost contemptuously by Les Green. Shortly afterwards, the influential Willie Carlin, the closest thing to a certified dwarf in the first division, was somehow permitted to power in a header from Hinton's corner.

The second half brought little respite for Spurs, and a magnificent team move orchestrated by Carlin ended with O'Hare driving a superb strike beyond Jennings. Another flowing move saw Durban nod in a fifth, as a delirious crowd regaled their heroes with 'We've got the best team in the land...' They weren't far off it, and Nicholson was fulsome in his praise of Derby's football afterwards. A new force, propelled by a vibrant new managerial power, was most definitely emerging.

Derby County: Green, Webster, Robson, Durban (Wignall), McFarland, Mackay, McGovern, Carlin, O'Hare, Hector, Hinton.

Tottenham: Jennings, Beal, Knowles, Mullery, England, Collins, Pearce, Greaves, Gilzean, Pratt, Morgan (Want).

Player Of The Month
Kevin Hector (Derby County)

Hector brought himself a degree of national attention by scoring forty-four league goals for fourth-division Bradford City in the 1965/66 season. A transfer to a club at a higher level was inevitable but, with no top-flight teams prepared to take a gamble, he instead signed for struggling second division side Derby County. Hector played a key role in transforming the club's fortunes after the arrival of Clough and Taylor, top-scoring with sixteen goals as they breezed to promotion in 1969, winning the title with seven points to spare.

Derby had already gone seven games unbeaten in an impressive start to life back in the first division, but September was the month where they showed their abilities to full effect. Hector began the month by heading the decisive goal in a thrilling game against leaders Everton, who would go on to become champions. Four days later, he scored a spectacular goal in a 3-0 victory against Southampton, confounding Jimmy Gabriel before hammering a left-footer past Eric Martin. Hector was on the scoresheet again in the famous 5-0 win against Spurs, scoring the second in a performance described as 'irrepressible'. His partnership with John O'Hare was causing problems for every defence they encountered, and a League Cup goal against Hull completed a prolific month for Hector who, like the rest of his team-mates, had settled immediately into first division football.

Hector continued to score freely throughout the season, hitting twelve league goals as Derby finished fourth, but things got even better through the 1970s with two title wins. Hector was a major contributor to the 1972 triumph with twelve league goals and netted a further thirteen as Dave Mackay's side came out on top in 1975.

Hector had won representative honours at Football League and under-23 level, but his England career was one of the shortest on record, comprising just two appearances as substitute. The first of them almost made him the most celebrated substitute in English football history, as he was thrown on by Sir Alf Ramsey with just two minutes to go in the fateful World Cup qualifier against Poland in 1973. The change had the mark of desperation, but Hector came close to becoming a national hero when his first touch saw him find space to power in a close-range header from a corner, only to see the ball rebound to safety from the knees of a Polish defender stationed on the goal line.

His international lifespan may have been uncommonly brief, but Hector had a stellar career with Derby, becoming their all-time record appearance maker as well as netting 155 goals for the club.

OCTOBER 1969

After five years of consistent improvement, Martin Peters had fallen out of form, to the extent that he had been dropped by Ron Greenwood. To the dismay of West Ham fans, Peters revealed that he was no longer happy at the club and would be seeking a transfer. Hardly the most emotive player on the field, Peters evidently felt that he wasn't properly appreciated. The irony wasn't lost on some journalists – his whole reputation had been built on stealth, on not being noticed, so this sudden craving for acclaim seemed out of character. Peters certainly wasn't unappreciated by Alf Ramsey, who called him 'not a good player – a great one.'

Pending receipt of the written transfer request, Ron Greenwood decided to leave Peters out of the side at home to

Burnley, insisting that all the player needed was rest. He may well have had a point: at the end of the previous season, Peters had played in all three home international matches, then five games in West Ham's trip to the USA, and four further matches on England's Central and South American tour. Nevertheless, the pre-match atmosphere at Upton Park was subdued as the fans contemplated life without one of their Holy Trinity, a man whose contribution to the club had been just as valuable as his two higher-profile colleagues.

Consolation was provided by Peters' replacement, an eighteen-year-old Bermudan called Clyde Best. With Burnley's defence putting Hugh McIlvanney in mind of 'a bunch of inebriated formation dancers', Best was given and gratefully accepted two simple chances to put his team in the clear. He later missed several great opportunities to complete a hat-trick, but the crowd were intrigued throughout by the performance of the raw youngster, one of just a handful of black players to have appeared in English league football. One of the others was West Ham's own John Charles, so it wasn't an entirely unusual sight for their fans, but nevertheless provoked a welter of press comment. 'Whatever would Alf Garnett feel about a Bermudan playing for his favourite team?' mused *The Observer*.

As far as Ron Greenwood was concerned, Alf would just have to get used to it, as the West Ham manager predicted confidently that Clyde would be followed into league football by a host of other 'coloured' players. 'Best shields the ball so well. He's so difficult to rob, and he's not been kicked up in the air so much that he's stopped doing it,' Greenwood said. 'Coloured players are full of suppleness and ability to adjust the body. They do it naturally. We've lots round here. Not that white players can't do the same. They have to work at it, though. The white player maybe can't make it look as lovely. But he can learn to do it.'

Greenwood's implicit acceptance that physical intimidation would inevitably inhibit talented players from doing what came naturally passed without comment.

After their reverse at Sheffield Wednesday, there was enormous interest in Derby's next fixture, at home to a seemingly revitalised Manchester United. Would their defeat prove to be a temporary setback or did it signal the bursting of a bubble? Clough's men answered emphatically, dominating the match with their teamwork and slick passing, and a 2-0 win was fair reward for their performance. United fans were less than impressed – many of them watched the game in stockinged feet as police made them remove their bovver boots at the turnstiles, and they regaled the referee with a barrage of abuse, diplomatically described by Eric Todd as depicting him as 'senile, blind, of doubtful lineage and certainly on Derby's secret payroll.'

Time and again, the increasingly impressive Roy McFarland snuffed out the menace of George Best, and the paucity of threat from other areas – with Charlton reduced to a deeper ineffective role and Law's injury absences becoming ever more prolonged – supported the impression that United were in danger of becoming little more than a one-man team. But what a man. Two weeks later, Best won United's match at home to Forest with a goal as skilful and spectacular as any he had ever scored, cutting back from the corner flag to the edge of the penalty area before crashing a shot into the top corner.

Best's status was now such that he didn't just win games on his own; his very presence put thousands on United's gates, home or away. But there were plenty of other clubs struggling to get customers through the turnstiles. In a bid to attract new spectators, Charlton Athletic offered additional entertainment for patrons for their home game against Portsmouth. Free bingo, together with the appearance on the pitch of a camel and a baby elephant, borrowed from a nearby zoo. If nothing else, it proved to be a sound lesson in knowing your audience. The gate was down by over 1,000 from their previous home match, as the reality quickly dawned that what was being offered wasn't necessarily the sort of thing to lure the less committed fans away from their Saturday afternoon in front of the wrestling.

Tottenham's dismal run of form continued with another home defeat, this time to Wolves. It was, however, a Wolves side showing themselves capable of troubling the best, with Mike O'Grady, recently recruited from Leeds, boosting a forward line already boasting the considerable talents of Derek Dougan, Dave Wagstaffe, Jim McCalliog and Hughie Curran. With Mike Bailey a driving force in midfield, Wolves had too much for Spurs at both ends of the pitch. A side usually noted for its invention and craft, this manifestation of Tottenham was condemned by *The Observer*. 'The determination of the Tottenham attacks was matched only by their tactical futility. Like some soccer charge of the Light Brigade, they came piling head down into the hard unyielding mass of defenders.'

Dougan, however, would soon be up before the beak following his dismissal against Everton the previous week. He would face an FA disciplinary commission which had again been in the firing line, this time by dishing out some severe punishments to lower-league players, some of whose families' livelihoods were jeopardised by the loss of as much as eight weeks' pay. FA secretary Denis Follows had dismissed the accusations of heavy-handedness, citing an enormous increase in cases brought before the commission as making sterner punishments essential if the increasing trend towards violent play and player misbehaviour was to be arrested.

Challenged with the suggestion that it would be more sensible and equitable for suspensions to be defined as a number of matches rather than a number of weeks, Follows attempted to defend the indefensible, stating that each commission was aware of forthcoming fixtures and could adjust the period of punishment accordingly.

Presumably these sages also had the power to foresee all future weather disruptions, as well as being experts in determining progress in cup competitions and the likelihood of replays. Using the previous season as a benchmark, a four-week suspension could have embraced anything between two and ten matches.

Follows was opposed to the standardisation of punishments, which would thereby obviate the need for the vast majority of committee meetings, as well as delivering a far more streamlined and visibly fairer process. Of course, it would also diminish the scope for these worthy retired gentlemen to have a day up in London and a nice all-expenses-paid lunch. Some may have been tempted to conclude that football was being run by out-of touch old duffers with nothing but self-interest at heart. *Plus ça change...*

Derby's sparkling start had been followed by a difficult month, as home defeats by Coventry and Manchester City were followed by a trip to Elland Road. Leeds duly put the pretenders in their place, but once again Clough's men earned plenty of plaudits for their football and their impeccable discipline. Clough had laid down the mentality with his players that disputing refereeing decisions was a futile and disagreeable exercise, and his team's acceptance of authority made a refreshing change from the increasing petulance and dissent so routinely seen elsewhere.

Partly because of this, and partly due to the vibrant media-friendly charisma of their young manager, Derby had become the darlings of the broadsheet media, garnering lavish praise for their performances and demeanour, whether in victory or defeat. And it wasn't just journalists – the Elland Road crowd saw them off to a tremendous ovation and a loudspeaker announcement lauded them for 'playing football, which is more than can be said for some sides who come here'. It was a sentiment that could seldom, if ever, have been replicated at other stadia when Leeds themselves were the visitors.

Leeds thereby remained hot on the heels of Everton, who racked up yet another win away at Coventry in a tetchy match. It appeared as though reports of the demise of Alan Ball's fiery immaturity had been somewhat premature – here he was described by *The Guardian* as behaving as though someone had just trodden on his train set. Royle's late goal gave Everton the points, raising further his hopes of inclusion in Ramsey's World Cup squad.

For Roger Hunt, however, the career trajectory seemed to be heading in the opposite direction, as he now found himself out of favour with Liverpool as well as with England. There was a little life left in the old and much-maligned dog yet, though – coming on as substitute against Southampton with just fifteen minutes to go, Hunt scored twice to ensure that the visitors' grisly brutality went suitably unrewarded.

Match Of The Month
4 October 1969, Division One: Wolves 2 Everton 3

Leaders Everton arrived at Molineux to face a Wolves side which, despite the recent and still assumed to be temporary departure of Peter Knowles, was emerging as an impressive and highly watchable first division force.

However, it was clear from the early stages how far they would have to improve to compete with the very best, as Everton totally dominated with their crisp passing and wonderful teamwork. Jimmy Husband's pace enabled him to burst clear only for Frank Munro to bundle him over, and Joe Royle had no time for subtlety as he thumped home the penalty. A crafty goal from Johnny Morrissey, cutting inside and deceiving Phil Parkes with an early shot when the keeper and almost everyone else was expecting a cross, doubled the lead.

Just after the interval, Hugh Curran forced home Mike Bailey's free kick, but the mood on the terraces, already ugly enough to have produced several scuffles and arrests, soon took a turn for the worse when Derek Dougan talked himself into an early bath, abusing first the linesman and then the referee. The decision sparked further trouble from a crowd evidently in the mood for violence, and several more troublemakers were led away as Dougan, already with a suspended sentence hanging over him, was left to contemplate the prospect of a lengthy ban.

Everton looked to have eased their way home when Colin Harvey slotted in a third, but Wolves matched their supporters' fight with a penalty from Curran giving them belated but ultimately forlorn hope. It was, however, their fans who would make the following day's headlines, with referee Keith Walker for the second week running needing a police escort off the pitch at the end of the game.

Wolves: Parkes, Wilson, Parkin, Bailey, Holsgrove, Munro (Walker), McCalliog, O'Grady, Dougan, Curran, Wagstaffe.

Everton: West, Wright, Brown, Kendall, Labone, Harvey, Husband, Ball, Royle, Hurst, Morrissey.

Player Of The Month
Peter Bonetti (Chelsea)

Bonetti's Chelsea career began in 1960 and he almost immediately became their first-choice goalkeeper. His position was seldom threatened until the arrival of Alex Stepney in 1966, but just three months later Stepney had departed for Manchester United, with manager Tommy Docherty having decided that Bonetti was the superior keeper after all.

Bonetti's club performances remained consistent enough for him to feature regularly in England squads, and when Banks suffered a temporary loss of form it appeared as though Bonetti might establish himself as number one choice for the 1970 World Cup. However, Ramsey kept faith with Banks and Bonetti travelled to Mexico in his customary back-up role.

1969/70 saw Chelsea enjoy their best season for over a decade as they established themselves as one of England's finest sides, and Bonetti's performances and reliability were instrumental in their ascent. October saw him keep three clean sheets which earned his team five points, as well as keeping out Leeds in a 2-0 League Cup win. However, it was the fixture in which he did concede goals, a 2-2 draw against a Derby County side which largely dominated the match, that Bonetti produced his most impressive display.

Initially seeming to dive the wrong way, he recovered acrobatically to save Alan Hinton's drive and then arched backwards to tip over Roy McFarland's header. Slender and agile, such athleticism was Bonetti's distinguishing feature, and even if his saves sometimes appeared more spectacular than was strictly necessary, he was a reliable keeper and enormously popular with the fans.

Bonetti had been a non-playing member of the 1966 squad but made his full England debut against Denmark in the same year. He won occasional caps in the run-up to the 1970 World Cup, but his international career will forever be remembered for and defined by his role in England's defeat to West Germany in 1970 when, deputising for the stricken Banks, he failed to keep out Beckenbauer's innocuous shot from the edge of the area. The extent of his blame for the other two German goals is debatable, but the game marked the end of his seven-cap international career and left Bonetti with an unfortunate legacy. Prior to that fateful day in Leon, Bonetti had conceded just a single goal in his six previous England appearances.

His Chelsea career continued unabated, as he helped them to win the Cup Winners' Cup in 1971, going on to record 700 club appearances by the time he left the club in 1979, his tally of games second only to Ron Harris.

NOVEMBER 1969

You just couldn't keep Derby County out of the news. Their recent results may have disappointed, but they had become a magnet for journalists and other media types. When Liverpool came to the Baseball Ground, Eric Todd noted that more and more critics from farther afield had come to take a first-hand look, 'adding further to the cramp and congestion in the inadequate press box at the Baseball Ground'. And, Eric observed, they would be returning home wearing awestruck expressions after witnessing a demolition of the visitors, whose 4-0 defeat was their heaviest for over four years. Bill Shankly himself was certainly impressed, stating matter-of-factly that when Derby play well, they beat any side in the country. He did, typically, observe that Derby keeper Les Green had been just as busy as Tommy Lawrence, which Eric conceded may well have been true, before adding delightfully that 'the main difference was that Lawrence had more bending to do...'

The boot was very much on the other foot the following week as Clough's men went to Highbury and were routed 4-0 themselves. Coming immediately after a 5-1 walloping of Crystal Palace, Arsenal's sudden goal-craziness wasn't so much uncharacteristic as unbelievable. It was widely assumed that Derby had merely suffered an off-day, but when they returned to the capital two weeks later, they ostensibly suffered a similar fate, going down 3-0 to West Ham. This, though, was a very different game, described by several reporters as the best match they had seen all season. With Peters happily if temporarily returned to the fold, West Ham displayed the sparkling form they were always capable of and he struck twice to help his team to the win. Derby had also played some superb football and had little luck in front of goal, but this latest reverse was another reminder that they weren't quite the finished article.

England's first game of nine as they built towards Mexico took them to Amsterdam to face a Dutch side which, despite their failure to qualify, were building a reputation of a force in waiting. Bonetti took the place of the injured Banks and made several good saves in an encouraging display, and there was an impressive debut for Liverpool's Emlyn Hughes. Their narrow victory, secured by Bell's fierce drive late on, was well received amid acknowledgement that the Dutch were a rapidly improving team and would be regrettable absentees from the Mexico World Cup. And no absentee would be lamented more than Johan Cruyff, first bringing himself to the country's attention when Ajax humbled Liverpool three years earlier but now clearly developing into a major world talent.

One of the features of the game, as in England's summer tour, was the facility for each team to utilise two substitutes. Domestically, despite the abolition of the 'injured players only' rule, the use of substitutes had still been predominantly to replace injured players, and on the occasions where tactical changes had been made they had almost invariably been on a like-for-like basis. The concept of using a substitute to change the shape of a team had yet to take hold, largely because with just one per team allowed, the possibility of a later injury made it too risky. In Mexico, two substitutes would be permitted and, given the draining conditions, their effective use was expected to be a vital factor.

However, in a testing match, Ramsey waited until the eighty-fifth minute to make his one and only move, replacing Lee with Peter Thompson. Ramsey again stated that he hadn't seen the need to make changes for the sake of it, but some journalists were of the view that experimenting in these warm-up games would help his decision-making when it came to the real thing. But Sir Alf remained as aloof as ever, refusing to be drawn on this and other issues relating to the match. Ramsey's relationship with the press had always been difficult, but there were increasing concerns that his almost open contempt for foreigners would be a real handicap when England arrived in Mexico. *The Sunday Times* had already observed that on his travels he tended to be more Alf Garnett than Alf Ramsey.

Writing his opinion piece in *The Observer*, Hugh McIlvanney acknowledged that as a Scotsman, he himself was regarded as a foreigner by Ramsey, but that when it came to gaining access to the manager he wasn't the only journalist 'reduced to scrounging around like destitutes waiting for a handout'. Sympathies for Hugh might have been restricted by his unashamed gloating when Scotland beat England's nine fit men at Wembley in 1967, or the headline 'Ramsey machine robs Scotland' after England's fully deserved draw thwarted the hopes of 130,000 rabid Scots at Hampden a year later. Equally, however, it was clear that Ramsey neither understood nor cared about the importance of public relations. It would ultimately prove costly both to England and to Ramsey himself.

If Sir Alf wasn't too bothered about integrating with foreigners, then at least his captain was. Pictured wearing a sombrero and a Linguaphone headset, Bobby Moore revealed that he was taking Spanish lessons so that he would have a decent working knowledge of the language by the time he arrived in South America. It will sadly never be known if he had the foresight to rehearse appropriate words for certain set-piece situations. *At the jewellers…*

Manchester United hadn't previously paid much attention to the Football League Cup, but were now hardly in a position to pick and choose which pots to chase. No European football, and already out of realistic contention for league honours, the competition represented a great opportunity to reacquaint themselves with silverware. For their quarter-final replay against Burnley, they selected a full-strength side, naturally including George Best. Unfortunately, this unscheduled additional game clashed with Northern Ireland's vital World Cup qualifier in Russia, and United – with Matt Busby rather than Wilf McGuinness cast as the villain of the piece – were widely criticised for denying both the Irish and in particular Best, whose chances to perform on the biggest world stages were few and far between.

Inevitably, United won and Northern Ireland lost, further igniting the club versus country debate. One got the sense that the person least bothered about the issue was Best himself, whose carefree attitude either enchanted or appalled, depending on your point of view and more tellingly your generation. 'I get on very well with birds and I'm not one to fight against that… it just wouldn't be possible for me to live like a monk to suit the demands of football…I know I would be a far better player if I became as obsessed with the game as some fellows are…'

Suggestions of a full-scale revival at Old Trafford were given a reality check with a 4-0 drubbing at Maine Road, where Colin Bell's imperious display was the centrepiece of City's performance and made Bobby Charlton look rather like yesterday's man. Charlton wasn't ready to be put out to grass just yet, though – the following week, restored to a more advanced role, he buried two thunderous strikes past Pat Jennings to help United to a 3-1 win.

A savage burst of frost and snow brought the largest incidence of postponed November fixtures since the war. The game at Rochdale was one of the survivors, but it proved hardly worth bothering, as the referee abandoned the game after an hour. Rather than being subjected to abuse, the referee's decision was greeted by warm applause from a crowd desperate to get back to the comforting glow of their fireplaces. A similarly early curtailment seemed likely at Portman Road, where the referee took the players off the field, but after a twenty-minute delay whilst groundsmen meticulously restored the pitch markings, the players returned to the fray to allow Ipswich to complete a 1-0 victory. And what else did West Ham deserve if four of their players were effete enough to take the field wearing gloves? Excusable for Clyde Best perhaps, but Moore, Hurst and Peters? World Cup winners? Men of national and international repute? Whatever was the game coming to?

Whilst Everton were enjoying an unscheduled rest, their neighbours lost vital ground, as Arsenal inflicted their first home defeat of the season. Meanwhile, at a frosty Maine Road, Leeds sought not only to keep the pressure on their Merseyside rivals but also to record their first win at the ground for thirty-three years. A scrappy game saw Leeds go ahead with a freak deflection before City equalised with a hotly contested penalty. When an injury brought a protracted hold-up in play, Lee and Sprake indulged in a bit of penalty practice, with Lee firing all his efforts home, to the delight and amusement of the home fans. It would be Leeds who laughed last, however, as a superb last-minute header from Mick Jones, almost from the edge of the area, arrowed into the top corner of Corrigan's net to deliver a vital win for his side.

The same day saw Derby's derby end in disappointment, as Clough's men suffered a 2-0 reverse at home to Forest. By now, it was clear that all was not well at the Baseball Ground, and their ferociously driven manager hadn't been shy in expressing his concerns that his ambitions for the club were not matched in the boardroom. In Clough's view, his team was ready to compete for major honours but in order to lift trophies, further investment not only in playing resources but also in improvements to the stadium and the playing surface – the poorest in the division – would be necessary.

Newspapers were full of speculation that this dynamic young talent might be lured abroad, with Barcelona amongst others cited as a possible destination.

Match Of The Month
8 November 1969, Division One: Arsenal 4 Derby County 0

Arsenal's gradual progress under Bertie Mee had been interrupted by a twelve-match winless run which had left the team in the bottom half of the table, but a resounding 5-1 win at Crystal Palace raised hopes of a revival. Meanwhile Derby, who had suffered a few setbacks after their spectacular start to the season, had come back to their sparkling best with a 4-0 demolition of Liverpool, prompting Bill Shankly to profess that they could beat any side in the country.

Derby initially threatened to further extend their list of victims, cutting through a cautious Arsenal on several occasions but unable to capitalise on the openings. The game's turning point came when Terry Neill limped off with an injury; whilst it may have made Arsenal more vulnerable at the back, it also introduced Charlie George into the action.

George made an instant impact, sweeping home a twenty-yarder just after the interval following a fine flowing move. With David Court having moved back to replace Neill and accommodate George, Arsenal's attacks now had far greater invention and fluidity. Sammels intercepted a poor backpass to double their lead, before George again made a tellingly impressive contribution, sliding a beautiful through ball to George Graham. Graham's square ball gave Sammels a tap-in and put the result beyond doubt. George Armstrong added a late fourth, leaving Derby well beaten with Brian Clough admitting that his team had been 'outrun, outfought and outplayed'.

It was a reminder that Derby were still a work in progress and an indication that Arsenal, contrary to usual appearances, really were capable of playing creative, entertaining football, at least when Charlie George was on the pitch.

Arsenal: Barnett, Storey, McNab, Court, Neill (George), Simpson, Robertson, Sammels, Radford, Graham, Armstrong.

Derby: Green, Webster, Robson, Durban, McFarland, Mackay, McGovern, Carlin, O'Hare, Hector, Hinton.

Player Of The Month
Colin Bell (Manchester City)

Signed from second-division Bury in 1966, Bell had consistently excelled for City ever since their promotion later that year. He was voted the club's Player of the Year in their 1968 championship season and was a prominent influence in their triumphant FA Cup run the following season. Bell won his first full England cap in 1968 and became a regular in the squad thereafter. Still only twenty-three, he had improved consistently year by year and there seemed little that he couldn't do. Highly accomplished in every facet of the game, his skills were amplified by his extraordinary running power, which saw him feature regularly in both penalty areas during the course of a match.

This month saw him demonstrate the full range of his talents. In a typically difficult struggle against a dour Southampton side, it was Bell who made the difference with a magnificent strike, his thirty-yard drive arrowing into the top corner past the flailing Eric Martin. A week later, when United arrived for the derby, Bell was once again City's star man, his two goals the centrepiece of a dominant display in which he totally overshadowed Bobby Charlton, the man to whom he remained the understudy in Ramsey's England plans.

There were many who thought that Bell was already at the level to at least sit alongside, if not replace, Charlton as a regular starter, and he did his claims no harm with a fine display in the friendly in Amsterdam, his late strike seeing England to victory over the emerging Dutch side. As well as scoring three times over the two legs of City's Cup Winners' Cup tie against SK Lierse, Bell even had time to show nationwide TV viewers his prowess at indoor football, being voted player of the tournament in the *Daily Express* five-a-side championships as City comfortably took the trophy.

Having helped City win the League and Cup Winners' cups, Bell was a shoo-in for the Mexico squad but started only one game, the 1-0 win over the Czechs. He twice came on as a substitute to replace Bobby Charlton, the second occasion famously being during the 3-2 defeat to West Germany. Bell brought much-needed energy to a tiring England side, orchestrating a series of attacks which, but for some extraordinary refereeing, would have brought England the win they deserved.

After Mexico, Bell cemented himself into the England side, a regular starter for Ramsey, Mercer and Revie, and would have won far more than his forty-eight caps had it not been for a terrible knee injury in November 1975, cruelly coming at the time when he was producing his best form in an England shirt.

Prior to his injury, Bell's City career had continued to flourish and although the side were unable to reach the heights they had achieved in previous seasons, his performances and goal output remained highly impressive. His eventual return to first-team action more than two years after his injury provided one of Maine Road's most emotional days. It was clear, however, that Bell's mobility had been permanently impaired, and he was forced to retire in 1979. Widely regarded as City's finest ever player, Bell has a stand named after him at the Etihad Stadium.

DECEMBER 1969

The season's first Merseyside derby was more than just a domestic dispute – it would have a significant bearing on the league table as the halfway point approached. A frantic first half saw Ball try to win the game on his own, to the detriment of his team's performance. The match was decided within a few minutes of the restart. Emlyn Hughes' header put Liverpool ahead before

Sandy Brown created one of the most memorable moments in derby history by thundering a spectacular header into his own net. Liverpool's ultimate 3-0 win not only revived their own title chances, but also further enhanced Leeds' hopes of becoming the first side for eleven years to retain the crown.

The League Cup semi-final draw brought the two Manchester clubs together for a tussle which would be seen by over 126,000 spectators over the two games. In the first leg at Maine Road, United put in a far more spirited display than in the recent league encounter, and as the game moved towards injury time the teams were level at 1-1. Then Ian Ure snaked out a long leg to bring down Franny Lee as he stormed into the area, and Lee kept his nerve to bury the spot-kick, giving City a slight advantage to take to Old Trafford.

Meanwhile, meticulous as ever, Sir Alf brought together a squad of no fewer than thirty players for the friendly against Portugal, with the clear inference that here was his Mexico long-list. Those whose absences were most conspicuous were the Chelsea pair of Hollins and Osgood, together with Manchester City's Mike Summerbee. The feisty Osgood had already been quoted in print as describing himself as unsuitable for Ramsey's England, a surefire recipe for exclusion given the manager's distaste for mavericks and his sensitivity to criticism, however subtly implied. The players were all required to travel to London on the Monday before the game, at least giving them the chance to tune into Sunday evening's *Monty Python's Flying Circus* and enjoy the Dead Parrot sketch. One can easily envisage Bobby Charlton turning to brother Jack during a break in training and asking quizzically: 'Pining for the fjords…?' Or maybe not.

After their many outstanding displays in 1966, Portugal were welcome return visitors to Wembley, but the game was far from the glorious spectacle the teams had produced in that memorable semi-final. By the end of the game, dear old Hugh reckoned that 'the more neurotic England supporters were thinking of cancelling their round trips to Mexico and instead booking one-way tickets to Beachy Head'. As one of few, if any, football writers to repeatedly include suicide references in his reports, some of his loyal followers must have been to send letters to *The Observer*… 'For God's sake, please don't send this man to Highbury ever again…'

A terribly disappointing match was decided by Jack Charlton's header from a corner kick routine straight out of the Leeds United textbook, although England's margin of victory would have been greater but for Francis Lee's comedy penalty miss, as he sliced his shot into the lens of one of the startled photographers seated ten yards wide of the goal. Hughes and Bonetti retained their places and both again performed well, but sporadic jeering and slow-handclapping from the crowd indicated that this hadn't been one of the team's finer evenings.

It wasn't one of the crowd's better nights, either. The most disturbing feature of the proceedings was the disproportionately severe reaction to fouls committed by the opposition's two black players.

Such was the all-pervading influence of Alf Garnett and *Till Death Us Do Part* that the show formed the press's natural reference point for everything that would come to be known as political incorrectness. 'Johnny Speight had written the script for a large proportion of the crowd,' said *The Times*. Racial tensions within the UK continued to escalate, but the relatively small number of non-white players in league football had been regarded more as a novelty rather than something to draw a more sinister response. This was alarmingly different: the Wembley crowd had given a disturbing taste of the far worse things to come in the decades ahead.

If few black players featured on the pitch, the same was certainly true on the terraces, despite the burgeoning numbers of immigrants in urban areas. This was hardly surprising – the game wasn't in the blood of the Asian or West Indian communities and with football matches renowned for hooligans, the last thing immigrants already hassled enough in their daily lives needed was to be exposed to the guaranteed presence of gangs of yobs minded towards violence.

It was a big four days for Manchester United. A visit to Anfield would be followed by the second leg of their League Cup semi-final against City. Phase one could hardly have gone better, as a rampant United tore Liverpool apart, their 4-1 victory sealed by a Charlton drive which ranked amongst his most spectacular. Their confidence for the City game was further enhanced by the confirmation that Colin Bell would be an absentee, and the second full house of the tie confirmed that the League Cup had really arrived. A thrilling match ultimately produced a dramatic 2-2 draw, which saw City edge through to a Wembley date with West Bromwich Albion.

Everton's return match with Derby County again produced some beautiful football, even if Alan Ball's late goal was the only one of the day. Making his home debut was Keith Newton, whose transfer from second-division Blackburn made it easier for him to continue to catch Alf Ramsey's eye.

As Christmas approached, the range of football-related presents for younger football lovers was wider than it had ever been. And the scope for star players to make a few more bob from endorsing them was increasing accordingly. Alan Ball lent his support to Soccerama, claiming that he had never played a better game. And he probably hadn't, as this new board game gave its players the chance to simulate life as a manager, having to balance budgets, be astute in the transfer market, cope with injuries and suspensions, and pick teams to deal with specific opponents as they tried to lead their clubs to glory. Although primitive in comparison with what was to come, it was nevertheless the first step on the road towards the advent of the all-conquering Championship Manager over thirty years later.

When it came to endorsing products, George Best remained the main man, and one of the new lines to earn his approval was 'Stylo Matchmakers'. One of the variants of this new range of football boots contained the revolutionary concept of side lacing, allowing the boots to look uncommonly stylish as well as providing a totally smooth covering for the instep, meaning that those long-range powerdrives were much more likely to go exactly where you intended. Alas, the manufacturers had overlooked the fact that the concept of side lacing was revolutionary for a reason. It didn't work. The asymmetric design created enormous stress on the non-laced side, and youngsters thrilled to receive the super-trendy boots in their Christmas stockings were soon reduced to tears when they literally fell apart at the seams after being subjected to a few twists, turns and tackles.

The 1966 World Cup had been the first to be accompanied by dedicated souvenir merchandise, but the items made available scarcely scratched the surface of the ranges which were now becoming available. The emergence at clubs large and small of souvenir shops or 'boutiques' offered an ever-expanding range of items, with the previous staples of scarves, bob-hats, badges and rosettes being joined by cufflinks, key rings, wallets, ashtrays, ties, bedside lamps… and, crucially, replica kits for boys. And only for boys, it clearly being thought inconceivable that any self-respecting fully grown adult would entertain the idea of wearing a football shirt other than to play football in. It would be many years before replica shirts became man-size, but when they did…

After a day spent wearing and playing with their new acquisitions, Britain's youth could then settle down to the first *Morecambe and Wise Christmas Show*, as the BBC had promoted Eric and Ernie from their previous role as participants in *Christmas Night with the Stars* to having a show of their own. It proved to be quite a good decision.

Benny Hill got the ITV Christmas Day nod, relegating Tommy Cooper and Ken Dodd's Diddymen to the Boxing Day programme. Their Boxing Day schedule also incorporated a special edition of the strangely popular sitcom *Nearest and Dearest*. Hylda Baker and Jimmy Jewel were the stars of this pickle factory-themed abomination, but the show's main attraction was a character called Walter, a pitiful mute pensioner with chronic bladder problems. Walter's only contribution to the show was to respond to Hylda's 'Have you been, Walter?' by contorting his savagely wrinkled features into either an agonised grimace or a disturbingly grinning gurn, according to whether or not he had recently relieved himself. This is what passed for mainstream comedy in 1969. The *Monty Python* team were pushing at an open door.

Don Revie would by then have been wearing an agonised grimace of his own as Leeds had suffered their first defeat since August in a 2-1 Boxing Day reverse at Newcastle, although one doubts if anyone dared enquire 'Have you been, Don?' on the coach journey back to Yorkshire. His team at least had a chance of redemption just 24 hours later when they took on Everton at Elland Road, and two goals from Mick Jones were sufficient to outweigh Alan Whittle's late reply. The game was a tough, physical affair, with Everton more than Leeds' equals when it came to getting stuck in. A game of over forty-five fouls saw Everton commit seven of the first eight in a display which was more Academy of Violence than School of Science. The pressure at the top was evidently beginning to tell, and based on their performances in big cup games over recent seasons, pressure was something that Everton struggled to cope with.

Chelsea's impressive recent form saw them move up to third, though still well adrift of the top two and generally considered too flaky to be realistic contenders. They looked a decent bet for a cup run, with Peter Osgood showing his class more consistently than at any time since his recovery from a broken leg. He ended the year with a majestic display at Selhurst Park, scoring four times as a hapless Palace were brushed aside and left to contemplate the strong possibility of an instant return to the second division.

Match Of The Month
17 December 1969, League Cup Semi-Final Second Leg: Manchester United 2 Manchester City 2 (aggregate 3-4)

After Franny Lee's late penalty had given City a 2-1 first-leg lead, the teams came to Old Trafford with the tie perfectly poised. City's narrow advantage was balanced by the team changes from the first leg, with Bell now missing through injury whilst United welcomed back Denis Law. The tie's second crowd of over 63,000 settled down to an encounter which most agreed was too close to call.

City took an early lead when Bowyer forced the ball home after efforts by Young and Lee had been blocked, and it looked briefly as though they might have an easy ride. United's response was spirited, and when the unlikely figure of defender Paul Edwards made a surging run through the middle, he latched on to Crerand's pass and shinned a twenty-yarder which dipped viciously over Corrigan's dive to put his team back in the tie.

Law's return had been quiet, but with half an hour to go he produced a vintage piece of anticipation when Corrigan spilled Best's shot, whipping the ball almost off the keeper's toes to flash it into the net in front of a jubilant Stretford End. United briefly had the ascendancy as they sought to get in front for the first time in the tie, but the game was decided in City's favour by one of the strangest goals in derby history.

When City were awarded a free kick twenty yards out, referee Jim Finney signalled clearly that the kick was indirect. Lee, however, took a sprinter's run-up and drove the ball directly at goal, where Stepney instinctively dived to save. The keeper could only parry the shot out to the waiting Summerbee, who joyously swept the ball home to send City to Wembley. Debate raged for days afterwards. Shouldn't Stepney have let the ball pass harmlessly into the net? But what if the ball had taken a slight deflection en route? Was it a clever ploy by Lee or just a fluke?

Whatever, City had again overcome their rivals to further enhance their status as Manchester's top dogs although, within a month, United would exact a measure of revenge in the FA Cup.

Manchester United: Stepney, Edwards, Dunne, Stiles, Ure, Sadler, Morgan, Crerand, Charlton, Law, Best.

Manchester City: Corrigan, Book, Pardoe, Doyle, Booth, Oakes, Summerbee, Connor, Lee, Young, Bowyer.

Player Of The Month
Gordon Banks (Stoke City)

Banks signed for Leicester in 1959 after coming through the youth system at Chesterfield. He immediately established himself in the first team and won his first England cap under the recently appointed Alf Ramsey in 1963. By 1966, he was already regarded as one of the world's best goalkeepers and fully lived up to his reputation throughout the tournament as he helped England lift the trophy.

With a young Peter Shilton thirsting for first-team football, Banks was sold by Leicester in 1967, with manager Matt Gillies claiming that, at 29, 'his best years were behind him'. There were many managers who didn't agree but in an era when goalkeepers weren't valued as highly as outfield players, the asking price put off a number of clubs and it was left to Tony Waddington to sign him for Stoke for £52,000.

Banks' form for Stoke went through a couple of indifferent phases, and there were occasional suggestions that he could lose his England place, but he always quickly recovered his usual performance level and, as the countdown to Mexico began, had left no one in any doubt as to who was England's leading keeper.

December saw him in superb form for Stoke, conceding just a single goal in five games as his team ended the calendar year in sixth position. Their most notable result was a 1-0 win over Derby, in which Banks produced saves described as 'magical' by more than one reporter, but he also excelled in a 3-0 win over Sunderland and in securing a goalless draw at the Dell.

Banks cemented his worldwide reputation in Mexico primarily by making what is still regarded as the most famous save of all time from Pele's header, which instantly became an iconic moment in World Cup history. His legend was further enhanced by the game he *didn't* play in, as a generation of fans still steadfastly believe that England would never have lost to West Germany had Banks been in goal. Alf Ramsey clearly felt similarly, dolefully reflecting on Banks' sickness the day after the defeat. 'Why did it have to be *him*?'

Banks continued to perform at the highest level both for club and country, helping Stoke to win the League Cup in 1972 – still the only trophy won in their history – and remaining an automatic choice for England. However, he lost the sight of one eye in a car crash in October 1972 and was forced to retire from the game a year later.

Banks won 73 England caps and is regarded by many as the best goalkeeper not just of his own generation but of all time. Never flashy, his mastery of angles, anticipation and bravery were taken as read, and his capacity to produce saves which almost defied belief entertained and astonished spectators throughout his career.

JANUARY 1970

The FA Cup saw West Ham again founder against lower-league opposition, an occurrence so frequent that it barely merited the headline 'Cup Shock!' Their conquerors this time were second-division Middlesbrough. A more genuine surprise occurred at Bramall Lane, where Sheffield United edged past division one leaders Everton. Inspired by Alan Woodward, United tore into Everton from the start, twice striking the woodwork as West's goal was put under siege. When Everton broke away to win and convert a penalty, it appeared as though the Blades might have missed their chance, but Woodward set up goals for Gil Reece and Colin Addison to secure a famous victory.

Severe blow as it was for Everton, it served a positive purpose as, with no European football either, their sole focus would now be the championship. Meanwhile their main rivals, Leeds, looked set for another season of severe fixture congestion as they chased glory on three fronts, a situation exacerbated by the fact that the season had been shortened to allow preparation and acclimatisation time for the World Cup squad.

Other noteworthy cup performances saw Arsenal held at home by Blackpool and Spurs at Bradford City. The replays again illustrated the fact that underdogs usually only get one chance, as the big teams all made it through. The fourth-round draw threw up another Manchester derby but it was now another draw which was the main focus of attention, as the groups for Mexico were determined. And it was generally reckoned that England couldn't have had it much harder, drawing Brazil as well as two strong Eastern European teams in Romania and Czechoslovakia, both of whom had recently forced draws at Wembley.

Ramsey reiterated his confidence, pointing to England's excellence in the summer friendly at the Maracana, but not everyone agreed. Don Revie, hinting at the lack of patriotism which would manifest itself far more starkly a few years later, said: 'A South American side will probably win, and the best bet is Brazil.' Elsewhere, most English managers were at least publicly backing Ramsey's men to do it again.

Sir Alf's more immediate concern was the forthcoming visit of Holland, and he again named a thirty-man squad to participate in an extended 'get-together' prior to the game. Alan Oakes and Tommy Smith were the only two new names included whilst, despite his improved form, Peter Osgood continued to be ignored.

England's performance was such that the 75,000 at Wembley were moved to chant repeatedly 'What a load of rubbish!' interspersed with bouts of slow-handclapping. Debutants Mick Jones and Ian Storey-Moore acquitted themselves well, but the likes of Charlton, Bell, Lee and Peters were woefully out of form in a display which emphasised how important the missing Bobby Moore, Ball and Hurst were to Ramsey's plans. The Dutch, prompted by the ever more impressive Cruyff, were by far the better side, although they couldn't find a way past the reassuringly impressive Banks as the game ultimately drifted to a goalless draw.

Ramsey, as ever, gave little away. 'Frankly, it wasn't one of our better performances but there is no cause for alarm,' he said. The tabloids begged to differ, with The Man From *The Mirror* particularly affronted. 'Watching this disorganised, disorientated bunch of no-hopers sprawling pointlessly and patternlessly over the pitch was like being involved in some awful nightmare…England continued like some troupe of ninth-rate actors suddenly caught anguished in the spotlights of the Theatre Royal, Drury Lane, with their parts completely forgotten, looking desperately to some prompter in the wings.'

At least Ramsey had used both of his substitutes, bringing on Mullery for Lee and Hurst for Jones, but the changes failed to make any impact on opponents whose credentials had apparently diminished within two months from 'an emerging world force' to 'the part-timers of Holland, who could not even claim a place in the World Cup finals'. The imminent achievements of the Dutch at both national and club level perhaps make the result seem not quite so dreadful in retrospect, but with the World Cup just five months away, everyone bar Ramsey seemed to be getting rather fretful.

Ball's absence from the Holland game was due to a five-week suspension earned after accruing three cautions in the season's domestic games. The suspension, its severity increased as a result of his previous misdemeanours, extended to international matches, although he had at least been allowed to train with the international squad.

Another high-profile recipient of a suspension was George Best, who had been punished with a four-week ban for knocking the ball out of Jack Taylor's hands in the players' tunnel at the end of the League Cup tie at Maine Road. Charged with bringing the game into disrepute, the question was raised 'disrepute with whom?', since the offence took place out of sight of all but a very small handful of spectators. It was reckoned by Best's many apologists to be severe punishment for a small act of petulance, and his previous record – never sent off apart from in retaliation against Estudiantes after having been treated as a punchbag for eighty minutes – was hardly shocking.

Wolves' Derek Dougan was also well into his own six-week ban, and with so many of the game's major crowd-pulling stars again absent through the verdicts of the FA disciplinary commission, there were further claims of heavy-handedness. The FA remained defiant, reiterating the need to clean up the game, but there were an increasing number who felt that the severity of the sentences was the result of envious old men seeking to bring these popular young heroes down a peg or two. It was over two and a half years since Mick Jagger's imprisonment had provoked William Rees-Mogg's 'who breaks a butterfly on a wheel?' editorial piece in *The Times*, but the impression of authority delighting in crushing young creativity – especially when the victims were famous – still persisted.

The plethora of suspensions of star players also had a significant effect on gates. At Old Trafford, a United shorn of Best as well as the injured Law could draw only 42,000 for the visit of Arsenal, despite the visitors boasting their own new attraction. Conscious of their reputation as dour charisma-free grinders, Bertie Mee had made a most un-Arsenal-like signing with the £100,000 capture of Peter Marinello from Hibernian. It raised eyebrows, not least north of the border, where many observers felt that Peter Cormack and Pat Stanton would have been much better bets. Marinello's pretty-boy looks and flowing locks would certainly bring a few more photographers and female fans to Highbury, but would he be good enough to make a difference to the team?

He could hardly have got off to a better start, scoring within fifteen minutes of his debut, but United ultimately came back to secure the points, even if it was Marinello's face which would ultimately accompany the morning's match reports. There were parallels with Liverpool's signing of Alun Evans, another camera-friendly youngster whose contribution hadn't matched the column inches as he struggled to hold down a place in the side. Clubs were recognising the importance of glamour players in bringing fans through the gate, but how many of them could make a tangible contribution to the side?

Despite Best's continuing absence, there was never any question that United's next game would attract a full house. City's visit in the FA Cup gave United a chance to avenge their

League Cup defeat, as well as their recent league hammering at Maine Road, and they accepted it gratefully. City seldom threatened and once Willie Morgan had put the Reds ahead with a penalty just before half-time, the outcome was never in doubt. With a woeful Bell totally overshadowed by Bobby Charlton, a role reversal from the game at Maine Road two months earlier, City ended up well beaten, as two fine goals from Kidd cemented an emphatic victory for United.

With the round's most anticipated game proving surprisingly one-sided, it was left to others to provide real excitement. Third-division Watford accounted for Stoke City, and at Stamford Bridge Burnley came back from two down to earn a replay against a Chelsea side hotly tipped for cup success. Hollins and Osgood, the two Ramsey rejects, had put Chelsea into a strong position but Martin Dobson netted twice in the last ten minutes. And the watching John Arlott found support for the authority stance, observing that the FA's disciplinary drive had had a profound effect. He was delighted to report that the game had hardly featured a foul worthy of the name and that 'the pettinesses and gamesmanship which have made so much of our recent football distasteful were not to be seen'.

The replay, which saw the gates closed with over 32,000 inside Turf Moor, would have given Arlott cause to reconsider his conclusion. Burnley were well on top, before Chelsea responded with some brutal tackling, Harris and McCreadie to the fore. Houseman's equaliser with fifteen minutes to go knocked the stuffing out of the home side, and Chelsea romped away in extra time.

England's goal shortage at least gave hope to a number of strikers that a place on the Mexico flight could yet be secured. Jeff Astle did his cause no harm with a hat-trick against Crystal Palace and on the same day, Clarke, Osgood and Joe Royle all netted. Each had their advocates, but with the names of Lee and Hurst already inked in, how many back-up strikers would Alf require? One man certainly out of the reckoning was Jimmy Greaves, whose already minimal prospects were obliterated completely when, along with Alan Gilzean, Cyril Knowles and Joe Kinnear, he was castigated by Bill Nicholson for his performance in the FA Cup replay at Crystal Palace and unceremoniously dropped from the team. Even further from Ramsey's thoughts was Roger Hunt, whose long and record-breaking Liverpool career had come to an end with a transfer to second-division Bolton Wanderers.

The month saw the launch of yet another football weekly, *Striker,* the fourth new launch in less than two and a half years. The newcomer featured a column 'written' by Colin Bell who, despite his unassuming persona, was currently receiving plenty of publicity. He starred with Tony the Tiger in the Frosties TV ad, as well as featuring in the Granada sitcom series *The Dustbinmen*, where Graham Haberfield's Winston was cast as a Manchester City fanatic with a life-size cardboard cut-out of Colin in his bedroom. Slowly but surely, footballers continued to infiltrate other areas of popular culture.

Match Of The Month
10 January 1970, Division One: Chelsea 2 Leeds United 5

Chelsea's outstanding recent form had propelled them to third in the table, with some optimists even suggesting that they might be capable of reeling in the top two. However, when one of them, their increasingly bitter rivals from Leeds, arrived at Stamford Bridge, a severe reality check was delivered. As *The Observer* put it: 'Chelsea's delusions of grandeur disintegrated abruptly at Stamford Bridge yesterday…'

With Peter Bonetti absent with flu, Chelsea were forced to field Tommy Hughes in goal, and he didn't exactly cover himself in glory. Hughes had also had the bug but was deemed well enough to play, although later admitted to having been dosed up with antibiotics and even given a swig of brandy before the match. He played as though he had necked the whole bottle. 'It would take a holiday in Afghanistan to protect him from the aftermath of a performance that brought back memories of that other Scottish eccentric Frank Haffey,' *The Observer* added.

Feeble though Hughes had been, Leeds' supreme teamwork had in any event brutally exposed Chelsea's weaknesses and demonstrated how far they had to go before they could be considered serious title contenders. And yet, at half-time, things had looked so good…

Leeds went ahead when Clarke followed up Hughes' fumble but Chelsea responded impressively, being rewarded when Hollins powered through to lash a twenty-yarder past Sprake. And when Ian Hutchinson's prodigious long throw was headed down by Dempsey, Osgood swivelled to crash home a volley before turning to give Jack Charlton a verbal lashing. These two had plenty of history: Big Jack occasionally talked of his 'little black book' containing the names of opponents marked for retribution, and there was little doubt that Ossie was top of the list.

After Hutchinson squandered a great chance to extend Chelsea's lead, the game turned dramatically. Cooper's twenty-yarder was misjudged by Hughes to find the back of the net for the equaliser, before Giles slotted home a penalty awarded for handball. Bremner's close-range finish and Mick Jones' slick strike saw Leeds coast away towards the end, and their superiority was acknowledged by the crowd at the final whistle. It was a result which saw Leeds complete the double over Chelsea, but it wasn't quite the end of their rivalry for the season.

Chelsea: Hughes, Webb, McCreadie, Hollins, Dempsey, Harris, Cooke, Hudson, Osgood, Hutchinson, Houseman.

Leeds United: Sprake, Reaney, Cooper, Bremner, Charlton, Hunter, Lorimer, Clarke (Bates), Jones, Giles, Madeley.

Player Of The Month
Brian Kidd (Manchester United)

A product of their youth system, Kidd made his Manchester United debut in 1967 as an eighteen-year-old. He made an immediate impact in his first season by scoring seventeen goals, much the most famous of which was his header for United's third goal in the European Cup Final, a match played on his nineteenth birthday.

Kidd remained a regular but scored only one league goal in 1968/69 as the team struggled to recapture the form of previous years. Although there was no real improvement in results in the first half of the following season, Kidd had at least rediscovered his touch in front of goal. By the time January came, United's only hope of silverware was the FA Cup and, after edging past Ipswich Town, they were drawn to face Manchester City in the fourth round.

City had just beaten United in the League Cup semi-final as well as thrashing them in a recent league meeting, but this time it was United's turn to prevail. Without Best and Law, Kidd led their attack superbly and was rewarded with two tremendous goals, the second and United's third particularly memorable as he sprinted clear from the halfway line before lobbing the ball over Ken Mulhearn. It was the perfect occasion for Kidd to excel because, as well as restoring the footballing balance in Manchester, the game was witnessed by Sir Alf Ramsey.

Two days later, Leeds came to Old Trafford and Kidd was again outstanding, moving *The Guardian* to comment that 'Leeds had no one to compare with Kidd' and that United could do worse than build future sides around him. Kidd's performance was rewarded when his twenty-five-yard drive flew past Harvey to earn United a point from an unusually open 2-2 draw.

Ramsey duly included Kidd in the England squad for the home internationals in April, and after having earned eight under-23 caps, Kidd made his full debut against Northern Ireland. He travelled to South America as part of the twenty-eight-man party, winning a second cap in the warm-up game against Ecuador, but was one of the six players discarded before the tournament began. He would never be called up for England again.

Kidd remained with United until 1974, but with the team deteriorating he struggled to fulfil the promise of his early years. He was transferred to Arsenal, where he briefly rediscovered his scoring form, before moving to Manchester City two years later. His spell at City saw him form a productive partnership with Joe Royle, which saw Kidd's strike rate reach the highest level of his career as City narrowly failed to win the first division title.

Kidd's later career saw him cement a unique place in Manchester football history. Having played and scored for both sides in Manchester derbies, he went on to be part of the coaching staff at both clubs, in each case throughout a period where they won all three domestic honours.

FEBRUARY 1970

Something never previously seen in English football was tournament sponsorship, but now news came that agreement had been reached for the introduction of the Watney Cup, to be played before the start of the new season. The tournament would feature the two top-scoring teams from each division (other than those who had won championships, promotion or qualified for Europe) and each club would receive £4,000, with the FA and the Football League pocketing £25,000 apiece. An essential part of the agreement was that the games would feature on *Match Of The Day*, ensuring that the viewing public would be reminded of the dubious virtues of Watney's Red Barrel.

George Best's preferred tipple was doubtless rather more exotic, and whilst his enforced lay-off probably allowed him to indulge a little more than usual, he wasn't short of other things to keep him occupied. He was reckoned by now to have put his name to no fewer than eighty-seven different products, predominantly football- and fashion-related. He was also the go-to footballer for the promotion of hearty breakfasts in TV ads and, having previously savoured the delights of Cookstown sausages on screen, he now promoted the virtues of eggs, claiming in the not desperately convincing 'E for B and Georgie Best' campaign that he played much better football if he had eaten a plateful of eggs for breakfast.

George also found his way into scenarios which were normally the preserve of heart-throb actors, with the Fore aftershave advert seeing him pursued by an admiring bevy of beauties without even having to speak.

The world was also evidently eager to read what George had to say on life on and off the pitch. Apart from his 1,500 words in every edition of Jimmy Hill's *Football Weekly*, he had a regular column in the *News Of The World*, and the newly relaunched *Sun* came replete with a George Best page – 'today, next week and every week.' This was stardom of a kind never previously seen in sport.

The FA Cup fifth round took place only a fortnight after the fourth, reflecting the need to cram in the games so that the season could finish a couple of weeks earlier than usual. After his month on the sidelines, Best's comeback took place at Northampton. United's improved recent form had caused some to suggest that the team played better without his individualistic skills but, on a mudbath of a pitch so often the platform for giant-killings, Best reminded everyone what they had been missing by scoring six times in a mesmerising display. The following week saw the Egg Marketing Board report significantly increased sales.

United were joined in the quarter-finals by Chelsea, who thrashed Palace at Selhurst for the second time in two months and Leeds, who beat Mansfield. Liverpool were held at home by Leicester but produced a fine display to see off last season's finalists in the replay, on a rare night of joy for Alun Evans, who swept in both goals. Shankly was typically bullish after the game, claiming that 'the team had the look of cup winners about them'. The day's only surprise came with Derby's defeat at QPR, capping a difficult period for Clough's side, who were struggling to impose their fluent passing game on the heavier pitches.

Everton were also suffering in the winter mud as they showed few signs of benefitting from their relatively gentle fixture schedule. Their home game with Arsenal – which they had requested not to be televised due to concerns about overexposure – was another example. They fell behind to a goal from Charlie George only for their own new discovery, Alan Whittle, to hook in an equaliser. Radford restored Arsenal's lead but Whittle again equalised, cementing his position as an increasingly important member of the side and giving Everton a point they hardly deserved. For Arsenal, Marinello's impressive performance indicated that his signing might bring more tangible benefits than many had predicted. Everton, though, seemed to have lost their early-season authority and the return of Ball from suspension was eagerly awaited.

Leeds were now clear title favourites, but were unable to take full advantage of Everton's latest blip, themselves being held at White Hart Lane by a Spurs side still without Greaves, Gilzean, Knowles and Kinnear after the debacle at Crystal Palace. The four of them were instead to be found down the road, playing against Arsenal reserves in a Football Combination game at Highbury. Greaves' main contribution was to be booked for disputing a penalty decision as their team fell to a 2-0 defeat in front of over 12,000 spectators curious to witness their rivals' fallen idols as well as their own promising youngsters, most notably centre-forward Ray Kennedy. Kennedy and team-mate Eddie Kelly were soon rewarded with first-team debuts, and both scored in Arsenal's 3-1 win against Sunderland.

All too soon it was back to the FA Cup, with the tie of the sixth round expected to be at Loftus Road, where Chelsea were the visitors. A match which fully lived up to expectations saw Peter Osgood's hat-trick propel his team to a 4-2 win. Liverpool, however, had continued to give the appearance of a team in transition, and the ultimate indication that major surgery was required came with a dismal defeat at Watford, a side in a desperate struggle to avoid relegation to division three. Barry Endean's header delivered Watford's first ever cup semi-final appearance, as a defensive Liverpool set out their stall for a draw from the outset. Much more had been expected from the team, but where was the real star quality? Emlyn Hughes had injected energy and fire into the midfield, but Alun Evans continued to misfire and there was an ageing, past-their-best feel to much of the squad, with the likes of Yeats, Lawrence, Thompson, Callaghan, Hunt and St John struggling to recapture the glories of old.

Leeds and Manchester United also progressed, and found themselves pitted against each other in the semi-final draw. Chelsea's delight at being handed what looked a relatively straightforward passage to Wembley was enhanced when Alf Ramsey announced his team to face Belgium in Brussels two days later. At last, Peter Osgood would be given his chance.

Alan Ball's suspension was over, and he was instantly restored to the side against opposition which had also qualified for Mexico. And it was Ball who contributed most to what was England's best display of the season thus far, scoring twice in a highly impressive team performance. Conditions could hardly have been further removed from what they would face in Mexico, with much of the game being played in a snowstorm. However, it was a hugely encouraging night, with debutant Osgood playing a full part and being instrumental in setting up the first goal. Sir Alf himself expressed his view that 'Osgood had had a very good game' and returned home to rather more friendly headlines than of late.

Ramsey would have had mixed feelings on the news coming back from Brazil, where the Romanians, now known to be England's first opponents in Mexico, had just completed a very impressive tour. Their captain, Mircea Lucescu, had glad tidings about the form and shape of the Brazilians. 'Brazil,' he said, 'cannot win in Mexico. They have no chance. They play the old football, the football of the fifties. The tactical organisation and modern thinking of the European teams will leave them behind in Mexico. The players play to the crowd, for their own self-promotion. It is so different from the way England play. Their team is a combined, organised unit. I think England will win the World Cup.'

Brazil boss Saldanha was unconcerned by Lucescu's comments. 'The Europeans are not so perfect and we are not so terrible. Lucescu says that it is too late for me to change the way we play. But I won't even try. Why try to change the national character?' Once more, the prospect of a contest between European efficiency and South American flair and unpredictability was starting to whet appetites and, following their elimination by Peru, at least there would be no Argentinian brutality for England to counter.

A clear sign that Brian Clough had won the day with his demands for Derby to further upgrade in order to compete with the best came with the £110,000 signing of Terry Hennessey from neighbours Forest. Clough was at pains to point out that the signing in no way indicated that thirty-five-year-old Dave Mackay's first-team lifespan would be limited – rather, he committed to build a team around him, so that his tactical nous and leadership qualities would continue to benefit his colleagues. 'When Terry signs for us, Dave will be able to go on easily for another five years,' Clough said. It seemed just another of an ever-expanding portfolio of Cloughisms, but when Derby went to Anfield, Hennessey slotted in seamlessly alongside Mackay. In a superb team performance, Mackay was inspirational and Hennessey scored his first goal for the club. Shankly had immediately recognised the need to reinvigorate a team which so recently had had 'the look of cup winners about them', with Lawrence, Yeats and St John all omitted from the side which lost at Watford. Goalkeeper Ray Clemence was the most notable newcomer.

Match Of The Month
21 February 1970, FA Cup Fifth Round: QPR 2 Chelsea 4

Much the most attractive tie in the last sixteen was the West London derby between QPR and Chelsea. Billed as a clash of the great London entertainers – Rodney Marsh and Peter Osgood – there was also great interest in the precocious eighteen-year-old Alan Hudson, and Sir Alf took the opportunity to run the rule over the three of them.

With Loftus Road almost dangerously rammed to the gills, it looked a difficult assignment for Chelsea, especially when the game's first attack ended with Bonetti making a brilliant save to deny Barry Bridges. However, two goals in the first eight minutes removed any apprehension the visitors may have had, as Webb and Osgood put them firmly in control. When Venables slotted home a penalty to bring Rangers briefly back into the game – the kick retaken as Bonetti had been deemed to have moved too soon in saving the first effort – fighting broke out behind the goal and tempers frayed on the pitch, with Osgood displaying the less appealing side of his nature with a vicious tackle on Dave Clement. Osgood's caution, his fourth of the season, would give the FA's disciplinary commission further opportunity to flex its muscles, but he put that to the back of his mind by pouncing on Alan Kelly's fumble to restore the two-goal advantage.

Marsh, well shackled until now, then produced a moment of class and improvisation by putting Bridges through to cut the deficit, but the final word belonged to Osgood, whose delightful turn and finish completed his hat-trick and put Chelsea back in the clear. This time they stayed there, and the main question on everyone's lips, apart from who Chelsea would be drawn against in the semis, was whether Osgood had impressed Sir Alf sufficiently to force his way into the World Cup plans.

QPR: Kelly, Clement, Gillard, Watson, Mobley, Hazell, Bridges, Venables, Leach, Marsh, Ferguson.

Chelsea: Bonetti, Webb, McCreadie, Hollins, Dempsey, Harris, Cooke, Hudson, Osgood, Hutchinson, Houseman.

Player Of The Month
Martin Chivers (Tottenham)

Chivers made his Southampton debut in 1962 at seventeen years of age, almost immediately becoming a regular starter and prolific scorer. In 1965/66, his haul of thirty goals was instrumental in Southampton winning promotion, and the following season he quickly struck up a highly productive partnership with the newly signed Ron Davies. It was, however, Davies who got most of the goals and the headlines, and after a couple of years Chivers sought a transfer.

Spurs paid a record £125,000 to bring him to White Hart Lane, but with Greaves and Gilzean still close to their pomp,

Chivers struggled to make a real impact. However, after Bill Nicholson reacted angrily to his team's dismal FA Cup exit at Crystal Palace, the omission of the two strikers saw Chivers established as Spurs' main goal threat.

He took his opportunity with aplomb, two superb goals earning his team a point in an exciting game at Molineux before an outstanding performance saw him take all the headlines after Spurs' 1-1 draw with Leeds. His play was 'a revelation and a constant threat', according to *The Observer*, as Chivers frequently outmanoeuvred Jack Charlton to create openings for himself and his team-mates. Chivers was unfortunate to find Gary Sprake on one of his good days, and had to be content with forcing Terry Cooper to prod into his own goal. After another dominant display helped Spurs to a 1-0 win over Stoke, their first win in seven, Chivers was soon back on the scoresheet, his clean finish giving his team the points away at Newcastle.

The following season saw Chivers blossom into one of English football's finest strikers as he bagged thirty-four goals, including the two which won the League Cup Final. Spurs also finished third in the league and Chivers' outstanding form was rewarded with a first England call-up, for the game in Malta in February 1971. For the next two years, he was an England regular and achieved an impressive strike rate of thirteen goals in twenty-four appearances.

Back at Spurs, Chivers' form improved further still, with the 1971/72 season producing forty-four goals. Once again he showed himself to be a player for the big occasion, netting twice against Wolves in the UEFA Cup Final as Spurs brought home more silverware. Another League Cup winner's medal followed the next season as he added a further thirty-three goals to his career tally. Chivers had one more fruitful season with Spurs before the goals began to dry up as the team started to struggle, and he left in 1976 to try his luck in Switzerland. His record at Spurs – 174 goals in 367 appearances – stands comparison with all bar Jimmy Greaves and for two or three years he was the most feared and prolific striker in England.

MARCH 1970

Manchester City completed a three-year clean sweep of domestic honours when they finally overcame West Brom to win the League Cup, as the sides produced a thrilling spectacle on the worst surface ever seen for a football match at Wembley. In equally appalling conditions, Liverpool and Leeds played out a goalless draw at Anfield for a second successive year. Last time, it confirmed Leeds as champions; now, it meant that Everton, away winners for the first time in almost three months as they prevailed at Burnley, were back in pole position in a two-horse race, a point behind the champions with a game in hand. That game was a thrice-rearranged fixture at Tottenham four days later and, on a pudding of a pitch, Alan Whittle made yet another crucial contribution by firing an angled drive past Jennings to score the game's only goal and put Everton back on top.

White Hart Lane was also the venue for Chelsea's FA Cup semi-final against Watford and the pitch, if anything, looked even worse, allowing romantics to dream that the levelling effect would enhance Watford's chances of reaching Wembley. When they equalised Webb's early goal, there was a brief spell of hope before Chelsea's greater quality crushed their aspirations. Three goals in six minutes ended the tie as a contest, and Chelsea's 5-1 margin was the most decisive semi-final victory since the war.

At Hillsborough, no one expected anything other than a tight struggle between Leeds and Manchester United, and whilst the tie did indeed end goalless, it was a high-quality match with excitement at both ends. Although United were a team in decline, their star names were still capable of lifting them to occasional heights and, in what would prove to be their last serious tilt at silverware for six years, they took the game to their initially very cautious opponents. Leeds, however, became the dominant force as the match went on, and most observers concluded that the outcome was a fair one. A replay, however, was hardly ideal for Revie's team given their other commitments, and the news that Everton had completed a four-day double over Tottenham to extend their lead at the top made their task look even harder.

But Leeds knew nothing other than to plough on regardless. They saw off Standard Liege to reach the European Cup semi-finals, before winning at Molineux to keep within sight of Everton. Two days later, they took to the field at Villa Park for their replay with Manchester United. A superb match produced no goals in its 120 minutes but was of such quality that both teams received a standing ovation at its conclusion. Three days later, the teams reconvened at Burnden Park and at last produced a goal, with Billy Bremner's early effort proving sufficient to take Leeds back to Wembley.

It would, however, prove to be a Pyrrhic victory. Two additional gruelling matches had been crammed into an already heavily-crowded schedule and, with no scope for extending the league season, Leeds were left with more fixtures than anyone could reasonably be expected to cope with. Two days after finally reaching Wembley, injuries and exhaustion forced Revie to put out a severely weakened side for the league game against Southampton. It looked as though Leeds would get away with it until their energy drained away late in the game, when two own goals and a penalty saw Southampton take what were crucial points at both ends of the table.

There was consternation from Bert Head, manager of Southampton's relegation rivals Crystal Palace, but Revie insisted that he had acted on the advice of the club doctor. The physical demands of the cup semi-finals had put players at risk of injury and five of them had been rested. Even Leeds' most severe detractors would have had to concede that their schedule over the fifteen-day period was unmanageable. Saturday, Monday, Thursday, Saturday, Monday, Wednesday, Thursday, Saturday. Three of the matches were cup semi-finals and the rest of them potentially vital fixtures in the battle for the championship.

Two days after the defeat to Southampton, Leeds were faced with a trip to the Baseball Ground and Revie made the decision to sacrifice the league title. If the FA then saw fit to fine him, then so be it. His team of reserves were beaten 4-1, at least allowing the first-teamers to get a couple more days' rest before the first leg of their European Cup semi-final against Celtic.

Leeds' two defeats effectively handed the title to an Everton side that, with no European football and an early FA Cup exit, would end up playing sixteen fewer matches than their rivals over the course of the season. The formalities were almost completed with Everton's 5-2 win over Chelsea, mirroring Leeds' result some two months earlier. Not entirely coincidentally, Tommy Hughes was in goal for Chelsea and his catastrophic performance was again a major factor in the result.

The difficult relationships which Martin Peters and Jimmy Greaves had endured with their respective managers at last reached a conclusion. In a simple yet elegant solution, they swapped clubs in one of the most eye-catching transfers of the era. West Ham received £150,000 plus a striker valued at £50,000, which meant that Peters' £200,000 valuation saw him become the most expensive British footballer. Peters quickly scored on his debut against Coventry but, although he was the makeweight in the deal, there was greater focus on Greaves. The striker had a proud record to maintain – he had always scored on his debut at all levels for club and country – and as he stepped out at Maine Road in West Ham's claret and blue, few would have bet against him extending the sequence against a Manchester City side who had long since given up on the league in order to concentrate on cup glory.

Greaves didn't disappoint, needing only ten minutes to open his Hammers account with a typically calm finish, and he added a second for good measure. But the day will always be remembered for West Ham's fourth goal, scored by Ronnie Boyce with a forty-five-yard volley into an empty net as Joe Corrigan, having cleared the ball from the corner of the penalty area, ambled obliviously back towards the goalmouth. It was Corrigan's misfortune that the game had been selected for *Match Of The Day* coverage, and by his own admission it would take him some time to recover from the ridicule which subsequently came his way. Privately, though, he could see the funny side almost immediately, confiding to Geoff Hurst after the game: 'I was walking back when I suddenly noticed this ball in the back of the net. I thought "bloody hell, how come there are two balls on the pitch…?"'

At the bottom, the apparently doomed Crystal Palace suddenly awakened with victory at home to Southampton followed by a win at Manchester City, where Gerry Queen – hitherto most notable as the subject of the glorious 'Queen in brawl at Palace' headline – scored the only goal against a side with minds patently elsewhere.

The final chance for fringe players to catch Sir Alf's eye before the announcement of his World Cup squad was a game for the Football League against the Scottish League at Coventry. Players such as Emlyn Hughes, Brian Kidd, Jeff Astle, Ralph Coates and Roy McFarland were included, and Astle in particular impressed with two headed goals. Ralph Coates gave a typically energetic and enthusiastic display, but Brian Kidd's hopes took a blow when injury curtailed his evening just after half-time. He had played well until then, but had he done enough?

The answer came a few days later, when Ramsey revealed his squad for Mexico, initially comprising twenty-eight players, six of whom would be jettisoned once the tournament began. The biggest surprise was the inclusion of Kidd in preference to Mick Jones and Joe Royle. He had indeed done enough. There was also a space for Nobby Stiles, only recently recovered from injury but clearly regarded by Ramsey as an inspirational figure in the party, with his inclusion also sending a message to prospective opponents that England would be as robust as ever.

Match Of The Month
7 March 1970, League Cup Final: Manchester City 2 West Brom 1

Prior to the final, much of the attention had focused on the Wembley pitch, with heavy snow through the week rendering an already substandard surface close to unplayable. Two hundred schoolboys were drafted in to help to clear the playing area, and the FA Cup winners of the two previous seasons faced a stern challenge to produce a spectacle fit for a full house.

It was a challenge that both teams rose to with aplomb. West Brom made the perfect start, profiting from Corrigan's misjudgement to take the lead through the head of Astle. But City, having endured a severely delayed flight back from their midweek European game in Portugal, slowly got into gear and pressed Albion back for the remainder of the half.

The game's key moment came early in the second half when City, continuing to seek the equaliser, were caught on the break and Colin Suggett raced through. Later admitting he thought he would be flagged offside, Suggett took insufficient care with his finish, casually sliding the ball wide of goal. The linesman's flag had stayed firmly by his side.

Eventually, City's pressure told, with Mike Doyle firing home a low drive on the hour. Now, as legs tired on the cloying surface, it was time for Francis Lee to take centre stage. The last twelve months had seen him progress spectacularly to become England's most impressive striker, and here he played the match of his life, his relentless drive and energy continually forcing West Brom on to the back foot. Eventually, Lee and City got what they deserved, when Lee's beautifully manoeuvred cross was flicked on by Bell for Glyn Pardoe to turn home the extra-time winner.

Manchester City: Corrigan, Book, Mann, Doyle, Booth, Oakes, Heslop, Bell, Summerbee, Lee, Pardoe.

West Brom: Osborne, Fraser, Wilson, Brown, Talbut, Kaye, Cantello, Suggett, Astle, Hartford, Hope.

Player Of The Month
Bobby Moore (West Ham)

Bobby Moore's place in English football history is secure for all time, not just as captain of the World Cup-winning team but as the most accomplished and assured defender the country has ever produced.

After making his West Ham debut at seventeen in 1958, Moore soon earned international honours with the under-23 team before making his full debut in 1962. He immediately became a regular, becoming permanent captain in 1964, a year when he also captained West Ham to their FA Cup win. They followed up with the Cup Winners' Cup in 1965, and Moore's Wembley treble as captain was completed with the 1966 World Cup. Moore's ever-constructive use of the ball was illustrated by the two assists he provided for Geoff Hurst in the final.

At club level, West Ham routinely alternated between unmatchable brilliance and shambolic disorganisation, but were a football purist's delight. Renowned for their attacking flair and invention, it was left to Moore to marshal a frequently exposed defence as the team's style inevitably saw them produce goal-mouth action at both ends. Purple patches and disastrous winless runs were equally common and 1969/70 was a perfect example.

March began miserably with hammerings at Newcastle and Derby, and the Hammers were at serious risk of relegation. However, the month's remaining five games saw them concede just one goal as their accumulation of eight points ensured their safety. Moore, who so often seemed to be their only defender of any competence, inspired his team throughout the run with a series of polished displays.

A point against fellow relegation strugglers Ipswich was a disappointing result, but Moore at least ensured that West Ham's goal was never seriously threatened. Jimmy Greaves' arrival was celebrated with a stunning 5-1 win at Manchester City, before a vital goalless draw at Crystal Palace ensured that West Ham kept a margin above the drop zone. With Billy Bonds proving to be an unusually forceful ally, Moore saved his finest performance for the visit of Liverpool, and Pat Holland's goal secured the points. Their safety now fully secured, they breezed past Wolves with Moore frequently moving forward to prompt attacks in their 3-0 win.

Moore's England career continued to flourish, his performances seldom less than outstanding. Seemingly undeterred by the Bogota bracelet affair, Moore was at his imperious best throughout the Mexico World Cup, most notably in the classic match against Brazil. He continued to captain the side for the next three years, winning his 108th and final cap against Italy in 1973.

Described by many – including Pele, Franz Beckenbauer and Alex Ferguson – as the best defender they ever saw or played against, Moore's legendary status in the English game is now quite rightly marked by a statue outside Wembley Stadium.

APRIL 1970

The month began full of potential for records to be set. English clubs had qualified for the semi-finals of all three European competitions, and were all highly fancied to triumph. No country had ever before accomplished a clean sweep. Much the most anticipated tie was Leeds' European Cup clash with Celtic, predictably dubbed the Battle of Britain, but Connelly's goal gave the Scots a 1-0 win at Elland Road and meant that realistic hopes of English success rested in the other competitions. Manchester City's 1-0 reverse at Schalke left their Cup Winners' Cup tie finely balanced, but Arsenal took a commanding lead against Fairs Cup favourites Ajax, with a young Charlie George producing a fabulous performance, scoring twice in a 3-0 win at Highbury.

By now, Leeds had given up on the title but their merciless schedule beggared belief. Over the course of eight days, they had been obliged to play five games, with the centrepiece being the European Cup semi-final. Revie's team had built up a well of nationwide contempt over the previous five years, but even those who had continually damned them in the press couldn't help but feel an element of sympathy for their plight.

Everton duly wrapped up the title without fuss, beating West Brom 2-0 on the same night that Leeds had gone down to first-leg defeat against Celtic. Everton had needed only a point but once Alan Whittle had scored for the sixth successive match to put them ahead, the outcome was never in doubt. The league trophy was presented immediately after the game and paraded around the ground on a long, slow, joyous lap of honour.

Even though their main rivals had been severely handicapped, Everton's triumph was still an immensely worthy one, with this being their seventh win in succession. After struggling on the heavy pitches around the turn of the year, they had remained unbeaten since mid-January. They finished the season with sixty-six points, a tally which Leeds could only have equalled had they won every single one of their matches since their fixture congestion started to become an issue. Their midfield trio of Ball, Kendall and Harvey had allowed them to dominate games, Joe Royle now looked as though he would more than fulfil his initial promise and their find of the season, Alan Whittle, had not only contributed eleven goals but delivered many of them at critical times in crucial matches – four coming in 1-0 wins.

Derby County had also finished the season as they started it – in spectacular fashion. They recorded eight wins and four draws in their final twelve games to finish fourth in their first season back in the top flight, but their achievements were not to be rewarded with European football. Found guilty of 'gross administrative negligence', they were fined £10,000 and banned from European competition for a season. Derby's crimes included paying Dave Mackay to write articles in the club programme at £20 a time as well as failing to lodge certain players' contracts with the FA.

With the league settled, the FA Cup Final took centre stage and, with two finalists who openly despised each other, the level of anticipation was even higher than usual. The game was one of the most dramatic in Wembley history as Leeds, benefitting from the luxury of a full seven days' rest since their previous fixture, put in their best performance for weeks. They had much the better of the match, with Eddie Gray – who the previous week had scored a ridiculous goal against Burnley, dribbling past six men before firing home – running riot against David Webb. On a pitch largely bereft of grass, Jack Charlton's header crawled under McCreadie's boot before Peter Houseman's gentle shot provoked a trademark howler from Gary Sprake, gifting Chelsea an equaliser. Mick Jones looked to have settled matters as both teams tired, only for Ian Hutchinson's near-post header to restore parity almost immediately.

Extra time came and went without further score and at least there was no repeat of last year's scenes at the final whistle where, according to the *Playfair Football Annual*, the aftermath of the final had seen 'unseemly behaviour of gangs of television men fighting for on-the-field interviews'. The warring parties had been forced to accept a new code of conduct under which 'interviews will probably be mutual, with alternate questions for the two reporters'. And this indeed is how it turned out, after which both teams staggered round the pitch on a lap of honour. Leeds then went off to rest their limbs ahead of their visit to Hampden Park four days later.

They duly roused themselves for one final effort against Celtic, and Bremner's stunning goal saw them reach half-time with the aggregate scores level. Ultimately, however, the home side, roared on by a crowd of more than 136,000, dominated the second half, scoring twice within three minutes to leave Leeds with just the FA Cup Final replay to look forward to. Don Revie commendably made no excuses, conceding that Celtic had thoroughly deserved to go through, and several Leeds players would later state that Celtic were the finest side Leeds came up against in all their European campaigns.

The other English representatives fared rather better, with Manchester City producing their finest performance of the season – and, to some observers, their finest performance of the whole Mercer/Allison era – in demolishing Schalke 5-1. Schalke manager Rudi Gutendorf was moved to observe that his side had been thrashed by a team playing 'football from another planet'. Arsenal also came through in style against Ajax, restricting their opponents to just one goal in Amsterdam for a comfortable and highly impressive aggregate win against a side which would go on to win the European Cup in each of the next three seasons.

It had been intended that the home internationals would take place once the players' club commitments had all been fulfilled, but the unscheduled cup final replay plus European successes meant that those from Leeds, Chelsea, Arsenal and Manchester City still had crucial games to play. Don Revie asked Ramsey to allow Leeds players to be excused from duty for all three fixtures, and Joe Mercer followed by requesting that Bell and Lee shouldn't play in the Scotland game, four days before their final. Any intention Ramsey had of fielding his first choice XIs had been frustrated, but at least there would be more warm-up games before the team got to Mexico.

Frustration was even more in evidence after the first game, a 1-1 draw in Cardiff, where a poor display was salvaged only by a spectacular late equaliser from Francis Lee. The next game, at Wembley against Northern Ireland, was played out in a celebratory atmosphere, marking the 100th cap for Bobby Charlton, who duly got on the scoresheet in England's 3-1 win. The band played 'Congratulations', Charlton shed a tear as he led the team out and there were debuts for Coates and Kidd as Sir Alf again sought to assess some of his fringe players.

The sequence was completed by a 0-0 draw at Hampden, where Ramsey gave a surprising start to Peter Thompson, and noted that his team 'did not give as much as I expected'. In reality, there had been little intensity in any of the three performances, reinforcing the impression that these games had been almost an inconvenience. The shortening of the season and European commitments meant that players had crammed in matches with even shorter recuperation periods than normal, and would have been better served with a couple of weeks' rest rather than facing a trio of games against sides far more committed than they themselves would be.

The cup final replay – the first since 1912 – took place at Old Trafford, where a spectacularly savage encounter went to extra time before Chelsea ultimately triumphed. Leeds' season, so recently looking as though it could bring unprecedented success, had ended in bitter failure and exhaustion. On the same night, unseen by UK viewers other than for brief goal highlights at half and full time, Manchester City took their second trophy of the season by beating Gornik Zabrze 2-1 in Vienna's rainswept Prater Stadium. City's performance had merited a more convincing scoreline, and their fourth trophy in three seasons confirmed them as the era's most successful English club. As with their FA Cup-winning side, they had clinched the trophy with a team comprised wholly of English players.

Despite the result, there were minor irritations for Joe Mercer and Malcolm Allison to endure. Ironically, while UK viewers were unable to watch the match, it had been televised live in Austria, and this coupled with the appalling weather meant that a crowd of only about 12,000 – the bulk of them City fans – were present at the game. Mercer also expressed his dismay that both the BBC and ITV had chosen to give precedence to the FA Cup Final replay, a game which was, 'after all, just a qualifying competition' for the trophy City were striving to win.

The TV companies' decision emphasised the allure of the FA Cup and in particular the intrigue attached to the Chelsea–Leeds rivalry. Nevertheless, with ITV taking their customary hammering in the ratings, they might just as well have televised the European match. All their innovations and Brian Moore's exuberant commentary still couldn't get them to compete with the BBC. The advertising breaks and a cameraman who almost missed Hutchinson's goal in the first game can't have helped much, either.

With Arsenal coming back strongly to defeat Anderlecht at an emotional Highbury, thereby delivering the club's first trophy for seventeen years, English club football was in rude health indeed. The question now was not just whether its key players would be able to cope with the difficult conditions they would encounter in Mexico, but also whether they would be able to recover physically from what for many had been an exhausting schedule, the like of which none of their rivals would have been forced to endure.

Match Of The Month
29 April 1970, FA Cup Final Replay: Chelsea 2 Leeds United 1 (after extra time)

After the dramatic draw at Wembley, the sides travelled to Old Trafford eighteen days later. The level of enmity between the two sets of players was now at an all-time high. Personal feuds, not least between Osgood and Jack Charlton, were thinly if at all disguised and with so much at stake, it was inevitable that an ill-tempered encounter would ensue. But the violence went on to exceed all expectations, as the match became arguably the most brutal top-level encounter ever seen on these shores.

Many years later, David Elleray reviewed the footage and concluded that the referee could reasonably have dismissed as many as seven players. Whilst standards have changed markedly in the intervening years, the tolerance shown by Mr Jennings was incredible. It was almost as if he knew that the players were hell bent on going for each other right from the start, so decided just to let them get on with it.

It was easy to stereotype the contest as bruising, muscular Yorkshire thugs against the ball-playing fancy dans of Chelsea, but this was a Chelsea side more than capable of looking after itself. Ron Harris and Eddie McCreadie were obvious examples, but languid ball-players like Cooke and Osgood were always more than willing to leave a boot in. Eddie McCreadie's flying throat-high kick on Bremner was worthy of a custodial sentence, but the perfectly placed Mr Jennings happily waved play on.

Very occasionally football broke out, and from one such rare outburst an imperious run from the sinewy Clarke released Mick Jones to shoot emphatically across and beyond Bonetti and into the net. For the third time in the final Leeds were ahead; for the third time, they were unable to make it count. Chelsea equalised when Cooke followed a typically mazy dribble by floating a ball through for the unmarked Osgood to power home a diving header. These two beautiful, spectacular goals were completely out of context with the ugly brutality which had preceded them, but with the game now well into extra time, the winner was appropriately messy, Ian Hutchinson's long throw ultimately finding its way into the net via David Webb's shoulder. Not that Chelsea, or Webb, would have minded one hoot. Webb had been given a torrid time by Eddie Gray in the first game at Wembley and this was more than enough redemption. For Chelsea, the joy of lifting the cup for the first time in their history was made even sweeter by the sight of their bitter hated rivals broken and disconsolate on the turf, their heroic efforts over the last nine months having come to nothing.

Chelsea: Bonetti, Harris, McCreadie, Hollins, Dempsey, Webb, Baldwin, Hollins, Osgood (Hinton), Hutchinson, Houseman.

Leeds United: Sprake, Madeley, Cooper, Bremner, Charlton, Hunter, Lorimer, Clarke, Jones, Giles, Gray.

Player Of The Month
Charlie George (Arsenal)

Throughout the 1960s, it was difficult to find an Arsenal match report which didn't feature the word 'dull'. With Bertie Mee's side being founded on solid defence and all-round efficiency, there were few flashes of flair and colour to be found in their performances. When boyhood fan Charlie George swapped his spot on the terraces for a place on the pitch, it at least promised to provide Arsenal fans with something different.

George made his debut on the opening day of the 1969/70 season and held his place throughout the campaign. He scored the only goal at West Brom to give Arsenal their first win of the season and immediately became a fan favourite for his skill and attitude, as well as his 'one of us' background. When Peter Marinello joined midway through the season, Arsenal were in danger of becoming almost interesting, and their form in the second half of the season improved markedly.

Marinello's impact would prove to be fleeting, and it was George who would leave a lasting imprint on the club – beginning with this season. He had already scored eight goals coming into

April, and helped his team through to the semi-final of the Fairs Cup, although Arsenal were very much the underdogs as they lined up against Ajax at Highbury. George's early twenty-yard drive put them ahead, and with Ajax seemingly happy to hold on to a narrow defeat, a late Arsenal burst saw George's cool late penalty secure a commanding 3-0 lead after Sammels had netted a second.

Arsenal duly navigated their way through the second leg to set up a final against Anderlecht. After a 3-1 first-leg defeat, Arsenal won 3-0 at Highbury to secure their first trophy for seventeen years, with George playing a prominent role even though he failed to get on the scoresheet.

George surpassed even these achievements the following season, scoring many crucial goals in the league campaign and then the famous winner in the FA Cup Final, as Arsenal took the double and George cemented his place in club history. He stayed with Arsenal until 1975, although his impact was diminished by injury and ill-discipline, and moved to Derby County, where he picked up another league championship medal in his first season.

George's form earned him an England call-up and he made his debut against the Republic of Ireland in 1976. Revie's decision to substitute him after an hour saw George take umbrage, and this proved to be the player's only full cap. His career was continually dogged by injury, managing only 300 league games in a fifteen-year career, but his role in Arsenal's brief but spectacular renaissance in the early 1970s has ensured his cult status forever.

Summer 1970

England's warm-up games took them to the high-altitude destinations of Colombia and Ecuador. In Bogota, a tremendously accomplished performance saw England come away with a 4-0 win, in a match played at even higher altitude than any venue they would experience in Mexico. The Colombian coach was certainly taken with Ramsey's team, observing that 'England

impress me as a wonderful and powerful football machine...
compared with the 1966 team, this team has grown a lot.'

Next up was a game in Ecuador, where England again
impressed in a 2-0 win. With games in both venues also arranged
for – and won by – the 'shadow' XIs, it was generally reckoned
that the preparations couldn't have gone any better. A hiccup
was soon to emerge, with the accusation levelled at Bobby
Moore about the stolen bracelet, but after a tense few days all
was resolved and the squad assembled in Mexico fully intact.

And so on to a familiar and often-told tale. The tough battle
to overcome a negative, physical Romania; the clash with Brazil
featuring *that* save, *that* tackle and *that* miss by Jeff Astle; the
narrow win against Czechoslovakia to confirm the passage
through to the quarter-finals. And then the tale told more often
than any other, the defeat to West Germany and the end of
England's reign.

Many laid the blame at Alf's door for his substitutions. But
changes had to be made, with several players evidently struggling
in the heat and altitude. Bobby Charlton was certainly one of
them, his contribution in this match being more reputational
than physical, and Bell's introduction, just after Beckenbauer's
shot had crawled past Bonetti, gave England far more energy
in attack. Nevertheless, Helmut Schoen's changes ultimately
proved the more effective and it could be argued that this was
the first time that an important game had been won from the
bench, with German winger Grabowski taking advantage of an
exhausted Terry Cooper to stretch England to breaking point.

Looking at the footage again, one of the most striking
aspects is the refereeing in the second period of extra time. Juan
Coerezza, an Argentinian, had already caused raised eyebrows
when awarding the Mexican hosts an outrageous penalty
in an earlier group game. Now, he favoured the Germans
blatantly. Two decisions in particular stood out – when Lee beat
Schnellinger on the byline and dribbled inside to set up Hurst
to score, the goal was disallowed for an alleged infringement
which no one else saw or appealed for. Worse still, when Bell

turned past Beckenbauer in the area a couple of minutes later, the German captain's sliding tackle scythed him down for the most obvious of penalties. On a scale of zero to 100, this was 100. Coerezza, perfectly positioned, didn't look slightly interested and scuttled quickly away from the scene.

Argentinian anger at the Rattin affair in 1966 had festered ever since and with their side failing to qualify for Mexico, they didn't have the chance to take revenge in the conventional way. But Coerezza, their lone representative, had done the job for them. Immediately after he blows the final whistle, TV footage shows his face breaking out into a beaming smile just before he goes out of shot. 'That's for Rattin...'

England's defeat was cruel, unjust and undeserved. But we no longer ruled the world. And we never have done since.

Four Years that Shaped the Modern Game?

In 2016, the way the game is played, the way it's run, the way it's watched, the way it's reported, the way it's financed… all of these facets and more are unrecognisable from the period covered in this book. But the evolution of the game throughout those four special years can be seen to have started the progression towards so much of what we now take for granted in modern football, both on and off the pitch.

Sir Alf's bid to consign wingers to history evidently didn't work. Many top club sides carried on exactly as they had before. And even some of those who initially followed Ramsey's example would in time revert to their previous philosophies. At Chelsea, Tommy Docherty had been one notable early adopter of the 'wingless wonders' formula, redeploying Charlie Cooke as a midfielder and claiming that the days of the winger had gone forever. But eight years later, when Docherty revamped the Manchester United side following their relegation in 1974, the team's success was founded largely on the dynamic wing play of Steve Coppell and Gordon Hill. Wingers have remained an essential part of the game, even if most modern teams employ one rather than two, and the new breed work much harder and are more inclined to cut in than go down the line.

Ramsey's more telling legacy was that a team whose main attributes were hard work, fitness, teamwork and organisation could win a major trophy even when faced with opponents of greater technical quality. It immediately brought an enhanced focus on teams getting more out of their players, even the extravagantly gifted ones, and is a trend which has continued to this day. One of the common expressions around modern football is that supposedly superior teams must 'earn the right to play' – essentially that they must firstly put in the effort to tire their opponents, then use their extra quality to exploit the space which becomes available later in the game.

In 1969, Colin Bell, widely acknowledged as one of the fittest and hardest-working players in the game at that time, was monitored as covering 8,600 yards, or just under 8km, in a particular match. This was considered to be a remarkable figure, being almost exactly twice the distance Ferenc Puskas had been estimated to cover on that famous afternoon at Wembley sixteen years earlier. Yet in modern football, even those outfield players sometimes perceived as lazy by fans and pundits, unwilling to track back, often cover more than 10km. Even allowing for differences and inaccuracies in measuring techniques, the figures demonstrate graphically how the physical effort and fitness levels required of footballers has continued to escalate over the years.

The move to more defensive football really took hold in the late 1960s, with the low point probably being the 1968/69 season, when Leeds became the only champions in history to score fewer goals than they accrued points. Yet even then, they were still the division's third highest scorers. There were repeated suggestions for rule changes in order to make the game more attractive and the first action came with the move from goal average to goal difference, a minor change but one which on occasion has had a very significant impact in bringing trophies to teams which have focused on trying to score goals. This was followed in 1981 by the more substantive move to three points for a win, rendering the point secured by away teams hell-bent on keeping out the opposition a relatively less valuable reward.

However, after initially being deemed a success, the impact on tactics of awarding three points for a win has diminished. One point is still better than none at all, and a high proportion of away sides continue to set themselves up in a highly defensive formation, especially when visiting supposedly superior opposition. They are no longer allowed to use such robust physical methods to keep attackers at bay, but their levels of fitness and organisation are such that they can still often succeed. In a way, not much has changed from the late 1960s, with supporters of home teams now, as then, knowing they will be in for an afternoon of boredom and frustration unless or until their team can break down a massed defence.

One of the most important and far-reaching changes to emerge throughout the era was the introduction of tactical substitutes. Alf Ramsey may have been slower than some to recognise their potential, but by the 1970s they had become an integral part of the game. As the possibilities for them to change the pattern of a game became ever more apparent, substitutes were increasingly selected with a Plan B in mind. Some, such as David Fairclough at Liverpool, would even come to be defined by their role as substitute, 'impact players' who could make a crucial contribution as the game became stretched. Over the years, the number of substitutes permitted domestically and internationally, and the pool from which they can be selected, have gradually increased – as has the potential for managers to change games from the bench.

Rather than the 'not playing the game' attitude which initially greeted the concept of tactical substitutions, they are now seen as an essential element of modern football, and one of the attributes most prized in today's managers is the ability to analyse in real time the flow of a match and change the shape of their team accordingly. Other than their use for timewasting purposes, 1967's introduction of tactical substitutes has proved to have a far-reaching and hugely beneficial effect on the game.

Successful substitutions have, on many occasions, been said to have 'saved their manager from the sack', but such reprieves are often short-lived. Then, as now, many managerial dismissals were accompanied by outcry from the media: the big difference was that they didn't happen anywhere near so often. The late 1960s featured men such as Matt Busby, Bill Shankly, Harry Catterick, Bill Nicholson, Joe Mercer, Harry Potts, Ted Bates, Don Revie, Ron Greenwood, Tony Waddington and Joe Harvey – all of whom were or would become synonymous with their clubs, with tenures routinely exceeding ten years. In late 2014, Arsene Wenger was the only one of the twenty Premier League managers to have been in his job for over two years: excluding Wenger, the average time in post of Premier League managers at that point was just fifteen months.

Nevertheless, there was some evidence that directors in the late 1960s were giving managers less time to succeed and reacting to failure more quickly than before. A prime example came at QPR, whose dramatic ascent to the first division under Alec Stock via two successive promotions naturally raised the question of whether they would be able to cope in the first division. With injuries to key players, their task became harder again, but still they saw fit to dispense with the man who had brought them up from division three, winning the League Cup for good measure, after just a few difficult months. Johnny Carey at Nottingham Forest was another who suffered a dismissal which by previous standards seemed almost cruelly premature. So the prototype for the managerial merry-go-round had been built, even if it initially revolved in slow motion.

Slow motion was also a device which would transform TV coverage of football. *The Big Match*'s employment of Jimmy Hill for better or worse created the role of the television pundit, a move which in turn shaped the future of TV presentation. And the slow-motion action replay, which facilitated analysis of major incidents and in particular controversial refereeing decisions, was a vitally important tool in Hill's armoury. He received criticism for slating referees, even though ITV were at pains to point out that their analysis showed that the officials had been proved right 98 per cent of the time. That percentage is rather lower these days, as super-slow-motion replays from all conceivable angles frequently deliver evidence that even a perfectly placed referee couldn't possibly have seen in real time. But today's obsessive desire to show viewers what really happened in key incidents had its genesis in *The Big Match*'s primitive technology.

The saturation coverage of the 1966 World Cup was clearly the crucial first step towards the wall-to-wall football we see on TV today, and the trend towards riches pouring into the game from television had also begun, however modestly. BBC's *MOTD* coverage in 1966/67 cost them £33,000; by 1969/70 it had increased to £100,000. But the real big money lay in live coverage: even in 1967, the BBC tabled a bid of almost £800,000 to cover a season's worth of live games. Eventually, the money would talk.

As well as seeing football take its initial steps to receiving riches from television, the era witnessed the tentative first moves towards big-money sponsorship. The Watney Cup was deemed successful enough to continue for several years, and Texaco would soon follow suit by sponsoring an Anglo-Scottish competition. The Football League and FA would resist for many years overtures to sponsor their more important and well-established competitions, but there was an absolute inevitability that even for these great traditionalist bodies the price would ultimately be right. As it would be for the right for companies to have their logos emblazoned across the front of club shirts.

Footballers of the era were regarded as well-paid, which by the standards of the maximum wage era was certainly true, but in reality the pay of the average first division player was little more than that of a middle-manager in an office job. A comfortable living, but nowhere near enough to allow even top players to live off their earnings after their playing days were over. World Cup winners who didn't want to stay in the game were obliged to go into 'normal' jobs when their careers ended – Hurst and Peters into insurance, Wilson into undertaking, Hunt into the family haulage business.

However, the increased exposure given to football and footballers generated interest amongst marketing men and enabled top players to supplement their core income. George Best stood apart from the rest – the income from one of his modelling contracts in isolation doubled his basic £100 per week pay – but a host of other stars also featured in TV ads and product promotions in newspapers and magazines. In turn, agents had gradually crept on to the scene to represent those players seen to have worthwhile earnings potential. The seeds of the modern star player's image rights, multi-million pound endorsements and agents agitating relentlessly for transfers and better deals had been planted.

A particularly depressing development of the era was the advent of widespread hooliganism. By the end of the 1960s, some clubs had taken the first steps towards segregating fans within grounds but the overall situation would get much worse before it got better. It would take tragedy and legislation to force clubs to adopt measures to make their grounds safer. Fans' unruly behaviour extended to a series of pitch invasions during the 1970s, which in turn led to supporters being penned in on the terraces. The inability to escape from these pens cost ninety-six people their lives in the Hillsborough disaster and led inevitably to the all-seater stadia we see today.

The 1966 World Cup was the first to feature widespread merchandising and by 1970, the range of goods available to supporters – and the emergence of club shops for them to buy them in – was unrecognisable from the position only four years earlier. The mind-boggling range of products available from today's huge club superstores is a natural progression of this trend.

Whilst the era sparked trends which have influenced greatly the game as it is today, there are some developments which at the time could not have been foreseen. Everton's 1970 title win made them the fifth different side to take the title in five seasons. The sequence of spreading the spoils around would be extended by a further two years with the triumphs of Arsenal and Derby County. Seven different winners in seven years. The twenty-three-year Premier League era has produced just six different champions, a consequence of the rich getting richer, and burgeoning transfer fees putting superstar players out of the reach of all but the moneyed few. Leicester's remarkable surge to the title in 2015/16 – and the fact that the core wealth available to all Premier League clubs via TV money has increased substantially – has caused some optimists to observe that a new era of broader competitiveness might be upon us. It seems rather more likely that Leicester's triumph will prove to be a glorious one-off.

The eleven-season span between 1963 and 1973 saw eleven different sides win the FA Cup. The twenty-seven seasons from 1989 have produced just eight different winners, this being despite the fact that top clubs generally take the competition far less seriously, often fielding weakened and even second string sides. Protracted attempts by TV companies and the FA to bring the cup back to its old level of prominence have failed conspicuously, with the riches available from the Champions League meaning that achievement of a fourth-place finish in the league is seen as a significantly higher priority by club owners, even if not necessarily by the fans. It is difficult to envisage the position changing.

The other thing to have changed dramatically is the way the game is played, with many ex-pros mockingly referring to modern football as a 'non-contact sport'. Slide tackles which won the ball and took the man as well were totally fair in 1970 and well beyond – by the 2010s, the same tackles were frequently deemed to be sending-off offences. The moves have acted to protect and encourage skilful players, but the levels of defensive organisation are such that they still often struggle to impose themselves on games. Despite the occasional throwback – such as the Chelsea–Spurs game of 2016 – there are few occasions where the enmity between two teams is given the chance to express itself by way of physical violence. It's progress, of course it is, but who among us doesn't secretly yearn for a bit of good old-fashioned clogging to liven up a game in which the two teams' tactics are so carefully mapped out that it's almost like watching a chess match. But those days are gone forever, as are those *When England Ruled The World*. Gone, but definitely not forgotten.